SOUNDING THE MARGINS

Sounding the Margins

Collected Writings 1992 – 2009

Pauline Oliveros

Foreword by John Luther Adams
Midword by Monique Buzzarté
Aftword by Stuart Dempster

Edited by Lawton Hall

Sounding the Margins: Collected Writings 1992-2009

By Pauline Oliveros
Foreword by John Luther Adams
Midword by Monique Buzzarté
Aftword by Stuart Dempster
Editing, compilation, and page design by Lawton Hall
Cover by Nico Bovoso

Printed in the United States of America

Deep Listening Publications
P.O. Box 1956
Kingston, NY 12402
www.deeplistening.org

ISBN-10: 1-889471-16-X
ISBN-13: 978-1-889471-16-7
Library of Congress Control Number (LCCN): 2010934427

To the history of the future.

For Douglas Oliveros Nightengale,
born October 25, 2009.

Contents

FOREWORD

On her 21st birthday, Pauline Oliveros received from her mother a gift that changed her life: a reel-to-reel tape recorder.

Listening to a recording she made of the sounds outside her window, Pauline immediately recognized that the microphone had heard things that her ears had missed. This epiphany led her to the simple but demanding practice she has followed ever since:

> *"Listen to everything all the time and remind yourself when you are not listening."*

This discipline became the foundation of Pauline's life work: listening, improvising, teaching, expanding the capabilities of musical instruments—sounding the margins of music.

For Pauline, music is rooted in sound and in listening. This may seem like self-evident proposition. But practiced with Pauline's uncompromising integrity, it's surprising how radically it challenges conventional orthodoxies.

Pauline is profoundly curious and open to new sounds, new ideas and new experiences. Her irrepressible enthusiasm is evident in everything she does—in her music, her teaching, and in the writings in this book.

Pauline is a generous, expansive and ageless spirit. She is a mentor, teacher, inspiration and role model to countless musicians all over the world. But anyone who would dismiss her as a sort of New Age guru is missing the fierce intellect that burns within the woman and her work.

In the late 1990's, Pauline and I shared a teaching position alternating semesters at the Oberlin College Conservatory of Music. During those two years we were asked to propose a new core curriculum for the school. Pauline brought to that task the same energy she brings to everything she does. I was amazed at Pauline's uncanny knack for explaining the most radical artistic ideas on terms that made sense to skeptical educators.

Pauline has always been a leader in using new technology to make music. Yet for her, technology is not an end in itself. The technology she uses has always been in service to music, creativity and humanity.

Pauline is intrigued by the convergence of human and artificial intelligence, but she recognizes clearly the larger questions it raises: *"We must decide what a 50-year-old silicon structure is going to tell a five-billion-year-old structure of carbon before making irreversible physical changes."*

Of course machines are not a separate species. They are creations of human beings, reverberations and extensions of the human body and mind. And as she writes: *"It is the nonlinear carbon chaos, the unpredictable turns of chance permutation, the meatiness, the warmth, the simple, profound humanity of beings that brings presence and wonder to music."*

Pauline has dedicated her rich and active life to walking her talk. Just as she uses technology to expand the possibilities of music, Pauline believes that music has the power to transform human consciousness and society.

Technology holds the promise of helping us understand more fully the potential and the limits of our species in a "post-human" world. Perhaps the greatest and most imminent limit we face today is the potentially catastrophic effects of human-caused climate change. As human intelligence expands, augmented by technology, perhaps we will gain the understanding that will allow us to take our rightful place among the miraculous richness and diversity of life on the planet earth.

Pauline's practice of Deep Listening is grounded in two modes of attention: "focal attention" of the deeper resonances within ourselves, and "global attention" to the enveloping music of the world in which we live. Leaving the confined spaces of headphones, loudspeakers and concert halls, she often makes music in and with the larger-than-human world. This informs everything she does. Whether performing outdoors or indoors, Pauline listens deeply, encompassing in her music everything that is sounding.

Pauline explores acoustical space as a dynamic dimension of music, every bit as fundamental as pitch, timbre, intensity, density or duration. Through the practice of her art, she's come to believe that spaces in which we listen are every bit as important as the sounds we make. For Pauline, harmony is defined not by progressions of chords, but by the way we hear sounds together, in time and space.

With electronic processing and communications Pauline actively shapes the spaces in which she listens and performs. Using digital reverberation and delays, internet connections and other new tools, she creates virtual acoustic spaces that breathe and change as integral parts of the music. This is the heart of Pauline's Expanded Instrument System (EIS)—a continually evolving concept and toolkit that originated with her first experiments with that tape recorder, almost sixty years ago.

Ever since then Pauline has dedicated her life to sounding the margins, to expanding our awareness, to exploring the borders of music and life. As we cross over new borders again and again, what we thought was the margin turns out to be the center. We come to understand that wherever we may be we are always at the center of experience.

Pauline is from the generation before my own (I was born the year she received that first tape recorder.) But we're part of the same musical family—a long line of independent composers running from Charles Ives, Henry Cowell, Ruth Crawford Seeger and Johanna Beyer to John Cage, Morton Feldman, Conlon Nancarrow, Lou Harrison, James Tenney and Maryanne Amacher. Still going strong in her 70's, Pauline is a living treasure and a vibrant connection with this lineage.

Through her long, rich life fearlessly and joyfully sounding the margins, Pauline Oliveros stands as a singular figure, a central presence in the music of our time.

John Luther Adams

PREFACE

I am experiencing the long shadow of my existence.

This is the third book of my writings. I began with *Software for People: Collected Writings 1963-1980,* followed by The *Roots of the Moment: Collected Writings 1981-1995* and now *Sounding the Margins: Collected Writings 1992-2010.*

Like the previous two collections, the diverse articles in *Sounding the Margins* range from the poetic to the technical and reflect many of my interests, including my ongoing struggle to change the status quo of the position of women in music. They also include meditations on improvisation in its many varieties and a concern with the present and future of technology, both of which have served me throughout my career.

Yet though these writings reflect many of my interests and activities, there are many more that are not represented here. So the reader may want to know that in completing this book, I am already working on the next! Below I trace some of the influences on my work and mention some of the activities prior to 1992 that will be more fully documented in my next book:

The world of non-profit arts organizations is very important to me. My career began in 1960 with the group Sonics, which later became the San Francisco Tape Music Center (SFTMC), a prototype collaborative organization that was active until 1967. Since the SFTMC days to the present, my work and the work of my community of artists has been supported by a variety of non-profits. There exists an amazing network of small organizations and individuals throughout the world that support unconventional music and art. I am grateful for their hard work, presence, and support.

During the 1990's, I exercised all of my skills as a freelance composer, performer, producer, and administrator, devoting eight years to create, fund, and produce *Njinga the Queen King: The Return of a Warrior,* a pan-African opera, in collaboration with playwright and director Ione. Njinga was a great and demanding teacher as well as an evocative subject for my composing. Producing *Njinga* drew on my interest in technology, electronic music, diversity, and cultural fusion. My collaborations with Ione are ongoing and continuous.

During this time, after leaving my tenured position as Professor at University of California, San Diego in 1981, I was concerned with developing a non-profit platform as a home for creative artists and their work. Learning how to fund *Njinga* taught me how to realize this platform and forced the Pauline Oliveros Foundation (founded in 1985) to grow very rapidly.

Njinga had its premiere at the Majestic Theater at the Brooklyn Academy of Music in December 1993 with a run of eight performances. This major production occupied me from our first workshop at Yellow Springs Institute in Chester Pennsylvania 1991 until our last partial performance at Mills College in November 1998. The complete history of the production of *Njinga* has yet to be written and more documentation is forthcoming. However, a DVD from Mode Records (released in 2010) tells some of the story and documents the premiere BAM performances.

In 1988, I coined the term "Deep Listening" as a result of recording with Stuart Dempster and Panaiotis in the Fort Worden Cistern in Port Townsend, WA. Since then, I have continued to develop the practice of Deep Listening through more solo and ensemble recordings and performances, numerous workshops and retreats, and university classes.

In 2005, the Pauline Oliveros Foundation became Deep Listening Institute, Ltd. (DLI). I continue to serve as its Founder, Executive Director, and Trustee. DLI provides a platform for many younger artists and serves as a way to develop projects and to distribute recordings, videos, and writings. Today, the Deep Listening Institute holds the history of the Deep Listening practice and keeps expanding it throughout the world through publications, recordings, concerts, and Deep Listening Study Groups.

In the mid-1990's, funding began to decline for the non-profit arts organizations that supported my work because of attacks on the National Endowment for the Arts by Senator Jesse Helms and an increasingly conservative Congress.

At this same time, I was fortunately called back into academic work, beginning with a guest position at Mills College that turned into a regular fall-semester appointment as the Darius Milhaud Chair of Composition. This position was shared with Alvin Curran, who taught at Mills during the alternating spring semesters.

Other universities and colleges began to call me for semester-long teaching positions or residencies. Spring 1999 had me at Oberlin Conservatory, 2000 at Agnes Scott College, and 2001 as Artist-in-Residence at the University of Wisconsin, Madison. Between Mills in the fall and guest appointments in the spring, I was working full-time again after freelancing for fifteen years.

At the Arts Institute in Madison, I composed and produced another opera written and directed by Ione. *Io and Her and the Trouble with Him: A Dance-Opera in Primeval Time* had its premiere performance at the Union Theater in Madison with aerial dancer and choreographer Joanna Haigood as Io and vocalist Andrea Goodman as Memory/Io.

While still in Madison, I had another fateful call from Neil Rolnick, chair of the Department of the Arts at Rensselaer Polytechnic Institute (RPI) in Troy, NY. Neil had initiated the creation of Arts Department in 1981 and at the time, it was the only program that combined audio and visual arts in a single department. Previously, in the 80's and 90's, Neil had invited me to RPI to perform and present my work there during the early years of this program. One of these performances, titled *Njinga Interactive,* was a studio performance that involved PictureTel video conferencing, Internet Relay Chat (IRC), the campus radio station (WRPI), video, and live drumming.

On the phone, Neil explained the extraordinary circumstances of growth at RPI. President Shirley Jackson had secured an anonymous donation of $350,000,000.00, the largest single donation in history for any college at the time. With the donation, she sought the creation of a biotechnology center and the Experimental Media and Performing Arts Center (EMPAC).

As a result, the Arts Department was adding four new faculty members and—-to my great surprise and interest—Neil had called to ask if I would join the department.

This was a very exciting opportunity. I was attracted to the prospect of having diverse colleagues in the arts and the possibility of collaborations with engineers, architects, and information technologists. RPI, which is close to my home in Kingston, NY, is also an active research facility in art, technology, and science and has an advanced biotechnology center. I accepted the teaching position and have been on the faculty of RPI ever since.

It was difficult to give up my position at Mills College even though it took me away from home every fall. Mills' Music Department houses the Center for Contemporary Music (CCM), which was formerly the Mills Tape Music Center. I served as director of this program in 1966-7 after the San Francisco Tape Music Center received a large Rockefeller grant and was moved to Mills. The SFTMC, the first non-profit group to support my work, was an important place for the development of my tape and electronic music in the 1960's. It was relocated to Mills because the Rockefeller Foundation wanted the grant funds to be administered by a larger institution rather than an artist-run non-profit organization. My experience at the SFTMC served me well as did the director position at Mills. From there, I was invited to apply to the Music Department at the University of California at San Diego (UCSD) to establish an electronic music program for the graduate students there. The UCSD Music Department was new at the time and would consist mostly of composers and performers. My work at UCSD is documented in my first book of collected writings, *Software for People*.

I have continued my connection with the Mills College Music Department by teaching a two-hour course via Skype video chat each fall. This has worked well and I have great admiration for my colleagues at Mills and the students. There is a great community of artists at Mills as well as the greater Bay Area. Mills is one of the best places in the world for a young composer to learn in a creative environment.

Many years later, the threads between the SFTMC in the 60's, Mills College, UCSD, and RPI are now weaving together in the 21st Century. In another surprising turn of events, Johannes Goeble (director of RPI's EMPAC) proposed *Wow & Flutter—1961 <—> now*, a two-day celebration of the San Francisco Tape

Music Center. At that time, the EMPAC facility was under construction so the festival took place in the RPI Playhouse in October of 2004. My SFTMC colleagues Morton Subotnick, Ramon Sender, Anthony Martin, William R. Maginnis Jr. and I were brought together to recreate some of our pieces from the 1960's and to present new work as well.

EMPAC documented *Wow & Flutter* with a three-camera video shoot and high-quality audio recording. A DVD of this performance was included with the book *The San Francisco Tape Music Center: 1960's Counterculture and the Avant-Garde* (edited by David Bernstein, my colleague at the Mills College Music Department), which was published by the University of California Press in 2008. Bernstein wrote the title article for the book to help contextualize our music and art. Goeble was interested to show the origin of multimedia performance in our work. The book contains writings, interviews, and documents that had never before been collected and the DVD shows some of the legendary multimedia pieces by Sender and Subotnick (such as *Desert Ambulance* and *Mandolin*) that featured projected visuals by Tony Martin.

Wow & Flutter and the accompanying book and DVD helped establish a professional connection between RPI's EMPAC and the Mills College Music Department. Since joining the faculty at RPI, I have researched and developed ways to connect with my colleagues in California using high-bandwidth Internet2 so that we could continue to work together musically and otherwise. Though I am excited by my work and colleagues at RPI, I miss my colleagues, collaborations, and old friends (like Stuart Dempster) on the West Coast.

In 2002, I began collaborating with Brian Lonsway of the RPI Architecture Department. Brian's students created performable virtual sets that we used in collaboration with Scot Gresham-Lancaster at California State College, Hayward, via Internet2 technology. These sets created common virtual spaces for performers from Mills in California to share with performers at RPI. With them, we produced the real-time virtual performance *Peerings*, thus setting my dream of connecting California and New York into motion.

Since then, many more performances have been produced using both high- and low-tech means. *Sedimental Journey*, a celebration of 50 years of musical friendship between Stuart Dempster and myself, connected three participating sites using iChat AV software in 2005. Stuart performed from the DXARTS studio at the University of Washington in Seattle, I performed from RPI's iEAR studios in Troy, NY and the performance was viewed in the Concert Hall at Mills College in Oakland, CA. Two dancers under the direction of June Watanabe also improvised to our music on stage at Mills and on screen as video images.

In 2007, Jonas Braasch from RPI's Architecture Department joined the telematic performance research and we began weekly collaborations with Chris Chafe, director of the Center for Computer Research in Music and Acoustics (CCRMA) at Stanford University. Chris used these collaborations to refine his low-latency high-quality transmission software JackTrip for our rehearsals and performances. Using these technologies, we now have the potential to connect with performers in Asia, Europe, Canada, and the United States in three- and four-way ensemble performances.

My move to the RPI Department of the Arts has provided a rich environment for my continuing interest in the use of technology for music, teaching, and communications. Working together with colleagues and students in integrated electronic arts has stretched my intellect and given me a rich learning environment.

Currently, with the help of a National Science Foundation CreativeIT grant, Jonas Braasch, postdoctoral research associate Doug Van Nort, and I are creating a software agent that incorporates artificial intelligence into musical improvisation. The agent "listens" to live performers and analyzes their musical gestures to play along with the ensemble.

I am grateful that Deep Listening Institute, Ltd. continues to provide a platform for disseminating and publishing the results of so much activity that encompasses many years of my own work and the work of other artists. I offer *Sounding the Margins* as a pathway leading to the future.

ACKNOWLEDGEMENTS

I acknowledge and love the mysterious energy called music that we share across the world without knowing or understanding how this moving force has come into being. I continue my lifelong devotion to music with the hopes that widespread appreciation for music and music making can overcome the war-mongering impulses in man. Music is leading the cultural fusion that is taking place in our time in exciting and pervasive ways.

I acknowledge my beautiful life partner Ione and our many artistic and administrative collaborations. Ione has nurtured and supported all of our endeavors, both individual and collaborative.

I am grateful to the community of artists who support one another around the world in ways that are visible, audible, invisible, and inaudible. This ever-expanding network of artists is helping to change the world by making the art that they love.

Additional acknowledgements:

To all of my mentors and teachers

To Lawton Hall for compiling and editing *Sounding the Margins*

To John Luther Adams, Monique Buzzarté, and Stuart Dempster for their words

To Ione for her partnership and editing

To Al Margolis for his proofreading

To Lisa Barnard Kelley and Emily Halstein for their support

To the Deep Listening Institute

To all of the venues and sponsors who have made my work possible

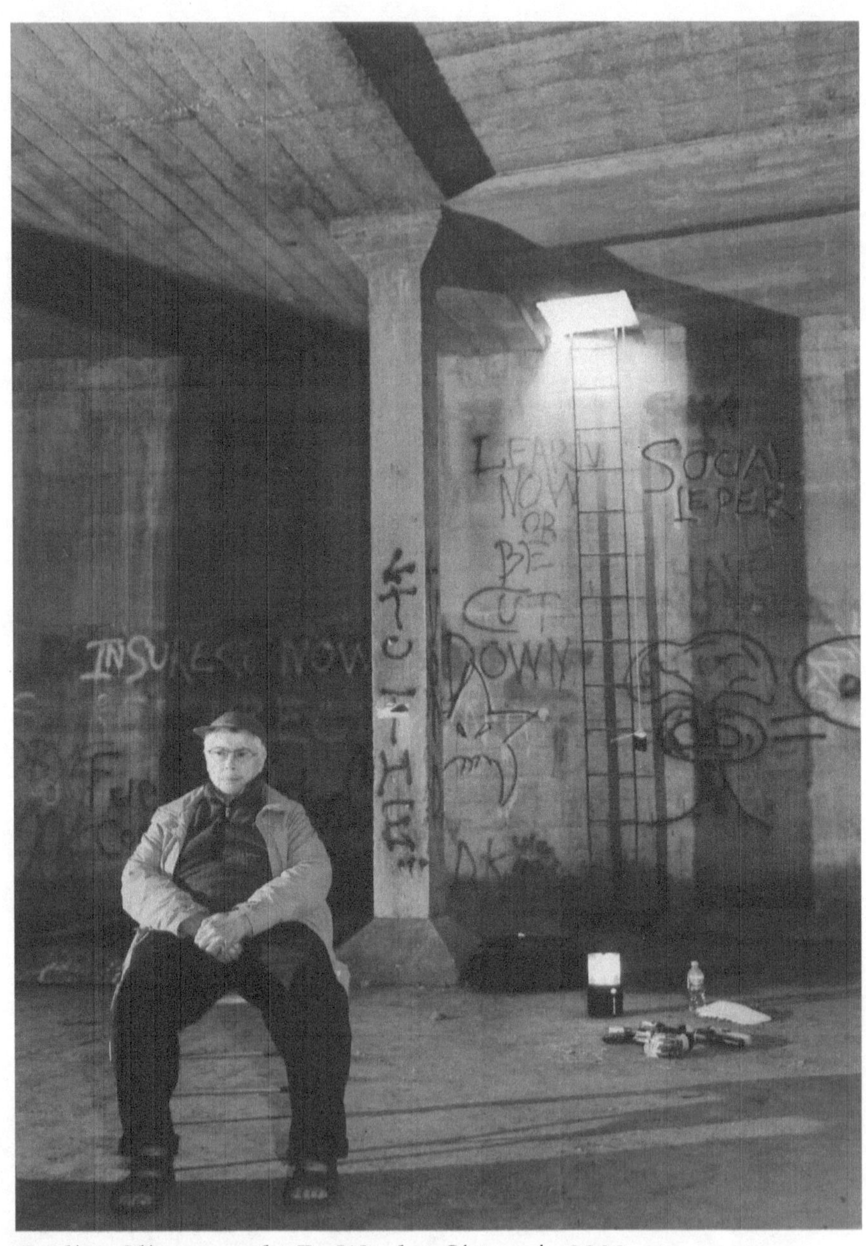

Pauline Oliveros at the Ft. Worden Cistern in 2009 – twenty years after the birth of Deep Listening. Photo by David Conklin

Death for JJ

March 1, 1992

Death

The body dissolving
The spirit loosening

Fright

The body dissolving
The spirit loosening

Pain

The body dissolving
The spirit loosening

Flight

The body dissolving
The spirit loosening

Rage

The body dissolving
The spirit loosening

Grief

The body dissolving
The spirit loosening

Awe

The body dissolving
The spirit loosening

Laughter

The body dissolving
The spirit loosening

Emptiness

The body dissolving
The spirit loosening

Ease

The body dissolving
The spirit loosening

Ardor

The body dissolving
The spirit loosening

Passion

The body dissolving
The spirit loosening

Solitude

The body dissolving
The spirit loosening

Reverence

The body dissolving
The spirit loosening

Equanimity

The body dissolving
The spirit loosening

Death

INTERACTIVE MUSIC

Published online in *NewMus MusicNet*,
www.newmus.net
April 1995

This essay is intended to elucidate the strategies used in my compositions designed to direct the attention of the performers. Included is a score for *Deep Listening Chorus*, a list of topics and questions for exploration, and a list of relevant scores from my catalog.

My work is either seen as a substantial contribution to the field of music or it is dismissed because it is not written in the conventional way and cannot be judged conventionally. It is dismissed because of a lack of written notes, or because participants are asked to invent pitches and rhythms according to recipes or metaphors. Musicians accustomed to reading notes and rhythms are often shocked by the bareness of the notation compared to familiar conventional scores, which direct their attention to predictable, repeatable, specific pitches and rhythms. I value the unpredictable and unknowable possibilities that can be activated by not specifying pitches and rhythms. I prefer organic rhythms rather than exclusively metrical rhythms. I prefer full-spectrum sound rather than a limited scalar system. My occasional use of scales and meter falls within this fuller context of sound-oriented composition.

My music is interactive music. It is interactive in the sense that participants take a share in creating the work rather than limit themselves to merely interpreting pitches and rhythms. I compose the overall forms and give guidelines for ways of listening and responding. These forms and guidelines, when appropriately applied, give the participants a creative opportunity to compose and perform simultaneously and to expand their musicianship.

The notational practices I employ to present my work include conventional staff notation, graphic notation, metaphors, prose, oral instructions, and recorded media. *Sonic Meditations*, for example, are notated as prose instructions or recipes. The notations for *Sonic Meditations* were presented in written form only after many trials with oral instructions among many different people. Even though *Sonic Meditations* are in print, I often vary or revise the wording I use to transmit the instructions in new situations.

My instructions are intended to start an attentional process within a participant and among a group which can deepen gradually with repeated experience. Here is an example of a piece for voices or instruments:

Three Strategic Options

Listen together. When you are ready to begin choose an option. Return to listening before choosing another option. Options are to be freely chosen throughout the duration of the piece. The piece ends when all return to listening together. Options:

1. Sound before another performer.
2. Sound after another performer.
3. Sound with another performer.

If performing as a soloist, substitute sound from the environment for another performer.

In order to perform *Three Strategic Options*, all players have to listen to one another. Attention shifts with each option. Sounding before another could have a competitive edge. One has to attentively listen for an opportune silence. Sounding after another requires patience. One has to listen for the end of a sound. Sounding with another takes intuition—knowing when to start and end. A definitive performance is not the goal—each performance can vary considerably, even though the integrity of the guidelines will not be disturbed. Style would change according to the performers, instrumentation, and environment, but the piece could be recognizable each time it is performed by the same group.

The central concern for all of my prose or oral instructions is to provide attentional strategies for the participants. Attentional strategies are nothing more than ways of listening and responding in consideration of oneself, others, and the environment. The result of using these strategies is listening. If performers are listening, then the audience is also likely to listen. In this body of work called interactive music, I have redefined the responsibilities of the composer, the performer, and listeners by asking that everyone share in the listening process—the gateway to creativity.

After trying one of my scores, many performers and audiences find that they have stretched their ears in new ways and that they can contribute imaginatively to the music. Furthermore, heightened listening may help musicians in their performance of more conventional music.

Even though it may seem impossible to judge the musical outcome of these pieces compared to conventional scores, the composition of guidelines and forms is a craft which takes as careful consideration as any score. It is important that the participants understand the directions. Making these directions clear is a challenging task for the composer. One wrong wording can cause resistance or confusion.

None of us who compose or improvise music can claim credit for inventing it. Music is a gift from the universe. Those of us who can tune to this gift are fortunate indeed—we interact with a powerful resource and connect with the billions of musicians who have preceded us, who are here with us, and who will succeed us. As musicians, we listen to make finer and finer distinctions in tone, sound, and rhythm. The slightest nuances accumulate and refine one's aesthetics. If we also listen to so-called "background noise", we better perceive our relationship to place—all sound provides us with information and forges connections. This is true for our daily lives as well.

The way one chooses to listen to music or daily life is a factor in the quality of one's life experience. Listening is a process that occurs at varying speeds. It can be like a bolt of lightning—all at once in the moment—or it can consist of intuitive guesses and thoughtful references to past experience.

Raw listening, however, has no past or future. It is the roots of the moment. It has the potential of instantaneously changing the listener forever.

Here is one of my practices:

> Listen to everything until it all belongs together and you are part of it.

* * *

For many years, I have led groups in interactive, sound-oriented music making. One of the simplest and most effective forms is *Deep Listening Chorus,* the instructions for which are on the following pages. People everywhere seem to need to make nonverbal sounds. It is a way to express emotions and to explore the unknown. People do it unconsciously and alone every day, but rarely consciously and in a group.

Because of this, most participants feel a sense of release after performing this piece that carries over to other activities and helps to activate the imagination or refresh the mind. Unrestricted vocal sound making is pleasurable!

No musical training is necessary, but a musical experience can and does happen.

Deep Listening Chorus

A form to activate community creative sound making

Commentary:

This piece is not intended as concert music. It is for a group of people to perform together as combined composers/performers/listeners in an agreed upon group activity. It is appropriate for a retreat, workshop, class or a get-together. This does not mean that an audience couldn't also enjoy the performance or hear it as art music. The present concert paradigm, though, restricts how such a piece could be presented and appreciated.

The Score:

1. Lying on the floor, heads or feet toward center and touching, listen/sound. Listen while sounding—listen while silent.
2. Listen to the whole field of sound. Let any sound heard whether inwardly or outwardly be a cue for relaxing or energizing as needed. This implies a global form of listening, which includes everything from the softest, loudest, nearest, most distant sounds possible to hear. Keep expanding to include more sound without assigning importance to any particular sound, except to cue relaxation or energizing. This form of auto-suggestion can also be used to accomplish goals. It can be done as a separate daily practice.
3. As a group, practice relaxation by scanning the body and releasing whatever tension is not needed. Send sound either mentally or vocally to the parts of the body that need releasing. Then bring consciousness to a pre-selected metaphor such as ice breaking up in the spring, the fullness of summer, the flow of electricity, etc. Each person helps to state the metaphor together simultaneously in an overlapping sound web using words, phrases and sentences at first, and then leading to a primarily nonverbal sounding. Words may weave in and out of the sounding, or not.
4. Anything goes if and only if you are listening.

A period of silence after the sounding is beneficial to help absorb the sensations, feelings and to assimilate the musical experience. After that, some people like to share their experiences, or not. *Deep Listening Chorus* often lasts for over an hour and a half.

There are many interesting questions and topics concerning the listening process to be explored by a *Deep Listening Chorus*. Following is a list:

> Super listening. Normal listening. Subliminal listening. What is interactive music? The composer/performer. One who makes and performs music. With self—with other(s)—with context/environment. Who is composing? Who is performing? What happens in the music? The ripening of technique. Open and closed languages. Limits, boundaries and borders. Games and gamuts. Scales and scales. The concert hall as an instrument. Sublime situations. Cautions and excesses. Leaving training / reprogramming for creativity. The Politics of Excellence. Demilitarization. High level strategy: Ways of listening / ways of performing. Strategy driven technique. Low level responses. Levels of awareness. Breath rhythm: Song. Heart rhythm: Dance. Gaia consciousness. Individual focus. Floating sounds. Musical territory. Poems of Freedom. Finding the still point: Silence, motion, interaction, relative, absolute. Developing language—reorganizing syntax. Sound Quest: sounding space—spacing sound. World of the part—part of the world. Role—function—part—whole. Letting go of old patterns—letting go of new patterns. Repatterning.

Other Interactive Pieces

The compositions listed below contain additional strategies for listening and responding at varying levels of musicianship:

- *Angels and Demons* for unspecified voices
- *Earth Ears* for unspecified instruments
- *El Relicario de los Animales* for 8 paired instruments, 4 percussionists, and voice
- *The Grand Buddha Marching Band* for unspecified voices or instruments
- *The Klickitat Ride* for unspecified voices or instruments
- *The New Sound Meditation* for unspecified voices or instruments
- *The Tuning Meditation* for unspecified voices or instruments
- *Traveling Companions* for 3 percussionists and 3 dancers
- *Rose Moon* for chorus, male and female soloists, and runner
- *Sonic Meditations* for unspecified voices or instruments
- *Tashi Gomang* for orchestra
- *The Wheel of Time* for string quartet
- *To Valerie Solanas and Marilyn Monroe in Recognition of Their Desperation* for small ensemble or chamber orchestra

Still Listening: Reflections on the Life and Music of David Tudor

with Erin Donavan and John D. S. Adams
MusicWorks Issue #70
Summer 1998

David Tudor came into my life—to my good fortune—during an intense period of my development as a composer in San Francisco in 1963. Much to my surprise and delight, I received an invitation to meet David at his request at the home of Olive Cowell. I was told that he was interested in my music. This interest was very important to me, as I knew what a wonderful musician he was. Little did I know that I was meeting a wonderful friend-to-be and that his encouragement would be central to my career.

David was learning to play the bandoneon at the time and expressed an interest in performing with me. He was staying in Berkeley with Maro Ajemian and Lionel Galston. I proceeded to compose a duo for accordion and bandoneon. We worked on it together along with Ahmed the Mynah Bird who insisted on imitating our phrases during the rehearsals. Eventually, it seemed only right to include Ahmed in the performance, so we did.

With David, I decided to organize a festival at the San Francisco Tape Music Center. We called it the Tudor Fest and it featured the music of John Cage, Alvin Lucier, Toshi Ichiyanagi and my *Duo for Accordion, Bandoneon and Possible Mynah Bird Obligato (See Saw Version).* It was during the preparations and rehearsals for this festival that David demonstrated his quintessential performance attitude: impeccable preparation, patience, respect for others, prodigious attention to detail, allegiance to sound, containment—listening intently to everything, and the ability to acknowledge the audience without calling attention to himself or being self-conscious. David would not begin any performance unless he was ready. This demonstration had a deep effect on me and all who participated in the Tudor Fest including John Chowning, Stuart Dempster, Steve Reich, Terry Riley, Loren Rush, Stanley Shaff, and Morton Subotnick. Recordings of this festival are in my archive—Special Collections in the library at the University of California, San Diego—Lynda Claasen, director.

[NB: These recordings now reside in the archives of the Center for Contemporary Music at Mills College. – P.O. 2008]

In 1965, David invited me to perform with him, Alvin Lucier, and David Behrman at the Case Institute in Cleveland, Ohio. This was my first acquaintance with Behrman and Lucier. Alvin performed his *Music for Solo Performer* and David B. his *Players with Circuits*. David Tudor performed my *Light Piece for David Tudor*, which included light projected into a prism that turned around and back as a spring wound down. Anthony Martin was the designer. *Light Piece* was an early drone piece with 4 channels of tape and piano. David's only instructions were to "play D-flat," which he did every which way: with a vibrator, an induction coil, a variety of mallets, sticks, and other techniques. All of the other pieces on the program were noise pieces, but my piece, which was fairly consonant, caused a minor stir in the audience that was alleviated when I raised the volume of the tape to overpower the shouting voices.

David tirelessly championed many composers by performing their works and becoming a mentor to other performers who were also composers and budding technologists. He helped to create the "audio art" genre as well as live electronic music. Many of the ingenious circuits for his compositions remain mysterious black boxes without schematic diagrams. He was dedicated to finding and using the inner and salient characteristics of materials and electronic circuits to make sounds. His inspiration for works such as *Rainforest* seeded many other works by those of us who performed with David and loved him for his generosity of spirit.

David gathered us to him in a loving way. He brought gifts from his extensive travels, he held dinner parties and cooked with the same performance attitude as he brought to his music. I treasure the many memories of chopping vegetables for his Indian cookery while the tangos of Astor Piazzola drove us on into the night as the fragrant aromas of spices rising mixed with laughter and provoked enormous appetites—it was also a lesson in patience!

After David left the planet on August 13th, there were extraordinarily unusual cloud formations during the early evening over the creek here in Kingston. A remarkably long, thin cloud hung low across the sky. In the distance, there were more such shapes alongside others—horizontal brush strokes and little puffs. Below, the water was like a mirror—quiet, peaceful, receiving the clouds lines and a small flock of floating white geese. It was very unique, like David. This beautiful natural scene will stay with me as a symbol of David's eternal journey. Though he is gone from the physical plane, his spirit is very much here.

STATEMENT

January 10, 1997

This statement was prepared for a press conference held at the American Federation of Musicians Local 802 in New York City on March 4, 1997. Local 802 hosted the press conference for the International Alliance for Women in Music (IAWM) and NOW-NYC (the Manhattan chapter of the National Organization for Women), who were joint sponsors of a demonstration outside Carnegie Hall at the Vienna Philharmonic Orchestra's New York concerts. This press conference occurred after the VPO voted to allow harpist Anna Lelkes to retroactively become a member of the orchestra on February 27, 1997, just before they arrived at Carnegie Hall.

The speakers at the conference were IAWM board member Catherine J. Pickar (who was also the official IAWM spokesperson on the Vienna Philharmonic Orchestra), NYC-NOW president Anne Conners, Abbie Conant (former principal trombonist of the Munich Philharmonic), and Pauline Oliveros.

The Vienna Philharmonic Orchestra's unethical exclusion of women and people of color is insupportable. The protest against this exclusion led by the International Association of Women in Music is a necessary step in changing such conditions in the performing musical arts. Great performers are obviously present in either gender and all colors and they can be players of any instrument.

In the light of this protest against the racist and sexist policy of the Vienna Philharmonic Orchestra, all who perform, compose, educate, publish and produce music also need to think again about what music is presented and taught. Who composed the music? How does one come to like music of any kind? How are opinions about music formed? What music is available in libraries for study and performance?

Including women and people of color in all forms of musical activity is an ethical and conscious choice to be made by all concerned. It is particularly incumbent on established musical organizations such as the Vienna Philharmonic, other established orchestras and institutions of higher education throughout the world to awaken to the effort of inclusiveness. This calls out for a reorganization of musical repertoire and more opportunities for composers to create new repertoire and for performers to play it and teach it. Once performers are integrated into musical ensembles that formerly excluded women and people of color, what music will they play? Ethics guide choices and raise consciousness. It is all too easy to continue an unethical tradition of exclusion without question. Music is the coordinating and synchronizing influence in all societies. It is obvious that integration has to take place through music and in the way music is taught and presented.

BREAKING THE SILENCE

Presented at Frau Musica (nova)
Cologne, Germany
January 1998

> *"And there appeared a great wonder in heaven; a woman clothed with the sun, and the moon under her feet, and upon her head a crown of twelve stars".*
>
> Revelations 12:1

Music is the most important coordinating, synchronizing, cultural force on earth. All societies recognize and respect the power of music. Music is used in the regulation of society in the service of the church, state and their educational institutions. Music is a basic tool of corporations in bringing their products to the market place. Music is also entertaining. However, music has many other functions and is a crucial mode of thought. Creative music or music that is newly composed or improvised can influence change by challenging habitual thought patterns. Change provokes further thought and dialogue. Thought and change of habit and dialogue brings resistance to outmoded social institutions. Thus creative music is often disparaged by threatened conservative interests.

The most positive function of music at this time could be for healing separations that cloud the spirit of humanity. For that reason alone, the creative input of women who are the traditional healers (like the ones burned at the stake in the 1600s) is more than ever needed. The participation of women in music throughout the history of world cultures has always been to assist rites of passage including birth, coming of age, marriage, and death. Women's role as respected keeper of these rites has been suppressed in favor of art music composed by men. The original function of art music was to entertain and aggrandize the aristocracy in countries such as Austria, Italy and others. How does art music function in our society today? What is it's value and to whom? How could art music composed by both women and men function in new ways?

Changing a paradigm is a rite of passage. The paradigm of exclusion will not change without the energy and participation of women—whether the composition of and participation in art music or any other kind of music. Women must really assume responsibility and take charge of this change. Our Western culture is suffering from the lack of spirit from music traditionally provided by women. It is not enough for women to buy into art music—no matter how attractive it is—and only become accomplished in the techniques and forms created and taught by men. The musical heroine of the new millennium must discover her own inner voice and seek out her own path in music. She must avoid participating in the competitive and cutthroat careerism that often goes with her field. She must answer the call of the lost music of women across the ages. Out of the united inner voices of many women will come the music of the millennium—the music that we need to find balance and harmonious relationships in our society. To achieve balance and harmony, it will be necessary to gather together, learn and promote high-level teamwork and strategy, network with each other, support each other and move toward healing the separation that so blatantly continues to exist—the separation of women from each other, from men and from the creative process and power of music. Creativity is a birth right for all human beings.

Women of many world cultures other than Western culture have created music from the earliest known times. Women were treated with respect as priestesses—keepers of rites and the makers of music for such rites. Women were most likely the first musicians singing lullabies to infants and wailing in grief for loved ones. Although some women composers through the centuries have found their voices, such as Hildegard of Bingen (a 900 year anniversary celebration of Hildegard is now under way), women of Western culture have particularly been discouraged from composing art music. Women's works have been disrespected, disparaged, suppressed or forgotten and excluded from performances and publication. With the destruction of Sappho's work, women were denied a model composer at the dawn of Western culture.

Two thousand years have elapsed since Paul's edict in the Bible proclaiming that women were to keep silent in the church. By extension, women were also to keep silent in all public institutions of the patriarchy. Women's silence has since been cruelly enforced by genocide, witch burning, and other murders; physical abuse such as rape, whippings, beatings, clitoridectomy and foot binding; psychological harassment such as ridicule, assignment to demeaning tasks, servile positions, poverty, denial of education and ownership of property, treatment as chattel, slavery and above all, denial of equality and freedom of choice. The residue in the collective mind of women from such treatment and the de facto continuance of physical and psychological abuse to this day is certainly a considerable force in women's fear to speak up and take charge of their lives and creativity. Though the intellectual paradigm concerning the freedom of women to participate actively in public life and music has changed and taken a more positive direction in our time, the fear remaining in the collective unconscious of women must be addressed and healed in order for real change at the emotional and psychological level to take place in our culture.

From the 18th century to this day, aristocratic iconography and patriarchal semiotics has deeply informed the creation and perception of Western art music. The composition of art music has been the exclusive territory of men. Until recent times, women have hesitated or feared to claim the title of "composer" for themselves even if they were creating music. The whole system of patronage for the composition, performance, publication and dissemination of music grew out of the first Viennese school. Women were excluded from this school. A male musical ghetto of "great" men was established. Though the audience was extended to the bourgeoisie, the second Viennese school continued the exclusion. Women were assigned to the "support group" of patronage and adoration. Contemporary male attitudes toward women have reinforced the dominance of Paul's edict. For example, here is a quotation from composer Alban Berg in a letter to Arnold Schoenberg concerning Alma Mahler—composer, widow of Gustav Mahler and principal collector for the Schoenberg fund:

> *"---I beg you dear Herr Schoenberg, not to take Frau Mahler's action too seriously. At bottom she knows—as far as a woman can comprehend it at all—who you are and she surely desires that these differences be cleared away. It's nothing but capriciousness, born of the moodiness of a woman used to dispensing favor and disfavor according to momentary caprice and whim. For love to turn to hate and*

hate to love, creatures like that need no greater reason than we need to decide between a light and dark tie. Maybe that is what Weinerger calls the amorality of woman. That would also explain everything else: the playful, unscrupulous ability of one and the same creature to adapt herself to the morality of a Mahler and the immorality of a Karpath ---"

The Berg-Schoenberg Correspondence[1]

None of the letters in *The Berg-Schoenberg Correspondence* reveal that Alma Mahler was also a composer. Kept in the shadow of her famous husband, the many references in the letters, including Berg's disrespectful comments about her and women in general, are all about Alma Mahler's role as principal supporter of the patronage of Arnold Schoenberg. Women were expected to take such roles and at times forced to do so by their circumstances and the importuning of men such as Berg.

Few women have managed to break their silence as composers without suffering ridicule, harassment, and lack of support. It takes continual effort to overcome the societal obstacles faced by women and indeed all excluded groups. As composers, our situation has only slightly improved in our time. It will be necessary to have festivals such as Frau Musica (nova) and much more to show the strength and vitality of women contributing to the creation of music. Women need to gather together to make music, to celebrate each other's work, to make strategies for change in their relationship to music, and to help each other heal the remaining fears left over from two thousand years of abuse. It will be necessary to continue to do this until women are completely integrated into the field of music at all levels.

The business of music has not changed enough and now it must change much more rapidly if we are to enjoy the fruits of our struggle in our lifetime. Despite the Women's Movement and the Civil Rights Movement, the male ghetto still prevails in music and is supported by the existing infrastructure of agents, managers, presenters, publishers, producers and patronage. Programs of art music still consist mainly of white male composers. The media rarely publishes features in support of women composers. Women's music is not a part of any standard repertoire for established musical organizations. Music educators rarely include materials about women composers in their writings and teaching, performers do not include women's music in their repertoire, nor do they teach their students with music written by women. There are exceptions, of course, such as the many musicologists who have adopted a feminist platform for their work. Those who work with enlightened attitudes concerning women in music must be recognized, noted and emulated.

Change is needed at the grass roots, fundamental level—in teaching, performing, creating, theorizing, historicizing and journalizing about music. Nothing less than a complete change in the field of music as a whole is necessary for equanimous representation. Women must overcome fears, find their voices, and break the silence imposed and sustained from the time of Paul's edict. They must find the strength, will, and compassion to help each other join together to organize changes to the whole field of music. Music can not go on as a lopsided affair belonging only to men. As music changes, so will the world as we know it. We need a balanced society with equal representation for both women and men and support for all composers and musicians.

* * *

Recommendations for how you can help to break the silence and change the paradigm of exclusiveness in music:

If you are a performer, always play music by women on your programs as well as music by men. Make your repertoire list available to others and teach your students to play music by women. Complain if contest repertoire does not include music written by women.

If you are a private music teacher, be sure that you have teaching materials written by women. The collective power of private music teachers is enormous.

If you are a professor, include women composers in your research and request your libraries to order publications of music by women. Include women's works in your theoretical analyses and writings.

If you are a journalist, write about the music of women. Keep a list of women who create music in your community or city. Find a way to publish the list or put it on the internet and link it to other such sites.

If you are a musicologist, rewrite music history to include women. Devote your research to women in music.

If you are an interested listener, by all means listen to music by women. Write letters to the musical organizations that you patronize requesting that they commission and perform music by women.

If you are a patron, commission works by women.

If you are a composer, give priority to community building over career building. Find ways to collaborate, serve the field and make it good for your colleagues as well as yourself. Question your relationship to the form of music you are writing. Are you listening to your own inner voice and answering it's call? Are you expressing what you need to express or what you have been taught to express by the canon of men's musical establishment? Of what value is the technique and form you have learned to the expression of what you feel and hear as your own voice in music? How would you like for your music to function in your community? In the world?

All could join the International Alliance for Women in Music to receive current information on all aspects of women in relationship with music, news of performances, composition and musicology, and for participation in initiatives to promote more performances and creation of music by women. http://www.iawm.org/

AURALIZING IN THE SONOSPHERE: VOCABULARY FOR INNER SOUND AND SOUNDING

From *Journal of Visual Culture*,
Vol. 11 No. 2

The Sonosphere is the sonorous or sonic envelope of the earth. The Biospheric layer of the Sonosphere is irrevocably interwoven with the Technosherical layer of the Sonosphere.

Humans sense the Sonosphere according to the bandwidth and resonant frequencies and mechanics of the ear, skin, bones, meridians, fluids and other organs and tissues of the body as coupled to the earth and its layers from the core to the magnetic fields as transmitted and perceived by the audio cortex and nervous system. (All of this with great variation of course) All cells of the earth and body vibrate.

The visual is favored over the aural in our culture. Thus we have fewer words in our vocabulary to express aurality. *Auralization* is a term coined by architect Mendel Kleiner for simulating the acoustics of rooms and buildings. This term is also apt for referring to inner sound and sounding, or sounds and sounding perceived subjectively through inner listening. Generally the word imagination is used with reference to all senses. Image of course is a visual term. So there is a cognitive dissonance when using "imagination" to refer to hearing or creating inner sound – for example a phrase of a new piece of music. This article introduces some vocabulary for discussing sound including the concept of the *sonosphere.*

I conceive of the *sonosphere* as beginning at the core of the earth and radiating in ever increasing fractal connections vibrating sonically through and encircling the earth. The *sonosphere* includes all sounds that can be perceived by humans, animals, birds, plants, trees and machines. Human ears are limited to approximately 20 Hz to 20 khz. However this range can be exceeded by some individuals and extended with the aid of technology.

Just as we can look out into the universe far beyond our seeing eyes with the aid of telescopes and into the micro world with microscopes we can listen far beyond and below the human range of hearing with microphones. We are of course protected from constantly hearing and perceiving the sounds of our body such as the sound of cells dividing, of blood flowing or neurons firing etc. However we can tune into these sounds voluntarily with the aid of technology.

Why would one want to listen to sounds beyond our human range? Or sounds below our threshold of hearing? Curiosity could be the answer and also for the possibility of expanding perception of the sonorous body that we inhabit. Perhaps new data could be collected for artistic purposes and for scientific and medical purposes as well. For example I ask musicians to auralize the sound of cells dividing as a sonic metaphor in the score to *Primordial Lift*. It could be helpful though to actually be able to hear the real sound as an example.

We live in a sonorous environment. Most of the time we shut out sound that is extraneous to our current purposes. It takes energy to ignore sounds. Our ears respond to sound involuntarily. It is the brain that processes sound to extrapolate meaning and take action.

I have faith in listening. Listening brings me to faith – faith that I can believe my ears as much as I can believe my eyes. Sound impacts my body and resonates within. Sounds keep returning to me as I listen. Our vocabulary limits discussing inner or mental sound and sounding or listening in dreams and day dreams. We need words that highlight the auditory cortex.

My appropriation of Kleiner's word auralization then can be used to refer to mentally modeling sound by remembering or by creating sound.. We need to know that this is possible in dreams as well as daily life. We can project sound in space or the sounding of a composition. We can auralize an improvisation. We can auralize a score without sounding a note outwardly. The body can and does resonate with such auralizations.

We need more words to access the richness of auditory phenomema and to express the meaning of sound and sounding. Here is a rudimentary list to add to our vocabulary so that instead of speaking of sound and sounding in visual terms we speak in auditory terms.

audiate	*phonascetics*	*reverberating*
audile	*phonate*	*reverberative*
auditive	*phonation*	*ring*
aural	*phonautograph*	*silence*
auralization	*phone*	*silentious*
aurality	*phonetic*	*silently*
call	*phonic*	*silentness*
call up	*phonics*	*silents*
dissonance	*phonogram*	*sonic*
echo	*phonogramic*	*soniferous*
inaudible	*phonographic*	*sonogram*
inaudibility	*phonon*	*sonor*
knell	*racket*	*sornorous*
noise	*randomness*	*sonosphere*
noiseless	*recall*	*stochasticity*
noiselessly	*resonant*	*subsonic*
noiselessness	*resonating*	*supersonic*
peal	*resound*	*telephone*
phon	*resounding*	*transonic*
phonal	*reverberate*	*unhearable*

There are more words to be discovered or invented and added to our vocabulary.

You might begin to notice how your attention changes when you use auditory terms instead of visual terms to speak about sound. Your dreams may become richer and soniferous. Your environment might come alive with sounds formerly unnoticed. The ear tells the eye where to look and the eye sometimes silences the ear.

Primordial/Lift

Pauline Oliveros
March 5, 1998

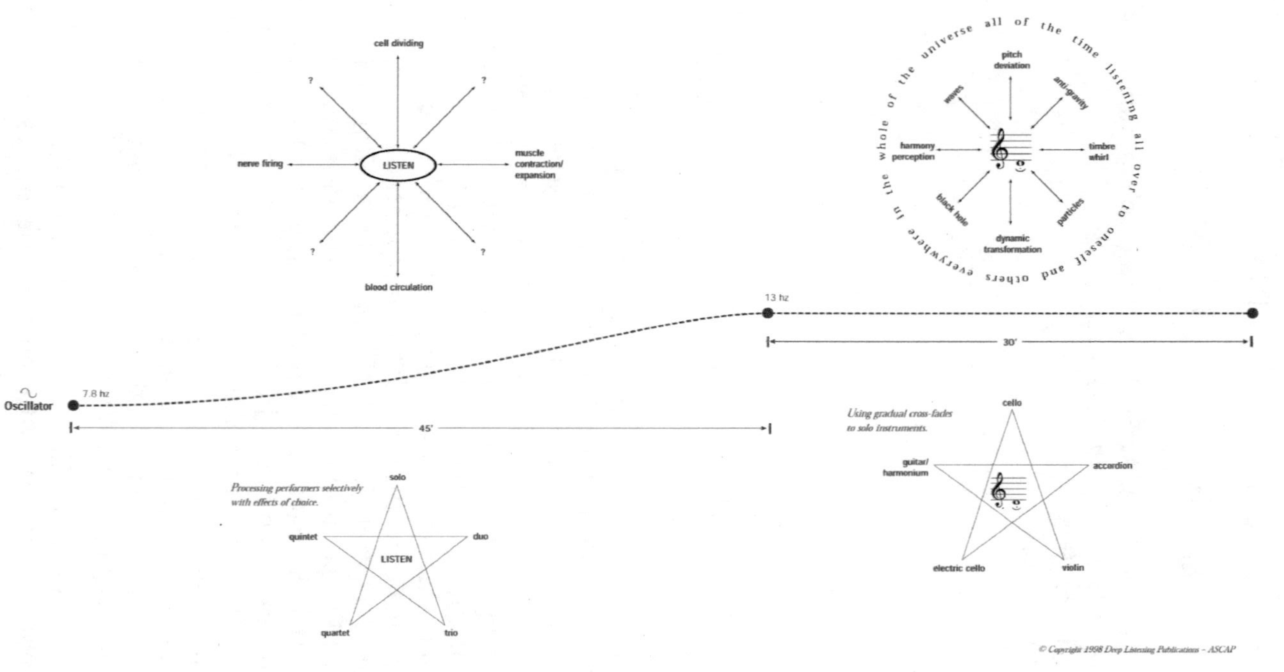

Deep Listening: Bridge to Collaboration

Keynote address, ArtSci98: Seeding Collaboration
Cooper Union, New York City
April 4-5, 1998
www.asci.org

Throughout the 45-year history of my professional career as a composer/performer, I have had the pleasure of many diverse collaborations with a wide range of artists, technologists, and scientists. Some of the highlights of my collaborations include evening-length works in dance with choreographers Merce Cunningham for *Canfield,* Deborah Hay for *Tasting the Blaze,* Susan Marshall for *Contenders,* and Paula Josa-Jones for *Ghostdance;* in theater with playwright/directors Lee Breuer for *Lear* and Carole Ione for *Njinga the Queen King;* with performance artist Linda Montano for *Living Arts;* with composer/performers Stuart Dempster and David Gamper for Deep Listening Band; with audio engineer Bob Bielecki for numerous sound design projects; with ham radio operator Dave Olean for *Echoes From the Moon* (where sound was sent to the moon on a radio frequency wave); and—more to the point of this conference—a ten-year study of attention with theoretical physicist and martial artist Dr. Lester Ingber from 1971-1981.

What is collaboration? For me, collaboration is joining or combining forces with another or others in interactions to produce work. A collaboration is a community of effort—preferably an equality of effort. Listening to one another in mutual respect is central to collaboration. Differences in the resources of collaborators are essential to the product. Each of us is the product of two human collaborators whose differences joined and combined in order to bring us into the world as new individuals. With listening and mutual respect, becoming parents is probably one of the most rewarding of collaborations.

I have been connected through my collaborations with hundreds of artists from many parts of the world. I so enjoy the nature and challenge of collaborations that I am in the midst of a ten-year program of collaborations. Beginning in 1991, as a celebration of my forty years of composing, I invited friends in six different cities where I had lived and worked to present something of their own via video telephone to help me celebrate. Each group in each city was connected by a telephone bridge and could see and hear one another through this early form of slow-scan distance technology. There was curator for each venue with a video telephone who oversaw a twenty-minute broadcast from each city followed by a six-city improvisation with all of the artists who wanted to participate. The three-hour celebration was organized by Joe Catalano and documented by his article "Electronic Midwifery" in Leonardo Music Journal[1]. In 2001, I expect to do another celebration—this time, for 50 years of composing. I am looking forward to collaborators from four continents via satellite communications with full spectrum-audio and video.

Collaboration with technologists has been a part of my work throughout my career. I have witnessed 45 years of sweeping, accelerating advances in the recording and computing technology used for music making. What we take for granted today in terms of recording and editing was relatively impossible at the beginning of my career. I am enormously grateful for the opportunities I have had to engage with new technologies and with the developing technologies of the future, such as the possibilities now opening to collaborate with other artists in different locations through the internet and internet broadcast.

As a composer, I have always been fascinated by whatever I hear. I am drawn to listening and have cultivated listening as a practice. My mother gave me an important tool in support of my interest in listening as a birthday gift in 1953: a tape recorder. It was one of the first consumer models to be made available on the home market. For musicians, the tape recorder has provided immediate rehearsal feedback as well as documentation of performances. The quicker the feedback, the faster the learning. Because of this, we are enjoying an unprecedented and phenomenal generation of musicians who have benefited from recording technology. Today's first-rate musicians can play almost anything in numerous different styles beautifully, with skills almost unimaginable 50 years ago. I admire the extended musical abilities that have been fostered by the use of tape recorders. Dancers have received similar benefits from video recording.

Shortly after receiving my gift in 1953, I placed the microphone of the recorder in the window of my San Francisco apartment and recorded the sound environment. Little did I realize the extent of the impact that this simple act would have on me. Although I thought that I was listening while recording, I was surprised to find sounds on the tape that I had not heard consciously. With this discovery, I gave myself a meditation: "Listen to everything all the time and remind yourself when you are not listening". Forty-five years later, I am still doing this meditation as the core of a practice that I call Deep Listening. Sustained listening is quite a task. Though hearing (if ears are healthy) is a continuous physical phenomenon and happens involuntarily when sound waves enter the ears, listening is intermittent and has to be cultivated voluntarily in its many forms. Surprisingly, many unenlightened musicians are hearing but not necessarily listening when they perform or compose. Listening is processing what we hear, for meaning, understanding, and direction or action.

Noticing the intermittent nature of listening through my own practice, I was increasingly drawn to encourage and promote listening for performers and students through my composing and teaching. Listening is rarely explored or taught even in music schools. Reading and writing skills seem to receive more emphasis by educators than listening skills, even though listening is equally important (and may indeed be more essential) for learning in all disciplines as well as music. I began to rely on listening in order to make music rather than on reading and writing. I gradually released the need to control pitch and rhythm through conventional notation in favor of the freedom to sculpt sound in time. Notation was no longer important to me when I began working on tape with electronic sound in the late 50's. Parallel to this development was my work in solo and group improvisation. Group improvisation was collaboration with a few like-minded colleagues. Our concerts of electronic music were liberally laced with free group improvisations—unheard of in concert music at the time. At the same time, Ornette Coleman and Cecil Taylor were similarly breaking free of charts and forms in jazz.

Today, we have a large, worldwide interest among musicians in freely improvised music. Boundaries between categories like jazz or classical music are dissolving. Musicians, with their phenomenal skills, are listening to one another and making music together as never before by creating new sound-oriented languages. In this way, musicians of different cultural backgrounds can play together.

In 1970, I began a body of work called *Sonic Meditation. Sonic Meditations* are recipes for ways of listening and sounding and are scores transmitted orally without conventional musical notation. I found that I could involve all kinds of people in Sonic Meditations whether or not they had any musical training. What mattered was an interest in participation, the cultivation of listening strategies, and willingness to explore sound. At the time, I was teaching composition and experimental studies in the music department of the University of California at San Diego. My *Sonic Meditations* flew in the face of traditional harmony and counterpoint and also of the complex notated scores of contemporary music.

My interests turned to the field of consciousness and the study of attention. Listening involves the direction of attention. There are two modes of attention: 1) focal attention, which corresponds to an all-or-nothing state—attention to one point and nothing else and 2) global attention, which corresponds to an open receptive state—attention expanded to a field. Focal attention is sharp and clear. Global attention is warm and fuzzy. The two modes work together as expansion and contraction.

I met the theoretical physicist and martial artist Dr. Lester Ingber at a conference on consciousness at UCSD. I recognized in a talk he gave on attention elements that supported my work. He was trying to describe human attention as a theoretical physicist. I was trying to describe listening as a composer/musician. Though our respective languages were vastly different, we managed (through listening to each other) to collaborate by sharing our discoveries for the next ten years. I created more and more *Sonic Meditations* and Lester described attentional processes with complex mathematical calculations. Lester was also a 5th Dan Karate master as well. I studied with him for 8 years and achieved the degree of black belt. My karate training with Lester was the key discipline that helped me to understand my own *Sonic Meditations* and the basics of listening.

In 1973, at the new Center for Music Experiment and Related Research at UCSD, I conducted an experiment with my *Sonic Meditations* with twenty people for four hours a day for nine weeks. I invited guests (including Dr. Ingber) to explore meditation, relaxation, and body disciplines and to perform *Sonic Meditations*. It was clear to me that listening was locked up by more exclusive attention to reading and writing. As simple as the instructions for *Sonic Meditations* are, it seemed necessary to do relaxation exercises as a bridge for the participants to feel free enough to participate. After engagement with sound-making, most people felt a deeper sense of relaxation and well being. Brain wave measurements and imaginal tests by a clinical psychologist at the beginning and end of the experiment supported the effects that *Sonic Meditations* seemed to have.

In the twenty-eight years that have passed since the beginning of my listening work, *Sonic Meditations* have been performed in many parts of the world and musicologists are writing about them with keen understanding. This is very satisfying to me. I feel that I have been heard—that some people are listening.

I resigned my professorship in 1981, moved to upstate New York, and founded my own non-profit arts organization, the Pauline Oliveros Foundation: Anchor for the Arts. The Pauline Oliveros Foundation is intended to promote the creation of new works and collaborations. It is a platform to continue my Deep Listening work. Deep Listening Band is a project of Pauline Oliveros Foundation. Deep Listening Band celebrates a decade of collaborative work this year—ten years after recording the album *Deep Listening* which is accompanying my talk. The recording was made in an abandoned cistern in Washington state. The reverberation time is forty-five seconds. This summer, I will lead the Eighth Annual Deep Listening Retreat at Rose Mountain in the Sangre de Cristo Mountains in New Mexico. Each summer, twenty people come together for a weeklong intensive devoted to listening as the bridge to creativity and collaboration. There is also an advanced retreat, a three-year certificate program which qualifies the certificate holder to teach Deep Listening workshops, and a five-year apprenticeship program which leads to qualification to lead a Deep Listening Retreat. These programs are intended to help the participants integrate Deep Listening with their own creative interests and professions.

In order to invoke the keynote and to end my talk, I would like to invite you now to try a *Sonic Meditation* called "Sounds from Childhood". This will be its third performance and the New York premiere of the piece.

Sounds from Childhood

Can you imagine a time in your childhood when you loved to make mouth noises?

Can you imagine freely making those sounds now?

In the next five or more minutes, make as many of those sounds as you want in spaces you hear and claim as your own.

A PERFORMER-CONTROLLED LIVE SOUND PROCESSING SYSTEM: NEW DEVELOPMENTS AND IMPLEMENTATIONS OF THE EXPANDED INSTRUMENT SYSTEM

By David Gamper with Pauline Oliveros
From *Leonardo Music Journal,* Volume 8
1998

Introduction

The Expanded Instrument System (EIS)[1] is a performer-controlled delay-based network of digital sound processing devices designed to be an improvising environment for acoustic musicians[2]. In its current configuration, each performer has appropriate microphones, a computer[3], and a collection of sound processing electronic devices[4]. Foot switches and "expression"-type foot pedals are interpreted by the computer to control the signal routing from the microphones among the sound processors, as well as control certain functions of the processors themselves. [Fig. 1] Each of these set-ups is referred to as an EIS station. [Fig. 2] Sound outputs from each station are distributed to speakers encircling the performance and audience space. On the computer's screen, the performer sees a display of the available functions to be controlled and their current state. [Fig. 3] This is critical, because many of these functions are actually controlled by a single foot pedal, which is switched to control the desired function. This "multi-function pedal" keeps the number of pedals confronting the performer to a minimum. There is also a separate function which allows the performer to store and recall sets of function settings. Although the labels for the functions are necessarily cryptic due to screen size limitations combined with readability constraints, they have proved to be readily decoded with a little practice. During performance, most functions are usually controlled by foot pedals and a foot switchboard[5].

The Expanded Instrument System emerged out of Pauline Oliveros' solo performance and composition work with tape and digital delays beginning in the late fifties[6]. One of her interests in developing the EIS was the effect of multiple delays on tone quality, observing that as the delays pile up, a virtual acoustic space is created that colors the sound of the instrument differently. Adding other processing to these delayed instrumental sounds, such as reverberation and other kinds of ambience effects, further transforms the performance space. The experience of improvising into the EIS is difficult to describe, but is certainly immersive and can be musically stimulating. Although this is inherent in playing into any long audio delay (the seduction of accompanying oneself is undeniable), the transformations possible with the more extensive sound processing of the EIS seem particularly fascinating to many. The EIS grew to accommodate additional performers and I was one such performer.

Oliveros was one of my composition teachers and my Master's thesis advisor at the University of California, San Diego in the early 70's. At that time, I also participated in her Meditation Project, an exploration of meditation technique in relation to music and musicians[7], which she integrated into her series of *Sonic Meditations* and the development of Deep Listening[8]. I had also been working with delays since getting my first tape recorder in the sixties. A natural partnership was formed when I began working with Oliveros again in 1989 and joined her Deep Listening Band performing on piano and winds the following year. At that time, all the sound processing in the EIS was centralized and manually controlled by two performers, vocalist Panaiotis and I, with the other performers (Oliveros, Stuart Dempster on trombone and didjeridu, and any guest musicians) having only limited control of their primary delays. The other performers sometimes wished they could change parameters or keep them the same when Panaiotis or I changed them. On the other hand, our mixing and routing duties meant that Panaiotis and I were sometimes not able to sound when we wanted. Although we experimented with various forms of distributed computer control, none proved usable in performance.

When Panaiotis left the group in 1993, it was evident that I could not operate the system alone. This immediate need to distribute control to the other performers drove me to conceive a configuration I could implement relatively quickly while using inexpensive stock MIDI equipment. The solution proved worthwhile to Deep Listening Band and adaptable to many other combinations of performers. Since then, I have extended the EIS to provide for guest musicians with limited learning time, adapted it to various compositional requirements, and have helped numerous composers and musicians explore it during extended installations and demonstrations.

Roots of Recent Technical Developments

My experience performing with Oliveros and others using the Expanded Instrument System has increased my understanding of how the requirements of performer control of a sound processing environment for improvising musicians differ from those of more strictly compositionally deterministic systems, even though the technologies may be very similar and improvisation may play a part. The most obvious difference is in wanting to be able to do anything possible at any possible time, although practical and aesthetic considerations tend to limit the range of possibilities. Improvising with variable delays and changing ambiance requires intense listening with minimal distractions of technical requirements. Having extensive choices when using the technology involved requires a clear, easily learned user interface. Since most instrumentalists' hands are fully occupied with their instruments, their feet often end up as the most precise and expressive means of independently operating controllers. These controller devices need to be kept to a minimum in spite of proliferating numbers of parameters to control. Scarcity of financial resources encourages use of existing inexpensive mass produced equipment, with customized devices added only when commercial markets do not provide solutions for coveted features. Since it is unlikely that a performer has continuous practice time on the EIS, it is important to only gradually add functions to be controlled in order not to confuse regular users with a frequently changing interface and configuration.

The Lexicon PCM 42 remains the primary delay of the Expanded Instrument System because it provides the warmest replay of acoustic sound of any processor that we know. It also features a voltage-controlled clock oscillator which allows a foot pedal to sweep the effective delay time over a three to one ratio of delay times of up to nine seconds. Since the advent of fixed sampling frequencies needed for digital input and output, this combination of smooth changes of delay time and related pitch bending has been designed out of digital delays of equivalent sound quality. Until another instrument achieves these features, the PCM 42 will remain our delay of choice. This also means that we are firmly planted in the analog signal domain and must make extensive use of analog signal routing[9].

With the addition of a Reson8 digital signal multi-processor computer, which runs a program designed to emulate some of the effects of the PCM 42, we were able to achieve computer control of modulation functions suggested by the manual controls on the PCM 42. Although we quickly discovered that the sound quality suffered somewhat, particularly with smooth modulations, there were other features which compensated. One is the ability to program complex and/or precise modulations not possible with the PCM 42.

In the previous configuration[10], modulation of the read/write speed of one of the delays was controlled through two functions: one a combination wave shape and depth; the other the speed of modulation. As with the use of the foot pedal on the PCM 42, this has the effect of modulating the pitch of whatever sound is being delayed. It soon becomes evident that leaving the depth and/or speed parameters unvaried often becomes very static musically. The modulation is more interesting when a more complex modulation function incorporating random variations is substituted. To implement this I programmed various modulation algorithms in which one chooses the algorithm (LMtype in Fig. 3) and then varies some aspect of it (LMctrl). The precision of control in the Reson8 program allowed me to use just tuning intervals in two types of step wise modulation functions. Because the algorithm "patches" are modular, I can easily modify or replace them. One algorithm (named LightningBox) is actually an editable (though not in performance) sequence of the other algorithms[11].

Previous experiments to bring computer control to the vintage PCM 42 delay meant giving up the direct analog foot pedal control, a form of control for which Oliveros in particular has developed a considerable technique. Recently I have designed, and Bob Bielecki has engineered an interface which may successfully implement this computer control. This interface, nicknamed the BGBox, is a hybrid digital and analog system using MIDI for convenient computer control, but retaining the smooth foot pedal control which is so much a part of the PCM 42's use as the heart of the EIS. Although the number of functions to control is greatly increased, I added a function for switching to additional multi-function pedal screens (the "Switch" function in Fig. 3) to keep the proliferation in check. Extending hands-free functional control to the PCM 42's has also enabled me to design simplified installations without the more cumbersome Reson8 while not giving up all of its advantages.

I have been circling the issue of "smooth analog control" for much of this section and perhaps now is the place to make a few additional observations. To date, Oliveros' and my experiences of attempts to duplicate the effect of a foot pedal plugged directly into a PCM 42 have not been satisfactory. I suspect that the digital domain has just not been fast enough to be smooth. The technical compromises needed to satisfy one of the subjective impressions of "smooth" or "fast" have meant that the other is degraded too much. Oliveros and I have also not had the resources to develop state of the art custom analog-to-digital controller conversion usable to our particular hardware configuration[12]. But our optimism is intact and further discussion and information would be welcome.

There are other areas of investigation that I hope will be incorporated in the near future, resources permitting. Foot pedals and switches as performance controllers for instrumentalists can surely be improved upon. I have experimented with small modifications which add some switching capabilities to a stock foot pedal and Bielecki is investigating instrument mounted controllers to allow free fingers to be used when possible. The capabilities of the BGBox interface encourages development of allowing a performer to record and save sequences of controller movements for playback at a later time. It can take several hours to set up an EIS that has been packed up for transport, no doubt partly due to my continuous tinkering and unwillingness to settle on a single configuration. A plug it in and play system might be possible if the physical configuration can be improved. But the Expanded Instrument System is sure to continue to evolve and be adapted to its users needs, with more clarity in the user interface and transparency of the technology.

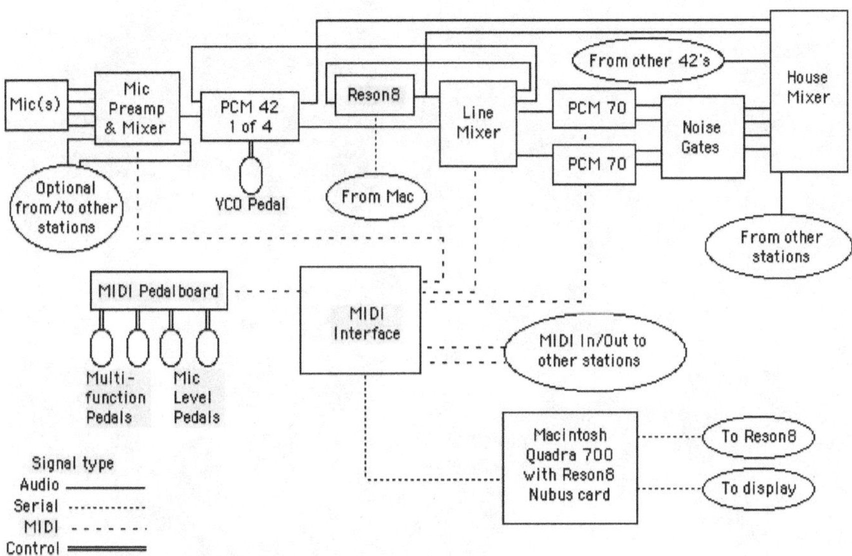

Figure 1—Block diagram of Oliveros' Expanded Instrument System station – others are similar conceptually. The PCM 42 is an analog-controlled digital delay from Lexicon. The PCM 70 is a MIDI-controlled digital effects processor, also from Lexicon. The Reson8 is an 8 processor digital signal processor computer, shared by all stations but programmed and controlled through a Nubus card in this station's Macintosh computer. The mic and line mixers are sections of a Mackie 1604 with OTTO MIDI control. In other stations, Niche ACM's (each a set of 8 MIDI-controlled resistors which can be mixed to stereo) are used. The MIDI pedal board is a Rolls MIDI Wizard footswitch board which also converts expression pedals to MIDI continuous controller data. The house mixer distributes outputs to speakers surrounding the audience.

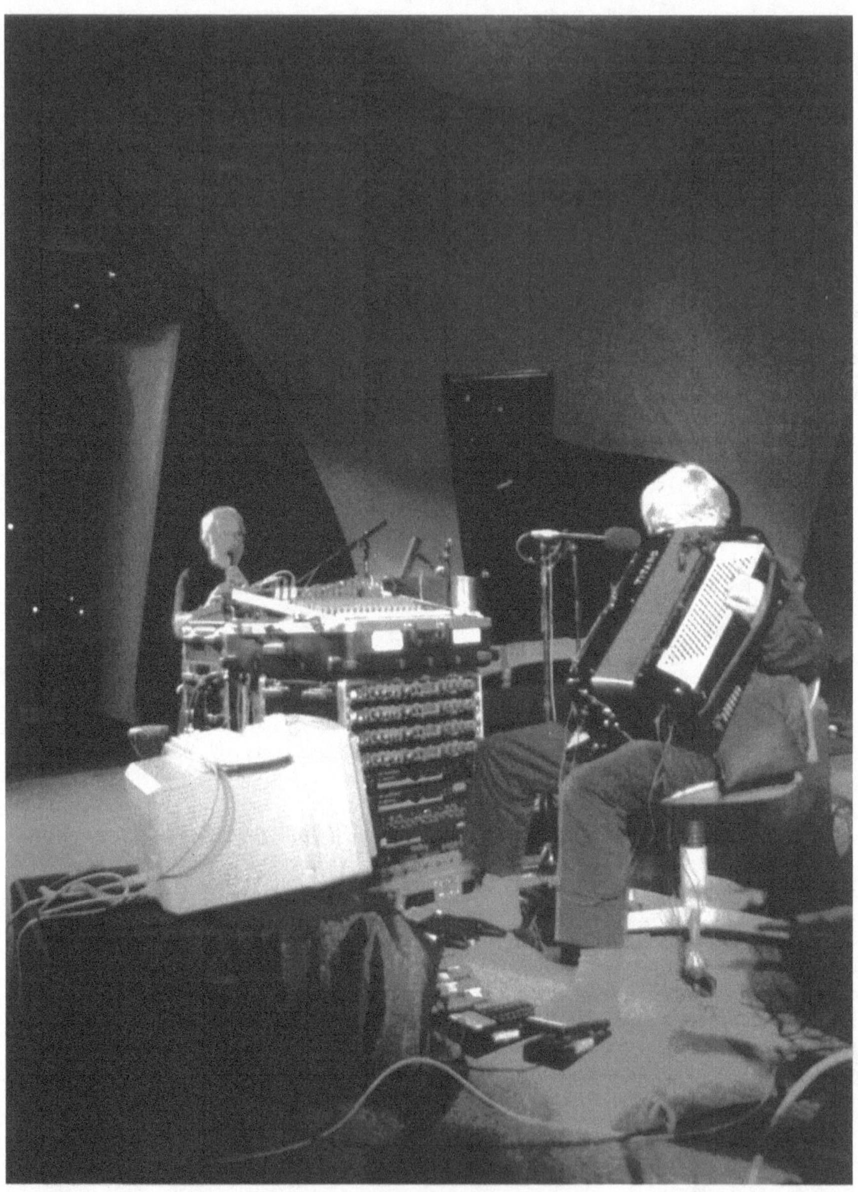

Figure 2—Deep Listening Band performing with the Expanded Instrument System at the Winter Garden of the World Financial Center in New York City. Oliveros is in the foreground with accordion with clip-on microphones and another mic for voice and small instruments. The equipment rack and automated mixer to her left and foot pedals, footswitch board and computer monitor in front of her, make up her EIS station. Gamper is to the rear with mic'ed piano and auxiliary mic fed to his own EIS station comprised of another equipment rack, mixer, and a laptop computer. (Photo: Gisela Gamper)

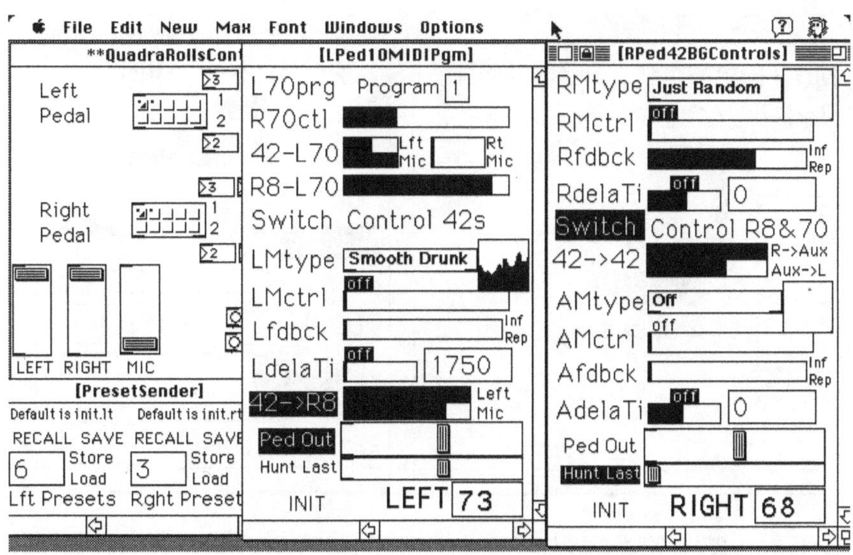

Figure 3—Computer screen read-out of a typical Expanded Instrument System user interface, programmed in Opcode's MAX. The upper left window includes readouts of the volume control pedals. The lower left window shows information about presets for the multifunction pedals displaying the last values of each function and the function being controlled.

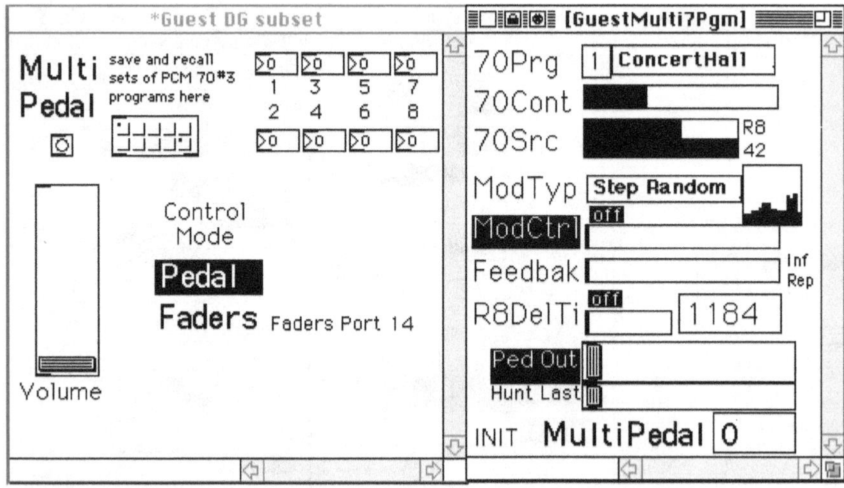

Figure 4—Computer screen read-out of typical simplified Expanded Instrument System guest station. Display and functions have been restricted to a single multifunction pedal (right window), but control of the functions can also be switched to a MIDI fader box for performers with a hand free.

Recent Uses in Performance

The core point of Oliveros' work is composing through listening and the Expanded Instrument System is one tool to enable that process. Pre-composition with the EIS is setting up a system that is responsive to instantaneous decisions which will be made while listening at the moment of performance. The resulting music (improvised composition) is not predetermined and could not be since it depends on what is heard and the ability of the composer/improviser to respond immediately. The EIS then serves as a fluid environment for the composer/performer.

Although I adhere to this form in performing with Oliveros and Deep Listening Band, in some of my other less improvisational music, the EIS allows me to quickly "breadboard" various configurations of sound processing which I then perform into[13]. My choices and decisions in this process of programming and configuring is also an important part of my work as a composer.

The current configuration of the Expanded Instrument System has proved to be flexible and extensible in a number of recent performances and recordings by Deep Listening Band (Oliveros, Stuart Dempster and myself). For each of the following, I was able to adapt the EIS with relatively small adjustments to the programming and patching.

In 1994, pieces by Ellen Fullman and Pauline Oliveros were commissioned for Deep Listening Band and Fullman's Long String Instrument installation[14]. Two week-long residencies allowed Fullman and I to experiment with adapting the EIS to her unique instrument. Fullman was especially taken by the ability to bend and sustain her tones. However, the mobility she needed to perform on her instrument made it impractical for her to operate an EIS station. I programmed my EIS station to allow her to use a subset of it limited to the functions she wanted to control. Her *TexasTravelTexture* combined the acoustically powerful Long String Instrument ensemble with Deep Listening Band with EIS and occasional EIS processing by Fullman. In contrast, Oliveros' *Epigraphs in the Time of AIDS* featured Deep Listening Band and Fullman as a quartet with EIS, with the other Long String Instrument players as a quiet underpinning.

On April 6, 1996 Deep Listening Band gave a three-site concert with Oliveros in Chicago, Dempster in Seattle, and me in New York linked over ISDN telephone lines by PictureTel audio and video via The Kitchen (New York, NY). Each remote performer had a small EIS station which could send MIDI through additional telephone lines to the station in New York, although unrelated technical problems precluded this at the time of the concert. The PictureTel technology introduces significant sound delays of its own. Although the delay based EIS processing was an appropriate match, the experiences of the audiences (and performers) at the three locations was interestingly different.

The number of discrete EIS stations is limited only by available equipment. Although each station can receive microphone inputs from other performers, guest musicians are often provided with a guest station simplified for the practice time available. [Fig. 4] One guest configuration I originally programmed for baritone Thomas Buckner, substitutes a set of faders for the volume control and multi-function foot pedals, allowing him to control these functions with his fingers. This configuration, which I further adapted to be able to switch between faders and pedals, was used during Oliveros' large, extended (four hours and thirty-three minutes) *Non Stop Flight* concert at Mills College on September 16, 1996[15]. Over the preceding week I had introduced a number of composer/performers to the guest station and each occupied it at various times during the course of the concert. I also programmed the system to send foot pedal data from all the stations to The Hub[16], who used it in their section of the concert. In addition, I added a third means of controlling the guest station, from the Hub itself, which could take over control of "EISing" their and other's sounds.

Another compositional approach was taken by Joe McPhee for his commissioned work *Unquenchable Fire* (1997)[17]. McPhee specifies that in certain sections, Deep Listening Band is to "EIS" the sounds of his quartet (two winds, 'cello and percussion) without themselves sounding. I distributed the microphones from each member of the Quartet to inputs of the Band's EIS stations and added a function to feed these signals into the EIS. Of course, this hearkens back to the earlier pre-1993 manifestation of centralized EIS control. The earlier compositions of Oliveros' *Pauline's Solo* and Gamper's *David's Solo* (both 1994), usually performed in succession, are a variation on this feature. Each piece features the named performer sounding and using their EIS station, with the other performer gradually adding additional processing through their own EIS station.

Recent Uses in Demonstration and Educational Settings

The Expanded Instrument System has proved itself in public demonstrations and in installations for study and exploration. When a musician, composer, or even a musically untutored child has the opportunity to experience the immersive sound processing of the EIS, it seem to lead many to new modes of listening and musical interaction. I'm sure this is a result of its long development and refinement as a working musical instrument, grounded in Oliveros' aesthetic, and with input from a wide variety of composer/musicians.

Where appropriate and logistically possible at a Deep Listening Band and other events where we are using the EIS, we sometimes have an "open mic" time before or after the concert. Children seem most interested and creative in publicly making sounds and hearing them transformed by one or more of the performers. The immediate feedback of hearing your own delayed sound all around you, whether further manipulated or not, can be exciting and enlightening. At one event, a jaw harpist filled the space with what developed into beautiful soulful music, far beyond idle noise making. At another, a child turned a spoken story into a drama with sound effects and music.

These "open mic" demonstrations are also opportunities to demystify the technological processes we are using in concert. We have always wanted performing with the EIS to be accessible to audiences as well as composers and musicians. There is no reason for this means of sound transformation to be obscure or esoteric. We try to keep the technology as transparent as possible and familiarity is one means to that end. The practice of Deep Listening Oliveros has developed (and for which the Band is named) is inclusive and melds the performer with both the performance environment and the audience as fellow listeners. To the extent that the audience becomes familiar with the sometimes surprising sounds coming from the speakers all around them, they can move beyond the novelty and connect with the music.

In November, 1997, I installed the Expanded Instrument System at Mills College (Oakland, CA) where Oliveros was teaching for the semester. During a weekend "Composing a Career" conference, sponsored by the Bay Area Women's Philharmonic, I demonstrated the EIS to small groups of composers and in the week following worked with three advanced music classes and many individual students and local composers. Oliveros and I noted a number of interesting observations which coalesced during this residency, including the following three.

Although everyone needs some period of instruction, musicians with even no experience with sound processing technology have been able to learn to operate an EIS station. Once they reach some basic level of proficiency, we are fascinated with the varied ways they proceed to explore music making. Kurt Erickson, a composer/performer at Mills College wrote to us:

> *With some initial trepidation, I recently had the opportunity to work with the EIS and I must relate how quickly those intimidations vanished once I started working with it. The thing that surprised me the most about the system was its accessibility and opportunity for immediate artistic gratification. While I can claim no mastery of the system, I found myself achieving some very gratifying results within just minutes. In fact, some of the out-takes from my time on the system were later used as the basis for an electro-acoustic composition. To say that it made me rethink my approach to composition would not be an exaggeration.*[18]

A performer with the EIS is able to extend and expand musical materials. One can produce a lot of material from simple sound sources. A composer disclosed to me at the beginning of a session that due to a long illness he had not been able to practice any of his instruments for more than fifteen minutes. He had had previous limited experience with the EIS and wondered if it could function as a sort of prosthesis. I left him after the training period and returned an hour later to find him still playing. Fortunately, the appointment following his didn't appear and he could continue for another hour and a half. He seemed elated that he had been able to make music again for an extended time.

Another composer/performer, saxophonist John Ingle, wrote us:

I am a skeptic when it comes to electronic processing of the acoustic sound of my saxophone. While I am interested in electronic music, I have usually been disappointed in the sound quality when I have had my sound processed in a real-time performance situation. Because of my interest in resonance, the harmonic series, and difference tones, I was eager to test the Expanded Instrument System. As an avid improviser, I found the EIS to be full of immediately gratifying musical possibilities, all in the "moment at hand" rather than through preconceived structures. In improvising with delay units, one must immediately deal with the preceding moment, or musical gesture. This can be a great tool for ear training, playing with a linear rhythmic pulse, and concentration. I think the EIS can be a powerful pedagogical tool for people of diverse musical backgrounds, from children to professional musicians. Because of the open-ended nature of the system, different artists can naturally get widely diverse results. While I used it as a "partner" in improvisation, one could also develop highly sophisticated through-composed works for instrumentalists and the system.[19]

From Oliveros' and my experiences at this and other similar residencies, along with the development of the new BGBox PCM 42 MIDI interface, we have been prompted to implement a small permanent EIS installation at the new Studio at Deep Listening Space in Kingston, NY (owned by the Pauline Oliveros Foundation.) I am developing a self guided tutorial to introduce composers and performers to the various control functions and overall operation of the interface. I also plan improvements to the programming interface which would allow experienced users to experiment with designing their own modulation algorithms and modulation sequences which could be applied to appropriate control parameters. Many have expressed interest in such a facility, and we expect a wide variety of compositions and performances will come from it.

QUANTUM IMPROVISATION: THE CYBERNETIC PRESENCE

Keynote address given at Improvisation Across Borders
University of California, San Diego
April 11, 1999

Musicworks Issue #75, Fall 1999

Included in *Sound Unbound: Sampling Digital Music and Culture*
Paul D. Miller a.k.a. DJ Spooky that Subliminal Kid, ed., MIT
Press, 2008

Dedicated to the memory of
Robert Erickson who encouraged
us all to improvise.

"In a hundred years there may be no clear distinction between humans and computers. There will be enormous augmentation of human perceptual and cognitive abilities through neural implant technology. Humans who do not use such implants are unable to participate in meaningful dialogue with those who do—knowledge is understood instantaneously through assimilated knowledge protocols. The goal of education and intelligent beings is discovering new knowledge to learn."

Ray Kurzweil, from *The Age of Spiritual Machines: When Computers Exceed Human Intelligence*[1]

What would I want from a "musician chip" if I were to receive the benefit of neural implant technology? What kind of a 21st century musician could I be? Humans, with the aid of technology, already see and hear far beyond the capability of the unaided senses. It's not long, according to Kurzweil, when such aids will be available at the internal, bodily level as implants, just like personal computers or digital assistants—external aids—are now. All of us improvisers could have new input from this "musician chip", which would also create new challenges. I'll return to the question of my musician chip after looking back across history for some reminders and highlights:

In 1900, the Gramophone Company advertised a catalog of 5000 recordings. The previous year, in 1899, the first magnetic (as opposed to acoustic) recording was made on a wire and thin metal strip. This human desire to record—to replicate and preserve sounds—has grown since then, such that 52,000 CD titles were produced in 1998 alone!

Early jazz improvisation emerged after the Civil War and emancipation. Improvisation developed in parallel with radio broadcast and recording technology. It is thus not surprising that all styles and forms of improvisation have been empowered by recording. Recording is the memory and documentation of improvisation and testifies to an enormous creative effort by innumerable musicians. Musicianship for written forms of music has been empowered by recording as well.

The African aesthetic that melded with American and European dance music led to the birth of blues-influenced jazz in the 1920's. Ma Rainey and Bessie Smith mothered this music and rose to short-lived stardom as blues queens, migrating from the South to Northern metropolitan centers. Horn players of innumerable bands followed the lead of Ma Rainey, Bessie Smith, and other singers in a tremendous era of creativity and enterprise.

By 1930, 60% of all American households had radios. Improvised music spread through recordings and radio broadcasts. Music by Americans of African descent could be heard throughout the land and influenced all of American music. This enormous creativity was recognized and appropriated by the white entertainment establishment. The black-white exchange and interaction continued throughout the century and grew into the billion-dollar music industry which exists today.

In 1953, the first consumer model tape recorders were made available. This meant that musicians could record themselves at home or in their studios at any time. These recording devices are like "sound mirrors" and have caused musicianship to escalate with the aid of technology, such that today's musicians possess phenomenal performance skills in all styles of improvised or written music.

Since the 1970's, hip-hop has been a creative outlet for much of the world's youth culture. In the hip-hop medium, recordings are sources for improvisation. Rather than frozen historical objects, recordings become live material through DJ scratching and remixing.

The established American classical music institutions and conservatories tend to regard improvisation as a kind of "craft", subordinate to the more prestigious "art" of composition, even though it is well known that luminaries such as Mozart and Beethoven improvised regularly when they toured. Improvisation became a lost art and all but disappeared in American musical training establishments except among church organists or within occasional cadenzas in concertos.

The denial of the validity of improvisation has a racist tinge and origin. In America, in the first half of this century, improvisation grew mostly from jazz and blues—music from the heart of Americans of African descent—the disenfranchised people. After 1950, improvisation begins to appear in white avant-garde music through the influence of marginalized indeterminate or aleatoric procedures, jazz and blues, and recordings and live imports of non-Western music—disenfranchised music.

What's the purpose of creating music in performance without reference to memory or written form (a.k.a. improvisation)? The purpose varies according to the function of the music. One purpose is to enter into direct dialogue through sound with oneself and others. If the improvisation is creative, then new mental and physical patterns could be born—such as what happened with Ornette Coleman and Cecil Taylor when they broke from jazz traditions in the 50's and later Musica Electronica Viva and the San Francisco Tape Music Center, who broke free of classical music restrictions with improvisation. If the improvisation is historical such as replicating Charlie Parker, John Coltrane or the legacies of other great improvisers with no new elements, then the purpose is to affirm a tradition.

The improvising musician has to let go of each moment and also simultaneously understand the implications of any moment of the music in progress as it emerges into being. In historical improvisation, the course is charted or set by the conventions and codifications of the style —the Classicism of the music. In so-called "free improvisation" nothing is known about the music before it happens—this edge is the challenge for human and for machine intelligence. Unless the styles of the musicians improvising were already absorbed by the machine then what information would there be to calculate a response? If the outcome is known in advance it is not free improvisation, it is historical improvisation.

What does, in fact, happen when a creative musician makes new music? How can it be new or free? What is it free of? What could be new about it? What is happening with a solo improvising musician? a group? The soloist gives herself feedback and enters a dialogue with herself and musical space—the group stretches the possibilities for dialogue and new relationships come about creating a myriad of new possibilities even though the course of the music—new as it may be—will flow with ineluctable inevitability. The recorded legacies of innumerable musicians are waiting to answer these questions.

What would happen if a new musician chip were implanted in a human or a machine? All ranges would increased. Processing would be possible beyond known present human capabilities. What could be heard? Could a new musical paradigm include a new spatial domain? Moments of local sound—moments of moving sound with the ability to detect locations from light years away—defining new interdimensional spatiality? What would a spatial melody sound like—a pitch beginning on Saturn moving to Aldeberon to Sirius to Earth? Space related frequency and amplitude—multidimensional melody—color/space/sound melody. Who would be playing this tune? Who would be listening and where? Melody across space stretched out and also happening everywhere simultaneously. Space is the place—I hear you Sun Ra!

According to the article "Is Space Finite?" by Jean-Pierre Luminet, Glenn Starkman and Jeffery Weeks from the current issue of *Scientific American*:

"The universe may look infinitely large, but that could be an illusion. If space folds back on itself like the braids of a pretzel, it might be boundless, and light could spool around the cosmos endlessly.

The usual assumption is that the universe is, like a plane, simply connected, which means there is only one direct path for light to travel from a source to an observer. A simply connected

Euclidean or hyperbolic universe would indeed be infinite. But the universe might instead be multiply connected, like a torus, in which case there are many different such paths. An observer would see multiple images of each galaxy and could easily misinterpret them as distinct galaxies in an endless space, much as a visitor to a mirrored room has the illusion of seeing a huge crowd.[2]"

What if we could sound out, hear and perceive the shape of the universe by bouncing sound around the torus?

We don't have to be limited to the physical definitions of our perceptual ranges. What about imagination? Here is the challenge of the machine—the promise of hybrid human/machine forms through implants—the challenge of new beings with formidable powers of perception, memory, reasoning, and interpretation—non carbon-based beings created by humans to eventually replace humans. Are we creating new beings to replace humans or are we expanding our minds—making a quantum leap into the neural cortex to develop our own potential power?

In 1948, Norbert Weiner coined the word "cybernetics" meaning the science of control and communication in the animal and machine. The cybernetic presence is definitely with us. Kurzweil says in his time line, "10 years from now (2009) human musicians routinely jam with cybernetic musicians." This is a shallow statement because there is no revelation concerning style, complexity or form. In fact, many musicians are already improvising with machines programmed to respond to improvised input. Will Kurzweil's cybernetic musicians be self-determining in 10 years?

In 1977, the first desktop computers from Apple were made available. Musicians and hobbyists continued to work out programs to make and play music in their home studios—away from Bell Labs, Princeton, Stanford and other institutions for computer music research.

Improvisation also developed and merged with new forms of interaction made possible by machine intelligence. Computers expanded the reach of solo as well as group improvisers. The work of Laurie Spiegel, David Behrman, Warren Burt, Joel Chadabe, George Lewis, Elliott Sharp, Jim Tenney, Deep Listening Band, Chris Brown, The Hub and many others comes to mind.

By 1990, computer hard disc recording and editing became available. A powerful and revolutionary combination—the merging of recording and computing. What a wonderful tool for the creative musician!

"In twenty years, virtual musicians with their own reputations are emerging". We need to know what constitutes a musician. How will humans—with or without implants—compete or collaborate with the cybernetic presence? I don't feel comfortable with the notion of surgical implants. I hope that some non-invasive reversible form may be available.

"Thirty years from now direct neural pathways for high bandwidth connections to the human brain perfected. There will be a range of neural implants to enhance auditory and visual perception and interpretation, memory and reasoning". What would be enhanced? What and how would such powers be measured and valued and by whom? What about imagination? What kind of improvisation could and inevitably will result?

Music and especially improvised music is not a game of chess—improvisation (especially free improvisation) could definitely represent another challenge to machine intelligence. It is not the silicon linearity of intensive calculation that makes improvisation wonderful. It is the nonlinear carbon chaos, the unpredictable turns of chance permutation, the meatiness, the warmth, the simple, profound humanity of beings that brings presence and wonder to music.

In 1937 the Church-Turing Thesis stated that "All problems that humans can solve can be reduced to a set of algorithms, supporting the idea that machine intelligence and human intelligence are essentially equivalent".

In Star Date 2336 we find a machine intelligence—minus human emotions that evidently don't reduce to a set of algorithms—at work on the Star Ship Enterprise. *Star Trek's* android Lt. Commander Data is an idea of the future predicted by the Church-Turing Theory. Data solves problems and is a sentient life form with the same rights as other life forms. His ultimate storage capacity is 800 quadrillion bits and his total linear computation speed is 60 trillion operations per second. Data can remember every fact he is exposed to and can imitate voices so perfectly that he can even fool the computer of the Enterprise into thinking he is someone else. *Star Trek's* Data has performed as a classical musician on several episodes. His classical musician chip allows him to perform any music superbly, having absorbed all known styles and all available recorded interpretations of written music. The musician who learns to perform classic forms and idioms is a conservative who affirms and preserves tradition. All of known music could be listened to, absorbed, analyzed, and interpreted by machine intelligence and be contained on a chip.

The composer is an organizer who designs and formalizes music prior to performance through notation. Computers already aid a variety of composer's design calculations. Computers can engage in rule-based composition, calculate and realize musical forms.

Experiments in Musical Intelligence by David Cope[3] describes the basic principles of analysis, pattern matching, object orientation and natural language processing. This system makes it possible to generate new compositions in the styles of various composers, from Bach and Mozart to Prokofiev and Scott Joplin. The program SARA (Simple Analytic Recombinant Algorithm) produces new compositions in the style of the music in its database. Already audiences are hard put to tell what music is composed by a human and what is composed by a machine All known styles of composition could be contained on the composer chip. Data could certainly handle all known styles of composition and historical improvisation.

Improvisor is a computer program that creates original music, written by British jazz saxophonist Paul Hodgson. Improvisor can emulate styles ranging from Bach to jazz greats Louis Armstrong and Charlie Parker—historical improvisation. What about the improvising musician as an evolutionary? What would an improviser chip have to include for Data to engage in free improvisation? To boldly go where no musician has gone before sounding through dimensions of space—of time? Finding new sounds and new sound relationships?

Data could probably analyze all known instruments for instrument makers, all performance abilities for performers and all known musical forms for composers. The edge though is the unknown of imagination for performers, improvisers, composers and instrument makers and the unification of all these roles.

* * *

We have now looked one hundred years before and several hundred years ahead of this 1999 conference Improvisation Across Borders.

What would I want on my Musician Chip? What skills should the 21st-century musician have? What could she know? On my musician chip I would like:

- The ability to recognize and identify instantaneously any frequency or combination of frequencies in any tuning, timbre in any tempo or rhythm, in any style of music or sound in any space.
- The ability to produce any frequency or sound in any tuning, timing, timbre, dynamic and articulation within the limits of the selected instruments or voices used. Maybe I would also like to morph from any instrument to any other instrument or voice. at will.
- The ability to recognize, identify and remember any music— its parts as well as the whole no matter the complexity.
- The ability to perceive and comprehend interdimensional spatiality.
- The ability to understand the relational wisdom that comprehends the nature of musical energy—it's form, parts and underlying spirituality—as the music develops in performance.
- The ability to perceive and comprehend the spiritual connection and interdependence of all beings and all creation as the basis and privilege of music making.
- The ability to create community and healing through music making.
- The ability to sound and perceive the far reaches of the universe much as whales sound and perceive the vastness of the oceans. This could set the stage for interdimensional galactic improvisations with yet unknown beings.
- I suppose it would be great to be able to print it all out as well in 3D color.

Are improvisers conscious? Do they have self-perception, self-awareness—the ability to feel? What is conscious improvisation?

For that matter, what is unconscious improvisation? The body knows what to do even if the small mind does not comprehend. The body "dances" the music—the nerves fire and the mind notices slightly after it happens. Conscious improvisation involves strategy—responding strategically even if the outcome is unknown. A strategy of conscious improvisation might be "play only if you are listening" or "trust the body to respond." This melds the notion of conscious/unconscious improvisation.

The capability of the human mind is unplumbed. We have far more capacity than we currently use in the neural cortex waiting for evolutionary expansion. Computers may actually instruct us in this process as we continue to merge with the machine intelligence that we are creating and interacting with. We must decide, though, what a 50-year-old silicon structure is going to tell a five billion year old structure of carbon before making irreversible physical changes.

Quantum computing is a revolutionary method of computing based on quantum physics that uses the abilities of particles (such as electrons) to exist in more than one state at the same time. Quantum computation can operate simultaneously on a combination of seemingly incompatible inputs.

By analogy or metaphor, Quantum Improvisation could mean a leap into new and ambiguous consciousness, opening a new variety of choices. Ambiguous consciousness would mean the ability to perform in more than one mental state simultaneously in order to reach or bridge past and future as an expanding present. There could be new sound combinations anchored by increasing order even though choices might seem incompatible. Such a quantum leap could mean that more of the neural cortex, the seat of creativity and problem solving, could be utilized in music making. Quantum Improvisation could find new ways to express and understand the relationships between mind and matter.

Ordinarily we use only a relatively small percentage of the neural cortex—this reflects the style of most content-oriented education in institutions, which limits and suppresses, rather than encourages creative problem solving. After enormous growth spurts in the brain by age 16, many people are no longer interested in creativity. Education—content-oriented education particularly—does not necessarily access the neural cortex. Rather, it is replaced by cortical learning, the classic learning of recognizable forms without encouragement or support for innovation, which requires creative problem solving. This situation is particularly true of music. Performance of traditional music is rewarded and encouraged rather than acts of creation. Performance and creativity both could be rewarded and encouraged.

What we need now is a complete program—an Improvatory of Music—for preschool through postdoctoral students in aural music, including all forms of improvisation and sonic traditions. As soon as possible, young children could be encouraged to improvise and create their own music. They could be introduced to sound gathering and listening strategies. This program would not replace traditional music learning but would complement it, enhance it, and make it possible for all people to participate in creative music making. An Improvatory would necessarily be interdisciplinary and include all of the arts and technology.

There exists now 100 years of recordings of the complete range of improvisational styles from historical to free. This is an ample documentation that could yield many fruitful studies for advanced degrees. Improvisational strategies could be introduced early and advance through graduate levels. Here is one example of an improvisational strategy: "Only sound what has not been sounded before".

Once an improvisation happens and is recorded and studied, it becomes historical. Too much replication can be destructive of creativity. Replication guarantees survival and perpetuation of form, but it can be dangerous when it takes the place of creative problem solving.

Music teachers in the Improvatory could encourage playing by ear as well as reading and writing music. The use of recording and computing could accelerate the learning of reading and writing music through intelligent courseware.

What would one learn at an Improvatory of Music?

- Basic listening skills, including the listening effect. Music only happens with conscious listening.
- Quantum listening—listening in more than one state simultaneously. If you are not listening, the music is not happening. A conscious observer is necessary. Conscious observation affects sound.

- Ways of sounding and listening—strategies.
- Starting from scratch—music by any means possible (i.e. bottle caps, found objects)
- Sound ecology—what happens in the environment?
- Sound gathering through recording
- Sound sensitivity
- Sound provision with live feeds from sonically stimulating environments such as ponds, oceans, natural soundscapes, the weather and many other sources including industrial and urban sites.
- Sound as intelligence.
- Relational techniques or relationality
- Relational organization
- Informality
- Egalitarian ethics
- Political structures
- Evolving open form processes
- Computing—Computers may push us or teach us about the mind and facilitate a quantum leap into unity of consciousness.
- Technology, especially tools for expanding the mind through listening.
- Instrumental research and development
- Acoustics
- Psychoacoustics
- Organizational strategy

Ideally, the space for an Improvatory would have an architecture that is supportive of the process. Chaos is a key resource in pushing evolution. Meeting places might provide an appropriately chaotic environment with reconfigurable levels, color, textures, sonorous objects, acoustics, recording opportunities and open spaces. There could be many choices to make.

This conference—Improvising Across Borders—brings a new dignity to a creative activity, which has been marginalized by the Western, established musical order. It is time now for an inclusive curriculum where improvised music is no longer ignored or denigrated. Borders between these activities should not only be crossed, but should dissolve. Degrees in both aural and written musics should be available equally. Aural music informs written music and vice versa.

Improvisation is a key process for creative problem solving and the expansion of mind that is needed to meet the challenge of the machine intelligence that we are creating. Improvisation is creative problem solving and is a portal to quantum thinking—thinking in more than one state simultaneously.

What is free improvisation? Nothing is known in advance of making the music. What's the algorithm for that condition? It may or may not be free of historical patterns or it may use historical patterns in new ways. Theoretically, free improvisation is totally spontaneous like the big bang of creation. Maybe the big bang was the first and only free improvisation. How about holding the possibility of the first unknown sound to begin an improvisation at an unknown time in a group of players who are all new to one another? Imagine then a crowd of creative people improvising together.

I thank the organizers of this conference for their courage and imagination.

ECHOES FROM THE MOON

Presented at the Höfe-Fest
Sankt Pölten, Austria
September 4, 1999

> *"I like how you use the moon as another element in the elaborate circuitry of your performance environment...there is the poetic image you create of one sitting at the edge of the earth, sending out sound through the emptiness of space to be reflected back off the moon, our closest planetary companion."*
>
> Douglas Cohen

Echoes From the Moon will receive its third performance on September 4, 1999 at the Höfefest in the City of St. Pölten, Austria. This performance will be a departure from the original work. Sound artist Andres Bosshard will create a "moon space" in which Pauline Oliveros will play her accordion while interacting with the moon. Her accordion sound will travel (via ham radio signal) to the moon and return, like an echo. The poet Ione will create a text to speak to the moon and help the audience members direct their voices to the moon, creating further echoes. Bosshard will use the open radio lines to create his "moon space" defined by the speaker installation. The audience members will be inside the "moon space" and hear the music and text created in this large spatial trio and chorus with Oliveros, Ione, Bosshard, and themselves.

Echoes From the Moon was created in 1987 with support from the National Endowment for the Arts. The idea for the project came to me in 1969 from watching the first lunar landing by United States astronauts on television. I thought that it would be interesting and poetic for people to experience an installation where they could send the sound of their voices to the moon and hear the echo come back to earth. They would be vocal astronauts.

My first experience of *Echoes From the Moon* was in New Lebanon, Maine with ham radio operator Dave Olean. He was one of the first HRO's to participate in the Moonbounce project in the 1960's. He and others sent Morse code to the moon and got it back, which allowed operators to increase the range of their broadcast.

I traveled to Maine to work with Dave. He had an array of twenty-four Yagi antennae that could be aimed at the moon. The moon is in constant motion and has to be tracked by the moving antennae. The antennae have to be large enough to receive the returning signal from the moon. Conditions are constantly changing—sometimes the signal is lost as the moon moves out of range and has to be found again and sometimes the signal going to the moon gets lost in galactic noise.

I sent my first "hello" to the moon from Dave's studio in 1987. I stepped on a footswitch to change the antenna from sending to receiving mode and in 2½ seconds heard the return "hello" from the moon. The sound shifted slightly downward in pitch—a Doppler effect caused by the motion of the moon moving relative to the earth, like the whistle of a train as it rushes past. I then played a duo with the moon using a tin whistle, accordion, and conch shell.

I am indebted to Scot Gresham-Lancaster who located Dave Olean for me in 1986 and helped to determine the technology necessary to perform *Echoes From the Moon*. Ten years later, Scot located all of the ham radio operators for a performance in Hayward, California, which took place during the lunar eclipse on September 23, 1996. Following is the description of that performance:

> *The lunar eclipse from the Hayward Amphitheater was gorgeous. The night was clear and the moon emerged above the trees in an orange mist. As she climbed the sky, her bright sliver emerged slowly from the black shadow—crystal clear. The moon was performing well for all to see and now we were ready to sound the moon.*
>
> *The setup for* Echoes From the Moon *involved Mark Gummer, a ham radio operator from Syracuse, New York, and Scot Gresham-Lancaster, the engineer and organizer for the*

project. Don Roberts, a Seattle-area HRO, and Mike Cousins at the Stanford Research Institute in Palo Alto, California were also involved with the installation.

Mark stood by with a 48-foot dish in his backyard. I sent sounds from my microphone in Hayward, California via telephone line to Mark and he, in turn, sent them to the moon with his ham radio rig. 2½ seconds later, he returned the echo from the moon. The audience cheered as each sound returned to the Hayward University Amphitheater.

*Later in the evening, Scot set up the installation so that anyone could talk to the moon using a telephone. There was a long line of people of all ages from the audience who participated. People enjoyed hearing their voices moon-processed return. There is a slight Doppler shift on the echo because of the motion of both earth and moon. This performance marked the premiere of the installation—*Echoes From the Moon *as I originally intended.*

With this setup, it was only possible to send short phrases of 3-4 seconds. The goal for the next installations would be to have continuous feeds for sending and receiving so that it would be possible to play with the moon as a delay line.

David Behrman and His Home-Grown Music

The Woodstock Times
September 26, 1999

"I do like to think of music as a healing art and as an aid to meditative states. The world is filled with busy noisy music and noise in general and I'd rather contribute to the quieter end of the spectrum most of the time."

David Behrman
August 1997

If you would like a lovely and stirring piece of music to drift with, meditate with, wake up with, or go to sleep with, try *On the Other Ocean* by New Yorker David Behrman. Composed with homemade electronics and software, this piece from 1978 still haunts me. Why don't we know as much about Behrman as Steve Reich, Terry Riley, and Philip Glass, the so-called Minimal fathers? Behrman, despite his many accomplishments as a composer, performer, software designer, record producer and writer, is rather retiring and a tad reclusive. He has championed many other composers instead of himself, perhaps without the reciprocity he so richly deserves for his art.

My first encounter with David Behrman was in a 1965 concert at Case Institute in Cleveland organized by the late David Tudor, the brilliant new music performer/composer and legendary associate of John Cage. The concert at Case Institute included *Players With Circuits* by Behrman, *Music for Solo Performer* by Alvin Lucier and my *Light Piece for David Tudor*. The community-minded Tudor brought the three of us together for the first time in this concert. The concert typified a development of composer/performers involved with live (rather than studio made) electronics encouraged and mentored by Tudor. Tudor became interested in the musical potential of electronics through his association with Cage. His transformation from virtuoso pianist to composer of electronic circuitry for music inspired many. The resulting music was mostly challenging for the audiences of the times and maybe these times too. Tudor brought Behrman, Lucier and myself together because of our interest in live electronics. Our association through the years of programs and collaborations continues to this day.

Behrman's fascination with electronic music was triggered by David Tudor and Gordon Mumma when they introduced him to battery-powered devices that could radically alter or greatly amplify acoustic sounds. From there, he created his own homemade music, making circuits prompted by letters from Mumma. Behrman enjoyed a sense of self reliance by making and performing his own music using homemade instruments that produced sounds that no human ears had experienced before and long before the popularity of the ubiquitous synthesizers of today. Because of this, his music retains it's unique flavor even to this day.

Behrman was a member of the Sonic Arts Union, a key group of composer/performers that included Alvin Lucier, Robert Ashley and Gorden Mumma. They loved traveling and performing together in the 60's and 70's. Their performances explored aspects of music that were outside the bounds of what contemporary music generally accepted. They were exploring homemade electronics and the nature of acoustics while crossing the lines between theater, poetry, visual arts, and music. At times, the Sonic Arts Union expanded from four to eight with the artists Mary Lucier and Shigeko Kobuta, the poet Mary Ashley, and the dancer Barbara Lloyd.

In the mid-70's, during his stint as director of the Center for Contemporary Music at Mills College in Oakland, CA, Behrman was one of the first composers to work with a microprocessor. He acquired the KIM-1 and began to program this elementary computer to replace the switching circuits he was using in his homemade electronic music devices. In the meantime, Apple Computer was being born in a garage somewhere in what is now Silicon Valley.

In addition to composing, Behrman was also an enthusiastic and active producer of recordings in the 60's for

Columbia's Music of Our Time series. He produced *In C* by Terry Riley, an acknowledged masterpiece of minimal music, *Come Out* by Steve Reich, *Night Music* by Richard Maxfield, my *I of IV*, and a compilation of choral music with electronics titled Extended Voices. These works continue to be cited in modern text books concerning 20th century music and are widely known from Behrman's recordings.

Behrman was a student of Wallingford Riegger. He learned "feisty independence" from Riegger and about independent American voices such as Charles Ives, Henry Cowell, Edgar Varese and John Cage. Riegger's students also included Morton Feldman and Robert Ashley. Behrman respected Riegger's music with it's "wonderful sense of sonority and rhythmic vitality".

At Harvard, where Behrman studied, his classmates included the pianist/composer Frederic Rzewski and composer/Greek scholar Christian Wolff. Rzewski and Wolff knew a great deal about European and American new music and influenced Behrman. Behrman remarks that "Frederic was always the first to order new scores by Karlheinz Stockhausen and Pierre Boulez and would get them way before the Harvard library ever did". Wolff made the suggestion to Rzewski and Behrman that they invite David Tudor to Harvard to give a concert. Tudor, a remarkable pianist, was the foremost interpreter of Stockhausen and Boulez as well as of the work of John Cage. Even though their music club could only offer a small fee, Tudor accepted the engagement and brought his friends Morton Feldman, Earle Brown, and John Cage with him. The concert that night expanded the minds of many of the Harvard students and a long and fruitful association was established between Tudor, Behrman and many others.

Behrman toured as composer/performer with the Cunningham Dance Company from 1970 through 1976 with David Tudor and Gordon Mumma. During that period, he assisted John Cage with several projects. Merce Cunningham commissioned him to compose music for Company repertory pieces in 1968, 1976 and 1984.

Much of Behrman's work since the late 1970's involves computer-controlled music systems interacting with people who may or may not be musically expert. He designs and writes most of the software for these systems. He loves making works which invite invention from skilled performers, too, such as Thomas

Buckner, Leroy Jenkins, Kazue Sawai, "Blue" Gene Tyranny, Stuart Dempster and others. "I like the idea of sharing in the creation of something and don't mind getting less than 100% of the credit for it. I like designing software which can be lifted off the ground—so to speak—by a wonderfully imaginative musician who does something with it that I would never have dreamed of." Among such pieces are *Unforseen Events, Refractive Light, My Dear Siegfried, Quick Silver*, and *QSRL*.

Behrman has also created sound installations with interactive music and graphics in collaboration with George Lewis. *A Map of the Known World* and *Algorithme et Kalimba* were exhibited at the Whitney Museum, the Museum of Contemporary Art in Chicago, the Hudson River Museum, the New York Hall of Science and the DeCordova Museum. Behrman's own *In Thin Air* with audience interaction was exhibited at the Addison Gallery of American Art, Ars Electronica in Linz and La Villette Science and Technology Museum in Paris.

Behrman completed a master's degree at Columbia University in 1963 and taught at Ohio State University, New Music in New Hampshire, Rutgers University and California Institute of the Arts. In the early 1980's, he designed educational music software as a consultant for Childrens' Television Workshop. He received a Japan-United States Friendship Commission grant in 1987-88 and a D.A.A.D. (Berlin) fellowship in 1988-89. He is a recent recipient of an Individuals Grant from the Foundation for Contemporary Performance in New York.

Behrman's music is delicious, organic, and homegrown—a testament to a creative soul contributing generously to our American culture.

David Behrman Discography

Leapday Night (with Takehisa Kosugi, Ben Neill, and Rhys Chatham). Includes *Leapday Night, Interspecies Smalltalk* and *A Traveler's Dream Journal*. Lovely Music, Ltd. LP/CD 1042, 1987/90.

Music from Japan by Kazue Sawai (koto). Includes *Navigation and Astronomy*. Classic Masters CMCD-1027, 1992.

Musique Submergides. Includes *Refractive Light*, Nova Era (Barcelona) NECD 2002, 1994.

My Dear Siegfried. Includes *My Dear Siegfried, QSRL, Viewfinder, A New Team Takes Over, Touch Tones, Pools of Phase Locked Loops*. Experimental Intermedia (XI) 129, 2005.

On the Other Ocean. Includes *On the Other Ocean* and *Figure in a Clearing*. Lovely Music, Ltd. CD/LP 1041, 1978/96.

Unforeseen Events (with Ben Neill). Experimental Intermedia (XI) 105, 1991.

Utopia Americana: Compilation of American Music. Includes *A Traveller's Dream Journal (EWR-LAX)*. Fritzitaliana (Turin) New Tone 6707, 1992.

Virtuosity with Purpose. Includes *All Thumbs* (with Petr Kotik and Ben Neill). Ear-Rational ECD 1034, 1991.

Wave Train (music from 1959 to 1968). Includes *Canons, Ricercar, Wave Train, Sounds for a Film by Robert Watts, Players with Circuits*, and *Runthrough*, Alga Marghen plana-B 5NMN.020, 1998.

Articles

Behrman, David and Anita Feldman. "History of Hooved Mammals." *Now Time* No.3 (Los Angeles), 1992.

Behrman, David. "Designing Interactive Computer-based Music Installations." *Contemporary Music Review* (London), 1992.

Fujieda, Mamoru and Toshie Kakinuma. "David Behrman's Electronic Art." Tokyo: Ongakugeijyutsu. August 1991.

Pollack, Howard. "A New Age and a New Left: David Behrman and Frederic Rzewski." *Harvard Composers: Essays on Walter Piston and His Students.* Scarecrow Press, 1992.

Evangelism in the Park

Oberlin College News
Spring 1999

Evangelism happened again in Tappan Square this past Monday. I was hoping for a good excuse to go outside when Corey Dargel called and asked if I would like to come to Tappan Square and do some improvising with an evangelical preacher named Brother Jed, who was going strong in the park. At first I declined as I am on deadline with a piece. Corey said he was going to get his toy pianos and was wondering how to go about the improvisation. I suggested that he take his pianos and accompany Brother Jed. Corey called Yvan Greenberg to come out too. By then, I realized that this was an opportunity not to be missed; I could do my work on the grass in the sun, listen to some Bible-thumping with accompaniment and dance, and get educated on several different levels. Maybe as a composer, I could learn some Evangelical educational strategies to educate my audiences. What could be better though than to go outside on a beautiful day?

God Loves and Creates Queers
by Corey Dargel, Yvan Greenberg, and Brother Jed Smock
a review:

Earlier in the day, as Corey passed by the spray-painted rock in Tappan Square, Brother Jed spotted his red nail polish and said, "What color are those nails?" Corey held them up so Brother Jed could see. "Red nail polish means that you are gay and spreading AIDS! Good thing it ain't black nail polish—black nails means that you are shooting kids and throwing bombs!" Corey blew Brother Jed a kiss and headed for the telephone to call me and get his toy pianos.

When Corey came back and began playing his toy pianos, Brother Jed said to him, "If you had a conscience you would know that playing the piano while someone else is talking is wrong."

I arrived in Tappan Square at about 3:45 PM. As I approached the site, I could see Brother Jed waving his arms and I could hear the tinkle of the toy pianos. Corey had two—one for each hand with very interesting tuning discrepancies. As I arrived, I could hear Corey's patterns clearly supporting Brother Jed's sermon.

"You students are only interested in lust, not love!"

"What is love, Brother Jed?"

"Love is self-denial."

"Can you tell us more about love?"

"Love is self-denial and helping others."

Corey held his ground with the accompaniment supporting the speech patterns. Brother Jed rose to the occasion and did some shouting, "All you Oberlin students are interested in is lust!"

The duo seemed to be locking in together very smoothly. It was no trouble to hear both of the performers clearly. I quietly worked away at the timings for my new piece, *Antigone's Dream*. [I have to deliver the CD by May 14.]

Brother Jed confronted a student who was reading a book nearby. "What are you reading that's more important than what I have to say?"

"Faust," said the student.

Brother Jed asked, "Are you going to have an exam?"

The student nodded. Brother Jed went into a parable about the real final exam that is coming to us all and how we had better get prepared for that! [He was laying into the fear thing real hard—Corey held steady with his accompaniment.]

Out of the corner of my eye appeared a figure. It was Yvan Greenberg dressed in all white, moving slowly across the green grass and passing near Brother Jed. He quietly, adeptly picked up Brother Jed's suitcase. Brother Jed yanked it away, yelling "Give me back my possessions, pervert!" and moved his chair closer toward Corey and me. Yvan continued his slow movement. He turned a right angle and was holding a white toy pistol straight out passing in back of Brother Jed at a distance of about 15 feet. [Brother Jed missed that one.]

Corey was really getting deeply into his patterns—the notes were flying, interlocking, and urging the obviously tired Evangelist on. By now [about an hour later], Orion Keyser had joined the music with whistling—nice timbral reinforcement and a captivating sound. I believe a kind of appreciation was developing here—Brother Jed seemed to realize that Corey's music was attracting people and also enhancing his presence and effect.

As Brother Jed was winding down, the students' performance was gathering more steam. He couldn't seem to muster the shouting style he once had and was beginning to mellow out and sit down more. I was tapping my foot in sync with the nice driving beat of the music. Yvan was in a crucified pose against a tree some distance back—a beautiful purity emanated from his relationship to the tree and the green grass all around his white robes.

Jarred McAdams began to ask some tough questions, trying to convince Brother Jed that not everyone who yells "Kiss my ass!" is a homosexual pervert. "Some of our best questions come from Oberlin students," said Brother Jed. By this time, his chair was only a few feet from Corey and the toy pianos. [Corey was really wailing!] Brother Jed seemed more and more relaxed and even had a slight smile on his face. He then opened his briefcase and brought out copies of his book, *Who Will Rise Up?: A Call to Confrontational Evangelism*, to sell to the students.

He showed pictures in the book to Oberlin students, focusing on "the little woman," explaining that he, at 56, was expressing himself physically with his much younger wife. [They met when she became a member of his congregation and he had explained to her how sinful she was.] Their union is not lustful like the majority of Oberlin students, Brother Jed shouted, "The primary purpose of sex is to produce human beings." Brother Jed and his "little woman" have five children and he wants to make more—"The wife and I need to populate the world with people who think like I do!" he concluded.

Well there you have it. Who educated whom and to what? Brother Jed walked away and Corey ended his piece.

[I loved it!]

SOUND OF HAND BY HUANG RUO: A REVIEW

Performed by David Schotzko, percussionist
Warner Concert Hall, Oberlin College
Spring 1999

"It is a piece derived from my studying on the Chan—Deep Meditation philosophy. In Chan, we believe that everything in the Universe has its own sound. If hands are playing on a drum, it is true what we heard is sound of drum, but isn't it sound of hands, sound of our ears, and sound of our eyes? Therefore, sound can be heard, also seen."

Huang Ruo's Program Note

After the big baffle which was set up behind the piano for the first two pieces disappeared into the basement—a magical moment as the organ pipes emerged over the stage of Warner Concert Hall—the rear door slowly opened and David Schotzko walked forward to center stage and stood on a podium, dressed simply in a black long sleeved shirt and pants. He only used his hands for this performance—no sticks or mallets.

Schotzko began with a standing meditation. One could hear a quiet, slowly swooping ambient sound originating from something unknown in the back of the stage. It continued throughout the first part of the piece. I could not identify what it was but it became a part of the piece for me. Schotzko concentrated and raised his right hand slowly, palm forward, in what might be interpreted as silent gestures from Chan practice. He fluttered his fingers with both hands in an interesting series of gestures.

During this gestural meditative beginning and before Schotzko made a sound, the rear door where he had entered slowly and dramatically swung open all by itself—was this the entrance of a Chan master? It seemed to be part of the piece—a possible effect of such concentration on the part of the performance meditation. Then the door slowly swings back to almost close by itself.

Schotzko began a beautiful variety of carefully crafted clapping sounds. The door opened again by itself. The clapping continued with echoes slapping back in counterpoint from the walls and floor, enhancing the music. Suddenly a figure rushed to the door from back stage and could be seen closing the unruly door. Here was a distinct interference—revealing what she probably thought was a mishap—a mistake—a wrong perception and action on her part and very poor timing—the door wanted to be open! I had accepted it as part of the piece. Her appearance was very noticeable, as was all motion on stage. My enjoyment of the possibilities that the door was letting the spirit of Chan in or out or letting "the sound be seen" was shattered then and there.

Ahh, well—it was a strikingly beautiful piece—beautifully scored by Huang and beautifully performed by David Schotzko. I liked it very much.

My only criticism is that perhaps Schotzo could have worn Tai Chi slippers so that the clapping when he circled the stage could have been heard without the unintentional sound of shoes clunking. Every sound heard or seen becomes crucial in such a performance.

A very nice recital!

Quantum Listening: From Practice to Theory (to Practice Practice)

Presented at the International Congress on Culture and Humanity in the New Millenium: The Future of Human Values The Chinese University of Hong Kong, January 8, 2000

MusicWorks Issue #76 (Spring 2000)

> *"Through the practice of meditation we can explore the depth of insight through the wisdom of listening and hearing."*
>
> Sogyal Rinpoche[1]

From childhood, I have practiced listening.

As a musician, I am interested in the sensual nature of sound, its power of synchronization, coordination, release, and change.

Hearing represents the primary sensory perception—hearing happens involuntarily. Listening, on the other hand, is a voluntary process that produces culture through training and experience. All cultures develop through modes of listening.

Deep Listening is listening in every possible way to everything possible to hear, regardless of what you are doing. Such intense listening includes the sounds of daily life, of nature, or one's own thoughts as well as musical sounds.

Deep Listening is a heightened state of awareness and connects the listener to all that there is. As a composer, I make my music through Deep Listening.

Deep Listening is active.

What is heard is changed by listening and it, in turn, changes the listener. I call how we process what we hear the 'listening effect'.

Two modes of listening exist, focal listening and global listening. Focal listening provides details through concentration on single sounds, whereas global listening provides context through concentration on the entire field of sound. When both modes are utilized and in balance with one another, the listener is in connection with all existence.

Listening shapes culture locally and universally.

Listening is directing attention to what is heard, gathering meaning, interpreting, and deciding whether or not to take action based upon that meaning.

Quantum Listening is listening to more than one reality simultaneously.

Listening for the least perceptible differences—perception at the edge of the new. Jumping like an atom out of orbit to a new orbit—creating a new orbit. Just as an atom occupies both orbits at once, one listens in multiple places at once.

Mothers do this. One focuses to a point and changes that point by listening.

Quantum Listening is listening in as many ways as possible simultaneously, while changing and being changed through the listening.

Quantum Listening leads back to practice practice!

I see and hear life as a grand improvisation. I stay open to the world of possibilities and to the interplay in the quantum field between myself, my community, society, the world, the universe, and beyond.

Our life improvisations will soon include the products of accelerated artificial evolution—hybrid humans, new beings born of technology, new challenges, consequences, dangers, freedoms, and responsibilities—all of this in addition to the life we already lead through the habits of our own natural evolution and traditions.

How will we meet the challenges of this rapidly evolving interactive culture—a culture that could give us freedom from perceptual, physical, and mental limitations?

Will we stop the evolution through destruction and annihilation or embrace it courageously and go forward into the new world it creates?

Here follows a brief history and description of my practice called Deep Listening. I describe Quantum Listening, a theory derived from the practice of Deep Listening. My composing, performing and educating is rooted in my practice and theory.

As a composer and performer, I have experienced a relationship with music technology that spans over half of the past century. Technology is changing and changing cultures more rapidly now than ever before. What used to take 300 years now happens in twenty minutes.

My teaching career stretches over fifty years from the first lessons I taught to my accordion students at age fifteen to the recent graduate composition seminars that I have given at Mills College, Oberlin Conservatory, and other institutions. Teaching has always been rewarding and engaging to me, and has nourished my career as a composer/performer.

When I taught a course entitled *The Nature of Music* to large classes of non-music majors at the University of California, San Diego, I wanted to engage the students in creative sound experiences. I began to compose pieces that would allow anyone to participate whether they could read music or not. By 1970, I had begun to compose *Sonic Meditations*[2], pieces based on the structure of human attention. *Sonic Meditations* gave my work a whole new direction. I began to understand how important listening is to creative music-making.

Compared to reading and writing, little attention is given to developing listening skills or to considering the nature of listening.

I have been training myself to listen with a very simple meditation since 1953, when my mother gave me a tape recorder for my twenty-first birthday. The tape recorder had just become commercially available and was not as ubiquitous as it is today. I immediately began to record from my apartment window whatever was happening. I noticed that the microphone was picking up sounds that I had not heard while the recording was in progress. After this realization, I gave myself the directive, "Listen to everything all the time and remind yourself when you are not listening."

I have been practicing this meditation ever since with more or less success—I still get the reminders after 46 years. My listening continues to evolve as a lifelong practice.

How we listen creates our life. Listening is the basis of all culture.

The quality and flexibility of listening skills is the foundation of musicianship. The essence of musicianship is the ability to discern the least change in pitch or tempo and relate that discernment to a field of ongoing sound or musical relationships.

For audiences, the greatest gift is rapt attention.

Composing *Sonic Meditations* led me deeper into my listening practice and to the notion that there were other important ways to relate to teaching that were different from the presentation to students of prescribed and measurable content. *Sonic Meditations* helped me devise ways to engage students in creative sound making. Processing the results with discussion led to content that came from the inside out (student to professor) rather than exclusively from the outside in (professor to student).

As my work progressed in composition and performance, I came to the notion of Deep Listening. In 1988, I made a recording in an underground cistern in Washington state with Stuart Dempster and Panaiotis, which was released in 1989 by New Albion under the title *Deep Listening*[3]. From my CD liner notes:

> *"Each composer represented in* Deep Listening *has a very individual style of composition. As we improvise together, and listen intensely to one another, our styles encounter in the moment, and intermingle to make a collective music. I call the result deep listening."*

After writing these words, many activities began to develop under the name of Deep Listening. In 1990, I published *Deep Listening Pieces*[4], which contains a brief explanation of my listening theory and pieces to practice and implement these theories. They involve two attentional processes—focal and global listening—and the interdependence of the two modes. The following year, I created and led the first Deep Listening Retreat at Rose Mountain Retreat Center with Tai Chi master and choreographer Heloise Gold[5].

I had already done research on attentional processes at the Center for Music Experiment at the University of California San Diego in 1973 and given numerous workshops based on my *Sonic Meditations*. This research is detailed in several articles in my book *Software for People*[6].

The Deep Listening Retreat gave me a wonderful opportunity to focus the material and to work more intensively with people. After five years, it was clear that advanced work was needed for those returning each year.

Based on a request from one of the participants, I decided to offer an advanced retreat and a Three Year Certificate[7] program for those who would like to teach Deep Listening and use it as a guide for their own creative development.

Poet and psychotherapist Ione joined Deep Listening as an instructor to offer Listening Through Dreaming[8], giving the participants the opportunity to practice listening in the retreat 24 hours a day.

As a team, Ione, Heloise Gold, and I unify our teaching with listening.

Consilient and common ground creates a whole learning situation. The retreat is always held in a beautiful natural mountain environment. Tai Chi and Chi Gong inform and ground the body in the ancient way of the Tao. Dream incubation and processing bring the aura of dreams into interplay with waking consciousness. Sounding and responding through Deep Listening provide new portals to creativity and unity with self and others.

What is Deep Listening?

For me, Deep Listening is a lifelong practice. The more I listen, the more I learn to listen. Deep Listening involves going below the surface of what is heard, expanding to the whole field of sound while finding focus. This is the way to connect with the acoustic environment, all that inhabits it, and all that there is.

For others, Deep Listening is a practice consisting of listening and sounding exercises and pieces I and others have composed since 1970. The results are processed by group discussions in workshops and retreats.

Deep Listening is for musicians as well as participants from other disciplines and interests. Previous musical training is not required.

The key to multi-level existence is Deep Listening—listening in as many ways as possible to everything that can possibly be heard all of the time. Deep Listening is exploring the relationships among any and all sounds whether natural or technological, intended or unintended, real, remembered or imaginary. Thought is included.

Deep Listening includes all sounds expanding the boundaries of perception. In this concept is language and the nature of its sound as well as natural sound and technological sound. And too, Deep Listening includes the environmental and atmospheric context of sound.

Listening is the key to performance.

Whatever the discipline, responses that originate from Deep Listening resonate with being—inform the artist and audience and make art an effortless harmony. Inclusiveness is essential to the process of unlocking layer after layer of imagination, meaning and memory down to the cellular level of human experience.

Hearing is the passive basis of listening.

Hearing is involuntary. Hearing protects us from unseen dangers. We can hear without listening. (Unconsciousness) We choose to listen inwardly or outwardly to the past, present or future. (Consciousness) Listening actively directs one's attention to what is heard, to the interaction of the relationships of sounds and modes of attention.

We hear in order to listen.

We listen in order to interpret our world and experience meaning. Our world is a complex matrix of vibrating energy, matter and air just as we are made of vibrations. Vibration connects us with all beings and connects us to all things interdependently.

We open in order to listen to the world as a field of possibilities and we listen with narrowed attention for specific things of vital interest to us in the world.

We interpret what we hear according to the way we listen.

Through accessing many forms of listening we grow and change whether we listen to the sounds of our daily lives, the environment or music.

Deep Listening takes us below the surface of our consciousness and helps to change or dissolve limiting boundaries.

Babies are the best Deep Listeners.

Think of the tremendous acts of attention and concentration that babies make to explore sounds and speak their first words, to learn language and communicate through listening.

Deep Listening is a birth right for all healthy humans.

As a blind person, the musician Stevie Wonder has listening abilities that persons with normal sight don't ordinarily develop.

Stevie Wonder is a Deep Listener as many blind people are.

With heightened listening ability one can detect the slightest differences in sounds. This enables acute voice recognition, echo detection, spatial location, etc. Such heightened listening substitutes auralization for visualization (or seeing) by creating sonic pictures, etc.

If you are a blind person, hearing is your means of sight, but such acute listening ability also could be cultivated among people with normal sight

If you were a deaf person hearing for the first time with a newly implanted bionic ear, how would you know what you were hearing? You would have to learn to interpret the sounds.

What if you could hear like a bat zipping and swooping around the night sky, or a whale sounding the depths of the oceans, or elephants sounding the earth?

What would it be like to attend a live concert with the ability to hear it anyway that you like?

What if you as a sophisticated listener could individually adjust and optimize the room acoustics for the music to your own taste?

What if you could equalize and mix an orchestra the way you want to hear it—while other listeners are hearing their own versions of the same concert?

What if you could cancel out any interference automatically so that only the music is purely audible?

What if such feats are possible as an internal and private experience? How could your experience be valued in relation to a community of interest?

What if your experience could be shared instantly in the present moment or later?

Audio engineers already do this; they have developed the art of recording concerts and usually have the best seat in the house for sound which they hear through headphones or near field speakers. The results of their listening can be shared through recordings.

All the technology for controlling the sound of concert acoustics exists already.

What if you could hear the frequency of colors?

Research on visual simulations and robotic sight has far outpaced research on hearing. Hearing has not seemed as important to scientists and technologists as seeing. One hears repeatedly that we live in a 'visually oriented society' even though the ear tells the eye where to look.

Those of us who are aurally-oriented are marginalized.

For example: The recent $165 million dollar Mars probe launched by NASA had a $15 microphone from a hearing aid module along as a hitchhiker. This was an afterthought although listening for the sounds of other worlds could yield data that might not come from cameras. We take cameras to the zoo, not tape recorders, and zoos are generally not open during prime sound time in the early morning or evening.

We need to be listening in all possible modes to meet the challenges of the unknown—the unexpected.

An unconscious negative attitude that makes hearing less important than sight developed in parallel with industrial age technology. Pre-industrial cultures depended on hearing for survival needs. Now unnecessarily loud motor sounds serve to let the operator know that a machine is working. Silent machines are possible but people seem to need the aural feedback even though it may contribute to the destruction of their hearing.

Why is industrial sound so often excessive?

Sound conveys a sense of power and connection to the machine operator. Sound is the mythos and symbolic representation of the need to accumulate power. It is unconscious "participation mystique" (C.G. Jung). The sounds of machines dominate and are a constant ubiquitous presence.

There is no courting of silence.

Urban sound levels continue to rise in a great cacophonic puzzle.

Those who operate machines can feel powerful—in control.

No part of the planet is untouched by machine sound. No wonder that the Youth Culture has embraced loud amplified music. How else could they feel heard extending their work to audiences as a powerful presence?

Technology has deeply altered the quality of life, both positively and negatively.

The devaluation of hearing through unconsciousness and ignorance has caused a serious imbalance in the quality of life. Suppression of listening is a consequence of this imbalance. Separation and alienation result. How we attend to this imbalance will have a profound influence on the future of human values. How we use the power of sound and music affects our values

We need sound designers and composers as consultants to city planning and noise abatement regulation.

Machines such as cranes, earth movers, pile drivers, etc. have amplified human muscle power enormously in the Industrial Age and enabled the large building accomplishments in the development of cities. We have machines that multiply and leverage our senses and our mental capabilities. In the 21st Century we will be grappling with who we are as extended humans—hybrid computer/humans and computer beings.

We already see and hear far into outer space and into micro space.

With the Hubble telescope we are able to see into galaxies from the edge of the universe. How thrilling it would be if we could also hear this too. How about launching a parabolic microphone on the next satellite to listen for the music of the spheres? With the electron microscope we can see atomic structures, but we could also listen to the micro-world, hearing a strange universe unfolded by Quantum Mechanics.

Research on hearing and repairing damaged ears increased after World War II—the need for ear protection in the work place had not been recognized earlier. Hearing loss is usually a slow, painless process occurring over many years and not necessarily detected until late in its progression. When veterans returned from battle with acoustic trauma, the more instant damage from the loud explosions of war motivated the Army to do new research on protecting and repairing ears.

> *"In 1978 the first person was implanted with a Bionic Ear. Rod Saunders went profoundly deaf because of head injury, and received the Bionic Ear when he was 48 years old. The prototype Bionic Ear (a cochlear transplant) proved to be a success and was commercialized in 1982. A range of improvements over the years as a result of the continuing research has led to additional benefits for people like Rod. Now over 20,000 people throughout the world can hear because of the Bionic Ear, including over 10,000 children."*
>
> Department of Otolaryngology,
> University of Melbourne[9]

> *"At least 28 million people in the United States suffer hearing loss. 60% have genetic hearing loss and the rest have damaged ears from industrial noise and loud music. At least 16 million are under 30 years old"*
>
> National Institute of Health[10]

Ignorance (more than accidents) causes ear damage which is currently irreversible. All the devices that are supposed to contribute positively to the quality of life are dangerous if they also produce sound levels at and above 85db and people have more or less continuous exposure to those levels.

Many people—especially young people—have no clue of the danger of loud music through headphones, or at a disco, or concert.

People are not necessarily aware of the occupational hazards of loud motors although some progress has been made.

Workplace ethics should hold employers accountable for such hazardous sound. Manufacturers should be accountable too.

Musicians need education about the dangers of their profession.

Audiologists should be consulted routinely and should hold positions as health inspectors. Just as restaurants must maintain cleanliness against infectious microbes, industrial workplaces should be free of continuous sound above 85db. Ear protection should be provided for employees.

Interpretation of our sense information (listening) and the sharing of this experience with each other is the basis of culture and our values.

For example, the members of traditional musical ensembles share knowledge through the experience of performing together, interpreting and creating repertoire and sharing it with audiences. Audiences participate by responding to the music. We rejoice in the pleasure of music that we know and love. Community develops around music. Critical response, discernment and education helps to shape and conserve musical values.

Unfamiliar contemporary music tests values, challenges habits, helps to create new thought patterns and expanded awareness. We need an Improvatory of Music[11] to balance the conservatory and promote the creation of music.

The youth culture, Generation X, is transforming music and creating new values across cultural divides. DJs are remixing the artifacts of recorded music cultures as performances. They are listening differently. They are deconstructing recorded music and turning recorded sound into live performance. The movement is powerful and reaches others instantly through the Internet as well as other media venues. Their listening and cultural flexibility is the future of music.

My own work is now presented live on the internet. Fifty years ago, I performed for the first time on another new media venue—television. Now in the 21st century the youth culture will navigate this new Internet venue.

We have arrived at the threshold of the 21st century with sense organs developed gradually by natural selection through the slow millennial process of evolution. We assume that as humans we hear in the same manner although not all ears have the same acuity. And, because we do not all share the same culture, we definitely are not all listening in the same way with the same attention.

Soon we will be faced with an unprecedented exponential acceleration in technology.

How do we understand normal hearing? What are we listening for?

Restoration of damaged sense organs and nerves will be possible. Regeneration of nerves may be possible also. For the first time there also may be a choice for enhancement of sense organs and for new perceptual abilities if our brains can handle the processing involved with the unfamiliar. When we cannot process complex information we tend to shut down our senses and retreat.

What if such retreat was impossible?

What if we could share our thoughts instantly over a network as computers now do? Such possibilities and amplified intelligence will present new challenges to our ethics and future human values.

What would you want to hear if you had a Bionic Ear that could let you listen to anything, anywhere any time?

As a musician would you like to focus on a particular instrument in an orchestra that seems inaudible? Or listen globally with the ability to equalize and optimize the sound of the whole ensemble canceling out any distracting interferences?

What does a bat hear as it swoops and dives through the air sounding its prey to locate it?

Would you like to zoom into a waterfall to hear individual sounds of the falling drops? Would you like to hear the sound of a cell dividing in your own body? The sound of blood coursing through your veins as you monitor your own health?

How about discerning the exact distance of sounds with an internal molecular computer?

What are the sounds of the gases in deep space?

All of this enhancement to hearing is already available with outboard equipment—microphones, amplifiers, speakers.

Surveillance by spies is quite sophisticated.

What if such equipment were available as on board internal equipment through microscopic ingested technology? (Never mind implants—they will be outdated.) How would you want to use your newly-enhanced ear power? How could humanity handle such power?

What is microscopic ingested technology?

"Nanobots are microscopic sized robots which will exist by 2030. Entering the blood stream Nanobots could scan your brain from the inside. Nanobots could swim through every capillary of your brain and take a high-resolution picture from inside."

Ray Kurzweil[12]

Note that Kurzweil doesn't posit nanobots that listen.

Nanotechnology is underway. The result could mean that new neural networks could be created and controlled within the brain. Nerves could be repaired. Brain extenders could extend your pattern recognition and memory. You would have the processing power of powerful computers or return to normal carbon based being.

"In a hundred years there may be no clear distinction between humans and computers. There will be enormous augmentation of human perceptual and cognitive abilities through neural implant technology. Humans who do not use such implants (or nanobots) are unable to participate in meaningful dialogue with those who do—knowledge is understood instantaneously through assimilated knowledge protocols. The goal of education and intelligent beings is discovering new knowledge to learn."

Ray Kurzweil[13]

What about spirituality?

To Kurzweil a spiritual experience is "a pattern of information."[14]

"Spirituality by definition means plummeting to the depths, getting down to the realm of experience. Spirituality is about

living deeply. It puts experience before everything else. It's about responding with passion, awe, reverence and gratitude to everything in life—including the grief, the pain, the suffering, the injustice. It's about tasting God, not just talking about God."

Matthew Fox[15]

We will need all the wisdom that we can possibly absorb to deal morally and ethically with the powers inherent in nanotechnology. Our battles with good and evil will jump to a new level.

Enter the Chip Monk[16]! Will spirituality evolve on a microchip with the programmed essence of the best of our world religions available to all? Could the Chip Monk be ingested to assist one's inner monk in the practice of deep ecumenism and the distillation of universal truth?

If you are a Buddhist, listening leads to the "Buddhaverse"; if you are a Christian, listening leads you to the word of God; if you are an artist, listening leads you to your material and to shape the material. If you are a scientist, listening leads you to theory and experiment.

If you are a spy, listening may lead you to prison.

We live in these conditions and our listening simultaneously perceives and shapes the moments that we live whether we are Buddhist, Christian, Islamic, artist, scientist, etc. Religion is a set of rules and regulations for a particular kind of listening. Style in art sets the way of listening.

Quantum Listening is listening to our listening. The field expands to embrace all kinds of listening with openess to all possibilities.

In 1990, the noted ethnomusicologist Ki Mantle Hood proposed the Quantum Theory of Music. When asked for the formula for QTM in 1994, he replied, "At present, our modus operandi is asking questions. We try to identify neglected, overlooked, not-always-obvious phenomena that relate in any way to the perception of music. That order of perception is only possible by participation."[17] Participation means actually experiencing all aspects of music creation and performance.

What is Quantum Listening?

Quantum Listening is listening in all sense modes to or for the least possible differences in any component part of a form or process while perceiving the whole and sensing change.

Quantum Listening leads you to notice that you are listening. Quantum Listening leads you to attention to a point—all-or-nothing focus which changes that point forever.

Quantum Listening leads you to an all embracing perspective of an ever-expanding field.

The Quantum Listener listens to listening.

Quantum Listening simultaneously creates and changes what is perceived. The perceiver and the perceived co-create through the listening effect. All sounds are included in the field. This creates potential, cultivates surprises, opens the imagination and approaches and even plunges over the edges of perception into the mystery of the universe predicted by Quantum Field Theory.

Quantum Listening is the ability to discern all that there is in a single moment —point in space (a transient) or a quanta.

> *"In the new physics of Quantum Field Theory, particles have an'aura" or a force field. Although it cannot be seen, its presence is felt. It conveys forces from one particle to another as they interact."*
>
> Steven Petersen[18]

Analogously, when one is listening to the whole field of sound without focusing on any one sound but expanding to include all sounds that can be heard—sounds seem to become interrelated rather than chaotic or meaningless—the field conveys forces (energy) from one sound to another.

The field seems to have a unified logic and form as if it were a composed piece of music.

A field carries the potential for manifesting a force. Particles of objects inside a field may change or move.[19]

The field of sound can be felt as potential force. There is active participation by the listener and co-creation of this form between the listener and sounds.

The field assumes meaning (potential force) and is transformed by the listener. The listener is also transformed by the field. If one is not listening in this expanded way then the form disappears into the background of consciousness—the field disappears—is meaningless, attention narrows, the potential lessens. This is analogous to the collapse of the wave function in Quantum Mechanics when a particle is observed and decides to change state.

Within the 'Listening Field' sounds which shift and change inside the field are the manifestation of forces which give rise to the perceived form. Listeners will hear the form slightly differently each from their own angle of observation in the field. Different listeners would have to occupy different locations in the field, thus their experience of the field would be different. This is no less true when listening to a piece of music in an audience in a concert hall.

A Quantum Theory of Music[20] would have to account for these slight differences in perception, their interaction and effect.

Each listener by the act of 'listening' affects the field and thus the form. The form affects the listener in a dance of reflections in the space between.

Listening performers feel the 'listening effect' as they are performing for an audience'.

This is focal/global listening with the added perspective of a 'witness" function.

This is listening to listening—layers of processing in the brain and body.

The skin listens too.

In fact the whole body listens in this heightened state of awareness. which can expand continually unless attention narrows (perhaps due to ego concerns) and there is the collapse of the wave function and a change in the field and it's potential.

In practicing Chi Gong, I have experienced listening with the palms of my hands to sense these electromagnetic fields. Since these are vibrations I call this sensing listening with the palms of the hands.

Simply imagining the sound of humming transfers immediately to the palms of my hands and manifests as healing energy.

There is a deep relationship between Chi Gong and Quantum Field Theory.

"Consciousness may be associated with all quantum mechanical processes...Since everything that occurs is ultimately the result of one or more quantum mechanical events, the universe is 'inhabited' by an almost unlimited number of rather discrete, conscious...entities that are responsible for the detailed workings of the universe"

E.H. Walker[21]

Can sounds be understood as particles?

"In a fashion analogous to auric fields, particle fields influence certain particles when near them."

Steven Petersen

Sounds near one another influence each other. Listeners near one another affect or influence one another with active listening.

"Particles have auras. This makes them like everything else in the universe, as the ancient Chinese viewed it."

Steven Petersen[22]

"Photons (light particles), do appear to process information and to act accordingly, and therefore, strange as it may sound, they seem to be organic"

Gary Zukav[23]

Particles behave like they have consciousness.[24]

"In fact, modern Quantum Field Theory suggests that what we call a particle is an 'energy knot' in the field... Thus particles are a flow creating the illusion of a form, made up of concentrated 'Chi'. Chi is similar to a cloud"

Hermann Weyl[25]

"When the Chi condenses, its visibility (or audibility) becomes apparent so that there are then the shapes (of individual things {or sounds}). When it disperses its visibility (or audibility) is no longer apparent and there are no shapes (or sounds). At the time of its condensation, can one say otherwise than that this was but temporary? But at the time of its dispersing, can one hastily say that is then non existent?"

Fung Yu-Lan[26]

Is sound intelligent? Does sound have consciousness?

Listen to sound disappearing.

This meditation that I practice takes one to the border of reality and virtuality. When do you stop hearing the sound? When does memory begin?

What we hear depends on the angle from which our ear receives sound. How we listen depends on our consciousness. Are we creating the sound that we hear by listening or is sound creating our listening? Is it co-creation between consciousnesses? Is the sound disappearing or am I disappearing?

Human values are developed through the experience of listening.

With practice, humanity could be transformed to a flexible culture of listeners.

Listening involves a reciprocity of energy flow; exchange of energy; sympathetic vibration: tuning into the web of mutually supportive interconnected thoughts, feelings, dreams, vital forces comprising our lives; empathy; the basis for compassion and love.

Yes, Deep Listening is the foundation for a radically transformed social matrix in which compassion and love are the core motivating principles guiding creative decision making and our actions in the world.

Quantum Listening is a 'simple' practice, open to all, which has profoundly rich and far-flung implications, for bringing to our world the two conditions the Dalai Lama illuminates in his recent book *Ethics for the New Millennium*[27], happiness and relief of suffering.

The practice generates theory.

Theory is perceiving structure—analyzing and explaining structure so that testing and experiments (practice) can be done. Theory directs practice and creates culture to practice practice.

Practice is a way of action—a set or sets of ways of doing or responding to gain experience

Listeners practicing cultural flexibility[28] would be aware of the profound interdependence of all beings and all things. A new music reflective of a new humanity with a high value on life could arise.

Tools of Change and Transformation

From *Open Source: Artists from the Institute for Electronic Arts* catalog from exhibition at the Central Academy of Fine Arts
Beijing, China
October-November 2001

Profound change in music and all the arts, driven predominantly by technology throughout the 20th century will more than likely increase at in an even more rapid pace in the 21st century.

Two inventions in the 20th century enabled the unprecedented change in the creation, performance, and dissemination of music—recording technology and the personal computer.

One hundred years of recording exposed musicians and the public to all forms of music in a global perspective—a mind-expanding development.

For musicians, the ability to record and immediately hear what was performed has enormously enhanced musicianship. Trained musicians can now play almost any form of music very well. This was not true before personal recorders were available.

20th century composers entered a new realm of creativity with electronic music. Experiments in electronic music began early and accelerated with the availability of magnetic tape recording. Organizing sounds by editing and splicing tape presented new forms for composers.

The second important invention was the personal computer, which provided a new means of controlling and organizing sounds. Computers enable composers to deal with more complex rhythms, sound mixtures, and forms.

The marriage of computing and recording has given composers and performers amazing flexibility in their compositions and performances.

Creators and performers of music are now on the brink of new challenges that will come from biotechnology in this century. According to scientist Ray Kurzweil, computers will have similar computing power as the human brain by 2010. It will be necessary to understand how to deal with ever more rapid change and complexity in music and the hybridization of computers and humans.

What is absolutely essential for being a composer or performer or indeed a person in the next decade or two is a serious ability to adjust to a continuous rate of technological change unprecedented in the history of our species.

SOUNDING THE MARGINS: A 40-YEAR RETROSPECTIVE OF THE WORKS OF PAULINE OLIVEROS

Presented by Meridian Music: Composers in Performance, the Pauline Oliveros Foundation, and Mills College
in celebration of Pauline Oliveros' 70th Birthday
Mills College, Oakland, California
May 31, June 1, and June 2, 2002

Introductory Note

Many musicians and artists from around the world are gathered here to honor and celebrate the life and work of an extraordinary individual, Pauline Oliveros, one of the most important musicians of our time. Each of us has been greatly affected by Pauline in one or more ways; as our teacher, mentor, role model, friend. Not only is Pauline a brilliant musician who has helped set many of the trends of contemporary music in the last four decades. Few composers have been as generous with their knowledge and time to younger artists. Perhaps more than any other female composer, Pauline has been out there on the front, so to speak, demanding that woman be treated equally. Besides all her academic credentials and musical genius, what those of us who are fortunate to be around her realize is that we are in the presence of a beautiful, compassionate, highly-developed spiritual being.

For the last 5 years, I have been incredibly fortunate to be a member of the Space Between, a trio with Pauline and my dear friend Dana Reason. For Dana and I, being on stage and on tour with Pauline in this setting has been the most valuable musical experience we could have desired. These "lessons" have been far more valuable than all the time we spent in music schools.

This festival is a small way of saying thank you, Pauline.

Philip Gelb

Letter

Dear Pauline,

Entering into the work of Deep Listening has opened new horizons in music and life for me and many others. Every encounter in making music is enriched thereby. Potential for creativity manifests and yields yet greater potential.

Let me take this opportunity to thank you for the privilege of participating in this life and work with you. In this festival we celebrate the deep joy in this music you have composed. So many pieces over what seems like a remarkably short period of years. This is such a treat to perform and to hear these works. Enjoy this embrace by this community you have helped create! New pieces are undoubtedly emerging. Intense light and happiness be with us all as we sound the margins! Now we move into the mystery of sounding in community and your gracious guidance as we all go on, on beyond, on beyond beyond!

Pax et bonum,

Tom Bickley

Pauline Oliveros Appreciation

"Sounding the Margins: A Forty-Year Retrospective of the Works of Pauline Oliveros" celebrates the achievements of one of America's foremost pioneers of experimental music. For more than a half century, as both composer and performer, Oliveros has cultivated a unique approach to the experience of sound. Early in her career she began to develop remarkably acute musical perceptions and an extraordinary aural imagination. In the 1940s when she first worked with a wire recorder, documenting her own performances and music from the radio, she quickly realized the revolutionary potential of this invention as a source of "musicianship feedback," a means to enhance listening skills and performance. In the early 1950s she worked with the first commercially available tape recorder, recording and listening to environmental sounds and later composing her first tape pieces in the 1960s.

Today Pauline Oliveros is among the world's leading composers. Through her music, writings, and teaching she has influenced generations of musicians by demonstrating that we are all free at any time and in any place to listen, in a musical way, to the sounds that are around us. Her musical pluralism embraces all sound and all music; as she explained in an essay written in 1978: "All of music speaks to me as music, no matter how diverse, no matter what its function might be, no matter how apparently simple or complex, no matter how it affects me emotionally or intellectually, and no matter what its origin: human, animal, artificial, or extra-terrestrial."

Oliveros views the multiplicity of sounds around us as a "a grand composition," a unified yet diverse sound field. She has devoted herself to developing and teaching perceptual skills capable of appreciating this global "sound environment." Her inclusive approach to listening parallels the work of John Cage, whose famous composition without sound 4'33"*(1952) provides us with an opportunity "to listen, in an aesthetic way, to what there is to hear." But Oliveros has taken this a step in a different direction, creating a technique which she calls "deep listening"—a praxis which focuses not only on the sounds of external environments, but also on the more ephemeral sounds of our innermost thoughts. She has also substituted Cage's musical anarchism, which leaves sounds alone "to be themselves," with an approach to listening and music-making based upon interactions between sounds, people, and the environments within which they coexist. To this end, she has created techniques for free improvisation for both musicians (working with virtuoso ensembles such as the Deep Listening Band) and non-musicians alike.*

Since Pauline Oliveros has played a leading role in the development of cultural life in the Bay Area, San Francisco is a fitting venue for our celebration of her contributions to the musical world. In 1957 her work as a young composer was featured on the listener-sponsored radio station, KPFA in Berkeley. Robert Erickson, who later became Oliveros' colleague at the University of California, San Diego, was the music director at that time. In 1961, she and Ramón Sender Barayón established an electronic music studio at the San Francisco Conservatory of Music. Together they produced a series of concerts called Sonics, the initial concert featuring group improvisations and early tape music by Sender, Oliveros, Terry Riley, and Phil Winsor. Later in 1961 Sender and Morton Subotnick founded the San Francisco Tape Music Center. Oliveros played a central role in its artistic evolution. Throughout its five-year existence (1961-66) the San Francisco Tape Music Center presented dozens of unique concerts of contemporary music; it also supported the development of new technologies, including Don Buchla's modular synthesizer—the "Buchla Box." There was an emphasis on breaking down disciplinary boundaries, especially between audio and visual media.

A grant from the Rockefeller Foundation provided an opportunity for the San Francisco Tape Music Center to move to Mills College in the summer of 1966. Oliveros became the first director of what was then called the Mills Tape Music Center and later re-named the Center for Contemporary Music. Her early tenure at Mills lasted only one year. However, in the 1990s, she returned to Mills as the Darius Milhaud Professor of Composition, where she has made an indelible impression as mentor, colleague, tireless advocate for women's music, and friend.

David W. Bernstein
Oakland, California
May 13, 2002

THE PROGRAM

Concert One
Friday, May 31, 2002 8:00 PM

Four Meditations for Orchestra (1971/1997)

Sounding the Margins Orchestra

Maggi Payne, flute
Diane Grubbe, flute
Tom Bickley, recorder
Philip Gelb, shakuhachi
Matt Ingalls, clarinet
Phillip Greenlief, soprano saxophone
Francis Wong, tenor saxophone
Jon Raskin, baritone saxophone
Vinny Golia, contrabass saxophone
Tom Djll, trumpet
Stuart Dempster, trombone
Monique Buzzarté, trombone
Toyoji Tomita, trombone
David Dove, trombone
Bill T. Roper, tuba
Sara Schoenbek, bassoon
Shoko Hikage, koto
Brett Larner, koto
Fred Frith, guitar
Mary Liz Smith, piano
Mathew Goodheart, piano
David Gamper, electronics
Tim Perkis, electronics
Angelique Van Berlo, free bass accordion
Jennifer Wilsey, percussion
George Marsh, percussion
Tom Nunn, homemade instruments
Gayle Young, Amaranth
Brenda Hutchinson, long tube instrument
Anne Hege, soprano
Karolyn Van Putten, voice, percussion
Daphne Chen, violin
Tara Flandreau, violin
Allison (AJ) Johnson, violin
Patty Liu, violin
Natalie Brecja, viola
Jorge Boehringer, viola
Hugh Livingston, cello
Anne Bourne, cello
Loren Dempster, cello
Matthew Sperry, bass
Chris Williams, bass
George Cremaschi, bass
Steed Cowart, rehearsal director

Variations for Sextet (1960)

sfSound Group

Matt Ingalls, clarinet
Hugh Livingston, cello
Diane Grubbe, flute/piccolo
David Bithell, trumpet
Carrie Weick, horn
Hadley McCarroll, piano
Jennifer Bailey, conductor

Variations for Sextet (1959-1960) is an example of Oliveros' early "traditional" works. It bears the influence of her mentor and teacher, Robert Erickson, a prominent author of acoustic theory and advocate of intuitive compositional methods. Oliveros stated that although her earliest works were composed using conventional musical notation and tend to sound like the works of Anton Webern, she created them by improvising rather than applying a rigorous intellectual technique. Written for flute/piccolo, Bb clarinet, Bb trumpet, F horn, 'cello, and piano, *Variations* explores her interest in timbre or sound color through her use of timbral gestures, rapid shifts in tone color, and radical shifts in rhythm.

Excerpt from *Io and Her and the Trouble with Him* (2001)

Written and directed by Ione
Choreography by Joanna Haigood
Set Design by Wayne Campbell
Pauline Oliveros, accordion
Performers: Joanna Haigood, Sheila Lopez, Suzanne Gallo

This Dance-Opera is a retelling of the Greek myth of Io told from a matriarchal perspective. It features aerial dancing, ancient spirits, magic spells and a sinister monster. It appeals to all who value the concept of freedom from oppression of all kinds. *Io and Her* will be available on DVD in 2003.

Improvisation (2002)

Pauline Oliveros, accordion	Margot Bevington, voice
Ione, spoken word	Ezekiel H. Talbot, guitar
Brenda Hutchinson, long tube instrument	Edward Schocker, glass instrument
Maggi Payne, flute	Brett Larner, koto
Anne Hege,voice	Jennifer Baker, trombone

Double Basses at Twenty Paces (1968)

Chris Williams, bass

Matt Sperry, bass

Alan Johnson, referee

Double Basses at Twenty Paces: a theater piece for two double basses, their seconds, and a referee (conductor) (1968) is perhaps Oliveros' best-known theater work. Oliveros, along with such notables as John Cage and Allan Kaprow, combined dramatic element with other traditional media. She stated that her theater pieces are "a study of theatrical elements treated like music . . . [so] that the gestures and objects have the same importance as sound." Oliveros' generally humorous antics, the conspicuous use of musical quotations, and her tendency to tailor the work to the performer's interests and abilities are the most conspicuous stylistic elements of her theater pieces.

Double Basses was written for bassists Bertram Turetzky and Allan Goldman. The action parodies a fencing duel and includes extended virtuosic bass passages from Dragonetti *Etudes* and Beethoven's *Fifth Symphony*.

Saxual Orientation (1998)

ROVA

Bruce Ackley, soprano saxophone	Larry Ochs, tenor Saxophone
Steve Adams, alto saxophone	Jon Raskin, baritone saxophone

This saxophone quartet was written for ROVA in 1998 with commission money from Meet the Composer. It is a structured improvisation with eight ensemble options. One of the options is a star pattern. It's a five-pointed star and at the center is the instruction "Just Listen", which is a central concept of Pauline's music. Each point of the star has directions to follow and each player plays the star independently. The other seven ensemble options range from a 23-note tone row to a key click rhythmic pattern. The options are performed in a predetermined order. The star pattern can repeat more than once.

Solo (1999)

Pauline Oliveros, accordion

Red Shifts (2000)

Monique Buzzarté, trombone

Tim Perkis, oscillator

Xopher Davidson, electronics

Red shifts, the systematic increase in the wavelength of all light received from a celestial object, is the shifting of individual lines in the spectrum of the object toward the red, or longer-wavelength, end of the visible spectrum. Most observed red shifts are the result of the Doppler effect; they are also produced by gravitation in accordance with the general theory of relativity.

The Space Between (1997 -)

Pauline Oliveros, accordion

Philip Gelb, shakuhachi

Dana Reason, piano

* * *

Concert Two

Saturday, June 1, 2002 1:00 PM

Sound Fishes (1992)

The Adem Trio

Gayle Young, amaranth

Anne Bourne, 'cello

Angelique Van Berlo, free bass accordion

Sound Fishes (1992) "Listening for what has not yet sounded, like a fisherman waiting for a nibble or a bite. Pull the sound out of the air like a fisherman catching a fish, sensing its size and energy—when you hear. When you hear the sound, play it. Move to another location if there are no nibbles or bites. There are sounds in the air like sounds in the water. When the water is clear, you might hear the sounds."

Improvisation (2002)

Timeless Pulse

Pauline Oliveros, accordion

David Wessel, electronics

Jennifer Wilsey, percussion

Quintuplets Play Pen: Homage to Ruth Crawford Seeger (2001)

Sarah Cahill, piano

Quintuplets Play Pen: Homage to Ruth Crawford Seeger was commissioned by Sarah Cahill in 2001. It is very unique in recent works of Pauline's in that it abandons her "usual meditative" style. Instead she emulates some of the interesting polyrhythmic ideas that were employed by Ruth Crawford.

Portrait of Tom Bickley

Tom Bickley, recorder and electronics

Portrait of Tom Bickley (2000) is a one specific version of the "Portrait of" series. Oliveros enters the performer's astrological and instrument or voice information into a computer program. The program was developed in 1987 with the assistance of Peter Ward and funded by the National Endowment for the Arts. The software generates sets of pitches for that performer. The performer renders a self-portrait using the pitch sets and a *Portrait* mandala. The mandala guides the performer through performing about aspects of life such as "dream" and "birth." Each performance begins and ends with "Stillness/Listen." The performer worked closely with Les Stuck at Mills College to create accompaniment and processing for sections of the mandala using Max/MSP software. *Portraits* have been created for many soloists and ensembles, including Malcolm Goldstein, Tom Buckner, and the Quintet of the Americas.

"Jaga Warrior's Tribute" **from** *Njinga the Queen King*

featuring Terry Baruti and Lorraine Bowser

with members of Adigun Sipho and Bana Ya Kongo

Njinga the Queen King, a play with music and pageantry, written and directed by Ione with sound design and original music by Pauline Oliveros and traditional music by the Njinga Players, premiered in 1993 at BAM'S Next Wave Festival. Njinga Mbandi, was the 17th Century ruler of Ndongo—the country that is now Angola—for 40 years and is considered to be that country's primary freedom fighter.

Improvisation

Ghostdance Trio

Pauline Oliveros, accordion

Shoko Hikage, koto

Toyoji Tomita, trombone

13 Changes (1986)

Chris Brown, computer
John Bischoff, computer
Tim Perkis, computer

13 Changes (1986) was composed for violinist Malcolm Goldstein. One of Pauline's numerous intuitive scores; the directions provide a series of images, some of them rather whimsical, (for example the eighth change, "Rollicking monkeys landing on Mars") for the musicians to explore sonically.

Improvisation

The Circle Trio
Pauline Oliveros, accordion
India Cooke, violin
Karolyn van Putten, voice and percussion

Tuning Meditation

Albany Community Chorus
directed by Anne Hege

Melinda Woodward	Chris Klein
Amy Gorman	Maia Ramsey
Alison Cardinet	Julie Hart
Mary Gillis	Roseann Fahner
Angela Kucherenko	Anne Hege

The *Tuning Meditation* (1971, 1980) is stylistically similar to Oliveros' seminal *Sonic Meditations* (1971, 1973). These meditation works characteristically do not require any special performance preparations or special musical training, and are intended to be performed over a long period of time. The *Tuning Meditation* exists in several versions: published versions exist online as the second movement in *Four Meditations for Orchestra*, and in printed form in the *Deep Listening Pieces* collection. Briefly, the performance directions consist of participants singing a long tone from imagination and tuning to someone else's long tone. *Crow's Nest* (1980), a variation on the *Tuning Meditation*, was a particularly remarkable performance of the *Tuning Meditation* as it was presented in the spiraled galleries of the Guggenheim Museum with a complement of one hundred singers.

Sonic Meditations

The *Sonic Meditations* (1971, 1973) are the earliest examples of Oliveros' most significant and original contributions to music literature–the meditation pieces. Oliveros' aesthetic emphasizes total freedom from such traditional compositional parameters as pitch, rhythm, style, technique, form, or the composer's "craft." Instead, each performance is allowed to evolve through a commitment to attention and a philosophy she terms "listening," first described in the preface to the *Sonic Meditations* collection. Among the most progressive aspects of "listening" within these works include the perception of acoustic phenomena, the verbal expression of subjective impressions, and the perception of how sounds affect the body.

The first *Sonic Meditations* were developed in 1970 in conjunction with the ♀ group, an association of women at the University of California at San Diego who shared an interest in free improvisation.

* * *

Concert Three

Saturday, June 1, 2002 8:00 PM

The Heart of Tones (1999)

The Sounding the Margins Orchestra

The Well and the Gentle (1983)

The Sounding the Margins Orchestra

Wind Horse (1989)

The Cornelius Cardew Choir

Sandra Yolles
Steven Tobin
Marjorie Tichenor
Maryliz Smith
Katherine Setar
Jonathan Segel
Jim Riley
Matthew Priest
Marianne McDonald
Bob Marsh (co-founder)
Aurora Mahassine
Cathryn Hrudicka
Penelope Houston
Brad Fischer
Leah Fenimore
Tim Duff
Tom Duff
Matthew Ross Davis
Dave Cowen
Beau Casey
Tom Bickley (co-founder and director)
Margot Bevington
Nancy Beckman

Wind Horse (1989) for chorus is a mandala of thirteen circles arranged symmetrically and connected by curving lines (see illustration). Each circle contains a word that describes a manner or aspect of sounding or listening. The circles guide the singers in creating a performance as they each follow the principle instruction "Remember that others are listening for you and responding to you."

The title is a direct translation of the Tibetan "Lung ta" the term for the colorful prayer flags which, according to tradition, release the prayers printed on them as they flutter in the wind. Ana Crucis Women's Choir (the oldest feminist choir in the US) premiered this score in July 1990.

Wind Horse exists also as a radiophonic work commissioned by New American Radio.

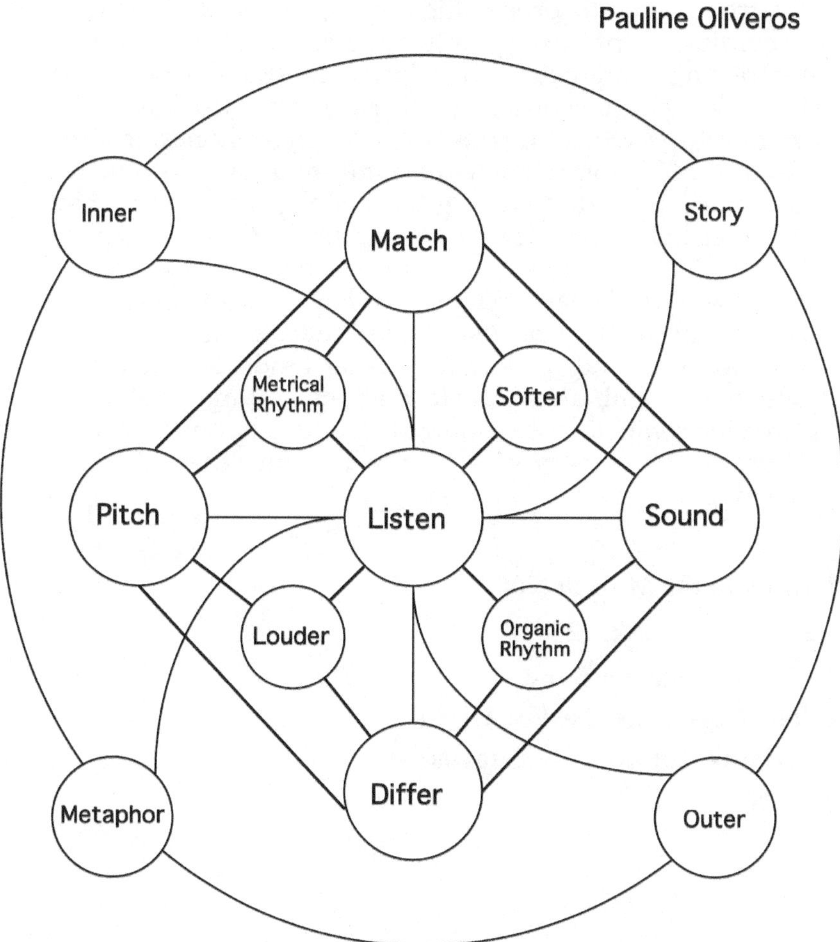

Margin Calls (2002)

Deep Listening Band

Stuart Dempster, trombone, conch shells, didjeridus, toys

David Gamper, keyboard, overtone flutes, found instruments

Pauline Oliveros, accordion, voice

The Cornelius Cardew Choir, Tom Bickley, director

Albany Community Chorus, Anne Hege, director

Regarding the technology used by Deep Listening Band at this concert:

The Expanded Instrument System (EIS) is an evolving electronic sound processing environment dedicated to providing improvising musicians control over various interesting parameters of electronic transformation of their acoustic performances. Performers each have their own setup, which includes their microphones, control devices and a computer with sound input and output. The computer provides the digital signal processing, which includes delays and ambiance, and translates and displays control information for this processing from foot pedals and switches. The musicians and their instruments are the sources of all the sounds, which they pick up with their microphones and subject to several kinds of pitch, time and spatial ambiance transformations and manipulations. No electronic sounds sources are used, only acoustic instruments and voices. Software for the EIS was developed by David Gamper.

Betting on the Margin (2002)

EISing on the Cake (2002)

Deep Listening Band
The Cornelius Cardew Choir
Albany Community Chorus

Solo (2002)

Pauline Oliveros, accordion

"Listening to this space I sound the space. Listening to the energy of all who are present I sound this energy. Listening to my listening and your listening I make this music here and now with the assistance of all that there is. I dedicate this music to compassion in this world now."

* * *

The Pauline Oliveros Birthday Potluck Picnic
Sunday, June 2, 2002 1:00 PM

The Grand Buddha Marching Band (1981)

The Grand Buddha Marching Band (1981) is another meditation work from the *Deep Listening Pieces* collection. Stylistically similar to Oliveros' seminal *Sonic Meditations, The Grand Buddha Marching Band* does not require any special performance preparations or special musical training, and is intended to be performed over a long period of time. In this work, the "band" consists of a group of singers or instrumentalists who form a tight, single-file, circular mandala form which spirals around a designated "drum major." Each marcher may make sounds spontaneously during the march, while "listening" and maintaining full awareness of the other marcher's performances. As the members become more distantly spaced, the marchers may speed up, slow down, or pass each other. The piece concludes when all performers have completely dispersed.

Biographies

Bruce Ackley, Rova Saxophone Quartet, was a founding member of Rova and has contributed to recordings by many musicians including John Zorn, Henry Kaiser, and Eugene Chadbourne.

Steve Adams, Rova Saxophone Quartet, studied at the School of Contemporary Music in Boston. He composed music for seven productions by the California Shakespeare Festival.

David Bernstein, roundtable participant, is a theorist, musicologist, and author specializing in twentieth-century music theory and analysis, and the aesthetics of the avant-garde. He is editor of *Writings Through John Cage's Music, Poetry and Art* (Chicago, 2001). Dr. Bernstein has taught at Mills since 1989.

Margot Bevington, voice, studied environmental science and music at Oberlin and is graduate student at Mills in music composition. She has worked extensively in the area of acoustic ecology. She sings with the Cardew Choir.

Tom Bickley, recorder, director of the Cardew Choir, festival co-producer, studied Gregorian chant, other medieval music, and African-American sacred music. He was among the first seven to receive the Certificate in Deep Listening. He is a native of Houston, now based in Berkeley, where he performs, composes and teaches music. www.metatronpress.com/tbickley

Anne Bourne, cello, has performed on the concert stage and recorded internationally with artists such as Jane Siberry, and composed music for film and dance. She holds the Certificate in Deep Listening and is the mother of young Willa.

Thomas Buckner is a baritone with a wide experience in a variety of musical genres. He is best known for his collaborations with contemporary composers and improvisers and has commissioned and premiered over 100 new works.

The Cardew Choir sings at the intersection of community and experimental music. This radically inclusive ensemble finds its roots in the work of English composer/performer Cornelius Cardew (1936-1981), his Scratch Orchestra, as well as Pauline Oliveros' Deep Listening, and is a blossoming of the vibrant music scene in the Bay Area. The first rehearsal was held in Berkeley on May Day 2001. The group was begun by Bob Marsh, Kattt Sammon, and Tom Bickley. It has performed works by Cardew, Kathy Kennedy, Joseph Zitt, and Pauline Oliveros. Members include both active musicians and performers who are just beginning to use their voices as singers. The choir welcomes new participants; enthusiasm necessary, prior experience not required.

Renee T. Coulombe is a composer, improviser and theorist; she is currently assistant professor of music theory and composition at the University of California, Riverside. Her compositions span across many genres and media, including instrumental works, electronica and digital works, and large-scale performance pieces incorporating dance, visual and theatrical elements. Her scholarly work encompasses many aspects of critical theory in music, including gender and sexuality theories in music, analyzing divergent musical repertoire including opera, punk, blues music, and electronica. She is a contributing editor to *Open Space Magazine* and associate editor of *Perspectives of New Music.* During fall of 2002, she will be a resident fellow at the humanities research institute "Improvisation in the Contemporary Performing Arts," convened by George Lewis.

Xopher Davidson, oscillator, is an engineer and composer. Formerly a non-representational painter, film auteur and loop technician, and curator, he is active in the groups Citizen Band and Mixture 151.

Stuart Dempster, sound gatherer, trombonist, composer, didjeriduist, et al, and Professor Emeritus at the University of Washington, has recorded for numerous labels including Columbia, Nonesuch, and New Albion. His New Albion recording *In the Great Abbey of Clement VI at Avignon* has become, in the words of one reviewer, "a cult classic." Also on New Albion is *Underground Overlays from the Cistern Chapel,* which consists of music sources for a 1995 Merce Cunningham Dance Company commission. His grants include: Creative Associate at SUNYAB (1967-68); Fellow, Center for Advanced Study, University of Illinois (1971-72); Fulbright Scholar in Australia (1973); NEA Composer Grant (1978); US/UK Fellowship (1979); Guggenheim Fellowship (1981). Dempster, a leading figure in the development of trombone technique and performance, published his landmark book *The Modern Trombone: A Definition of Its Idioms* in 1979. As a founding member of Deep Listening Band, he has toured extensively and produced the first three DLB recordings including the award-winning *Deep Listening* CD on New Albion, the first CD made in the now famous Fort Worden (Port Townsend, WA) cistern with a 45" reverberation time. Dempster is also known for soothing aches, pains, and psychic sores with his healing, yet playful, Sound Massage

Parlor. These and other environmental/site specific works, such as *SWAMI (State of Washington As a Musical instrument)*, have earned him a reputation as a composer/performer whose work is at once deep, meditative, and amusing. His multimedia collaboration with wife Renko Ishida Dempster, *Dream-Time-Pieces*, was exhibited at Seattle's Jack Straw New Media Gallery in 2000. As a founding member of ROOM, he has worked with this Seattle based movement, sound, and visual arts collective since 1998.

He is a regular performer with The Cathedral Band live/online at www.monroestreet.com/Cathedral/stage. Detailed discography, information on Sound Massage Parlor, and links to New Albion Records and Deep Listening Band available at http://faculty.washington.edu/dempster/.

David Gamper moves freely among the worlds of composition, improvisation, and electronic instrument design and construction. In his work creating performer controlled sound processing environments for improvising acoustic musicians including Deep Listening Band, he has directed development of the Expanded Instrument System (EIS) for the Pauline Oliveros Foundation. He has designed variations of the EIS for teaching, demonstration, recording, and for use by guest musicians in performance. The recording of a concert with Oliveros at the IJsbreker in Amsterdam has been described as "the pinnacle of the Oliveros-Gamper collaborations, music that through its depth, reveals ever more profound expression." His piece *Conch* (2000) was in the Whitney Museum of American Art's BitStreams exhibition in Spring 2001 and is included on the CD of sound art from that show. *See Hear Now* is Gamper's collaboration with Gisela Gamper which merges music and video into an immersing environment which transcends each medium. More information can be found at http://www.seehearnow.org/dgamper.

Diane Grubbe has appeared as soloist with the Sienna Music Festival in Italy, the San Francisco Concerto Orchestra, L'Orchestre de Notre Dame in San Francisco and the Calabasas Chamber Orchestra in Southern California, with whom she recorded the Vivaldi Piccolo Concerto for their CD, "The Baroque Concerto." An active chamber musician, Ms. Grubbe performs regularly on Bay Area concert series with her chamber ensembles Angelica, The Red Vine Trio and Octaves in Unison as well as on the East Coast and in Europe with The Elysium Art Ensemble, a mixed-instrument group which she co-founded. As an orchestral flutist, Ms. Grubbe has performs with numerous Bay Area orchestras including Napa Valley Symphony, Vallejo Symphony, Pocket Opera, Lamplighters and Cinnabar Opera Theatre.

Choreographer **Joanna Haigood** makes dances that use natural, architectural and cultural environments as a point of departure and often incorporate aerial flight. She cofounded ZACCHO Dance Theater.

Composer and instrument maker **Brenda Hutchinson** makes extensive use of language, stories, ambient and sampled sounds. She works with the Exploratorium and Harvestworks in New York.

Matt Ingalls, clarinet, composes electroacoustic music, leads the sfSound Ensemble and curates the ACME Observatory series in Berkeley. He studied at Mills, and the University of Texas.

Ione is an author, playwright and director. She is also an accomplished psychotherapist, specializing in myth and heritage, dream phenomena and women's issues. Her seminal work, *Pride of Family: Four Generations of American Women of Color*, is a *New York Times Notable Book*, and on the New York Public Library's List of 25 Books to Remember. Ione was a journalist for a number of years, and her articles have been widely published. She is the author of *This is a Dream! A Handbook for Deep Dreamers*. She is the director and playwright of *Njinga The Queen King: The Return of a Warrior* with music and sound design by Pauline Oliveros, premiered at BAM's Next Wave Festival in 1993. She is the director and creator of the story line for of *The Lunar Opera: Deep Listening For_Tunes*, premiered at Lincoln Center in August 2000. She is director and librettist of *Io and Her and the Trouble with Him: A Dance-Opera in Primeval Time*, premiered at the Union Theater, University of Wisconsin in April 2001. Other projects include: *Hotel Regina: A Video Opera* with music and sound design by Pauline Oliveros, and *Return To Egypt: A DVD Opera* with music and sound design by Andrea Goodman.

Allison Adah Johnson is a composer who studied at Stanford University (BA), the California Institute of the Arts (MFA), and is currently completing her PhD from the University of California San Diego. Her principal composition teachers have been Mel Powell, Morton Subotnick, and Chaya Chernowin. She studied Javanese gamelan with Djoko Walujo at CalArts and with Suhardi in Yogyakarta, Central Java. Her compositions have been performed throughout the US, Asia, and Europe and at the Frau Musica (nova) Festival in Cologne, the New Directions in Asian-American Music Festival in Santa Barbara, and at Feminist Theory & Music VI in Boise, Idaho, and her writings have been published by Studio Verlag and in *21st Century Music*. She has been a guest lecturer at Mills College and California State University San Marcos and currently teaches at Skyline College, Foothill College and Cogswell Polytechnical College in the Bay

Brett Larner, koto, studied koto in Tokyo under the master Kazue Sawai and holds a master's license from the Sawai So-Kyokuin. While active with the traditional and contemporary koto repertoire, Larner is primarily an improviser. He is a graduate student at Mills.

Cellist Hugh Livingston holds a doctorate in contemporary cello performance from UCSD, has been in residence at CNMAT at UC Berkeley, and performs in Mapa Mundi with Tom Bickley.

George Marsh, percussion, master improviser in a variety of styles, has composed for films and taught drumming and percussion at the UCSC and Sonoma State University.

Larry Ochs, Rova Saxophone Quartet, is a composer, and executive director of the Rova non-profit organization. He performs also in Maybe Monday with Fred Frith and Miya Masaoka, and is involved in many other innovative musical projects.

Pauline Oliveros, composer, musician, founder of Deep Listening. Pauline Oliveros' life as a composer, performer, and humanitarian is about opening her own and others' sensibilities to the many facets of sound. Since the 1960's she has profoundly influenced American music through her work with improvisation, meditation, electronic music, myth, and ritual. Many credit her with being the founder of present day meditative music. All of Oliveros' work emphasizes musicianship, attention strategies, and improvisational skills.

She has been celebrated worldwide. In the 1960's, John Rockwell named her work *Bye Bye Butterfly* as one of the most significant of that decade. In the 70's, she represented the U.S. at the World's Fair in Osaka, Japan; during the 80's she was honored with a retrospective at the John F. Kennedy Center for the Performing Arts in Washington D.C., and in the 1990's was presented with a letter of distinction from the American Music Center presented at Lincoln Center in New York. There is currently a plan for a global celebration of the 50th anniversary of her work in the year 2001. Oliveros work is available on more than 17 recordings produced by companies internationally.

Jann Pasler, roundtable participant, has published extensively as a musicologist and theorist in the areas of feminism and music and music in early twentieth-century Paris. She holds a Ph.D. from the University of Chicago and teaches at UCSD.

Maggi Payne is a composer, flutist, recording engineer/editor and video artist. At Mills College she is Co-Director of the Center for Contemporary Music, and teaches audio engineering, composition and electronic music.

Canadian-born **Dana Reason**, The Space Between, piano and roundtable participant, has performed extensively at international free-jazz and improvised music festivals. She is writing her Ph.D. dissertation titled *Playing like a Girl: Women Improvisors in the Second Half of the Twentieth Century* at UCSD.

Moira Roth, roundtable participant, is a feminist art historian and critic who writes and lectures extensively on contemporary art, and teaches at Mills. She is collaborating with Pauline Oliveros on *The Library of Maps*.

Edward Schocker, glass instrument, holds an MA in composition from Mills. He is active in the field of made/found instruments and alternate tuning systems. His dance-theater collaborations have toured extensively in Europe

Katherine Marie Setar is an adjunct instructor of theory and small ensemble performance at Chabot College in Hayward, California. She earned her Ph.D. and MA in music theory from the University of Southern California and her B.M. and piano performance from California State University at Northridge. Her awards include the USC Dean's Fellowship and a USC Teaching Fellowship in music theory. The main foci of her research consist of various approaches to music theory (these include traditional harmony, timbre theories, and acoustics) and the works of modern and post-modern composers. In addition to her teaching duties, she also works as a freelance accompanist, composer, and music instructor. Her publications include *Pauline Oliveros: Zhuren durch Improvisation, Watertank Software: Eine 'Interaction' zwichen Pauline Oliveros und einem halligen Raum* (1998) and *An Evolution in Listening: An Analytical and Critical Study of Structural, Acoustic, and Phenomenal Aspects of Selected Works by Pauline Oliveros* (1997).

The Space Between utilizes a unique combination of just intonation accordion with shakuhachi and piano, which immediately puts the trio in a special sonic space. The trio employs timbre and texture as their main structural units for composition and improvisation. As a result the discrepancy in tuning systems of the instruments becomes an advantage rather than a disadvantage.

Karolyn van Putten, voice and percussion, covers a wide variety of styles and settings. She has performed with Bobby McFerrin, Musica Divina, and Sisters of the Sound Continuum. She holds a Ph.D. in East-West psychology.

David Wessel, electronics, studied mathematics and experimental psychology at the University of Illinois and received a doctorate in mathematical psychology from Stanford in 1972. He worked at IRCAM in Paris and is the director of CNMAT at UC Berkeley

Jennifer Wilsey is a percussionist exploring the healing dimensions of sound through the use of percussion and voice. She received her musical training at the University of California, Santa Cruz.

Gayle Young, amaranth, is a composer, author and inventor of musical instruments and notational systems based in Toronto. She is managing editor of *Musicworks* magazine and is the biographer of electronic music pioneer Hugh LeCaine.

List of Donors and Contributors

All Souls Episcopal Church, Berkeley CA for rehearsal space

John Bischoff, Berkeley, CA

Anchor Brewing Company, San Francisco CA

Chris Brown, Oakland, CA

Marie Chouinard, Montreal, Canada

Austin E. Clarkson, Islington, Ontario, Canada

Mrs. Ernest Deffner, Titano

Kendall Jackson Winery, Santa Rose, CA

Richard Kerry, MA

Bun-Ching Lam, Poestenkill, NY

Raymond and Judith Levy-Sender, San Francisco, CA

Norman Lowrey, Boonton, NJ

Lisa Mages, Washington, DC

William Allaudin Mathieu, Sebastopol, CA

Dominique Mazeaud, Santa Fe,

Accordian

Laura Donnelly, Tucson, AZ

Margaret Dorfman, Palo Alto, CA

Pauline and Robin Dresher, Berkeley, CA

OP&WE Edwards Foundation, New York, NY

Bradley Fischer and Katherine Marie Setar, Fremont, CA

Floating World Studio, Columbia, MO

Foundation for Contemporary Performance Arts, New York, NY

Heloise J. Gold, Austin, TX

Daniel Goode, New York, NY

Lorraine Hansberry Theatre, San Francisco, CA

Andrew Hoyem, Arion Press, San Francisco, CA

Deborah Hay, Austin, TX

NM

Mills College, Oakland, CA

Gertrude Morse, Garrett Park, MD

Gordon Mumma and Michelle Fillion, Orinda, CA

Pauline Oliveros Foundation, Kingston, NY

Jann Pasler, Solana Beach, CA

Michael Payne, San Francisco, CA

Moira Roth, Berkeley, CA

T.P.T. Toyoji and Marianne Tomita MacDonald, Oakland, CA

J Taylor Van Horne, Los Angeles, CA

Katherine Walkup, Book Arts Dept. Mills College, Oakland CA

Long Zhou Chen Yi, Kansas City, MO

ZINA'S CIRCLE

From Digital Dialogues: Technology and Hand,
a collaborative symposium between the
M.I.T. Media Lab and Haystack Mountain School of Crafts
Deer Isle, Maine
September-October 2002

As a musician, I have always loved the feeling of energy that emanates from the palms of my hands after a performance. There is a pleasant tingling. At the conference, I wondered about the hands of the craftspeople and technologists and if they had similar sensations in relation to their practices.

For my session with the group, I decided to offer *Zina's Circle* from my *Sonic Meditations*. This piece emphasizes listening with the palms of the hands. All 66 participants stood in a circle with joined hands; left palm up (receiving from the participant to the left) and right palm down (sending to the participant on the right).

First, a light hand squeeze is sent around the circle as fast as possible—a test of reaction time—listening with the palms of the hands. Next, a whisper sound is added to the squeeze for sonic feedback. The listening is now layered with kinetic and audio signals. Some participants might respond more quickly to one signal or the other.

The rhythm of attention is perceptible as the signal circulates—sometimes it is seamless and sometimes there are gaps in reaction time. Occasionally, the signal disappeared and had to be initiated again when someone had a lapse of attention and broke the cycle.

If $1/10^{th}$ of a second is a normal reaction time for most people and there are 66 people in the circle, each cycle should take 6.6 seconds. Our first tries were closer to 12 seconds—pretty slow!

Next, instead of a whisper, an energetic "Ha!" accompanied the hand squeeze around the circle. In each cycle there is opportunity to shorten reaction time. With more energy in the sound, there is a fascinating pulsation—a weaving of voices and energy rippling around the circle.

Zina's Circle causes an oscillation of attention between open (or global) reception to focal action—hearing sound and squeezing hand.

At the end of an unbroken cycle, I asked the participants to release their hands gradually and bring the palms forward to sense the energy field between the palms as if it were a sphere that could be gently massaged. For most people there is a tangible feeling—as if holding a ghostly ball that tingles.

I felt that heightening the sensitivity of the hands could be a way of linking the technologists and craftspeople both literally and figuratively in keeping with the theme of the conference.

ATTENTION-NOTATION

The range of notational practices employed to present my work as a composer includes conventional staff notation, graphic notation, metaphors, prose, oral instruction and recorded media. *Sonic Meditations* are notated through prose instructions or recipes. The notations for *Sonic Meditations* were presented in written form only after many trials with oral instructions given to many different people. Even though *Sonic Meditations* are in print, I often vary or revise the wording I use to transmit the instructions in new situations.

Such instructions are intended to set an attentional process in motion within a participant and among the group that can deepen gradually with repeated experience. A definitive performance is not expected as each performance can vary considerably even though the integrity of the guidelines will not be disturbed and the piece will be recognizable each time.

The central concern in all my prose or oral instructions is to provide attentional strategies for the participants. Attentional strategies are nothing more than ways of listening and responding in consideration of oneself, others, and the environment.

Tripping on Wires: The Wireless Body—Who Is Improvising?

Keynote address given at Powering Up/Powering Down
University of California, San Diego
January 30, 2004

> *"By the time machines make a case for themselves in a convincing way and have all the subtle cues indicative of emotional reaction, there won't be a clear distinction between machine and human."*
>
> Ray Kurzweil[1]

We are in the transhuman age.

We are observing and participating in the hybridization of humans and computers—the merger, or what is referred to in scientific circles as *The Singularity,* predicted to arrive by the end of the twenty-first century. How has this situation come to pass? What is the underlying theme that drives humans toward this merger—the Singularity? What will our music be like in the later twenty-first century? Who will be creating this music and performing it, and who will be listening? How will it function and in what kind of society? How wide is the digital divide? Who will be left behind?

I have been tripping on wires—on stage and off stage—for half a century, during a rapidly accelerating technological change in music instrumentation. The body was the original instrument of choice for making music directly with voice, hands, feet, and body resonance. This has not essentially changed. However, when the technology for making musical sounds with early instruments (such as the Paleolithic bird bone whistle, one of the oldest instruments ever found) [cit] emerged, the body was extended into these instruments and became distanced from the process of music-making. Through the millennia, this distance has increased exponentially, until, with the inventions of recording technology and radio broadcasting, music could be completely disembodied.

I have lived for sixty-eight percent of the twentieth century and four percent of the twenty-first century. At this juncture, I have the perspective of seventy-two years experience with technological change, particularly with music technology. I have attempted over the years to enhance my musical understanding, abilities, and performance as a human by using the musical tools that are available to me as an extension of my body. As I continue to adopt new technologies as tools, I am participating in transhuman activity. Will I live to enter the posthuman age?

Little did I realize in 1942 that my fascination with the accordion at age nine would continue to this day and that I would re-tune and use the accordion with recording and electronics as I do now. It is humbling to realize how a simple technology, such as a small metal reed that vibrates freely when air flows through it (as in my accordion), has had a very lengthy presence in music history. Free reeds first appeared in ancient Asian mouth organs, beginning with the Chinese *sheng*, which was developed at least 4000 years ago . Their use in modern Western instruments, such as the accordion, bandoneon, and concertina, began in the mid-nineteenth century. These European instruments, unlike the Asian mouth organs, all distance the performer from his or her own breath. The bellows replace the lungs and the fingers that touch buttons and keys replace lips, tongue, and windpipe.

I was born into a time of disembodied music that I heard on the radio and phonograph. Recording had already existed since the late nineteenth century. Radio broadcast in America was only about twenty-five years old when I was born in 1932. Radio and recording grew rapidly and continue to be primary sources for exposure to wider and wider ranges of music than have ever been possible before. I took that music in my childhood for granted as I did the live piano music that I heard in my home each day. I did not realize how the wire recorder we owned by 1946 would evolve and be so important in my career and in the evolution of musicianship in general.

I have noticed how accomplished today's musicians are compared with musicians of forty or even twenty years ago. The young musicians that I encounter today can perform almost anything and are often adventurous and open to new work. Younger audiences are more adventurous and open, too. This capacity and openness was not so true in the past. I attribute this development to the availability of audio and video recording of performances, and of immediate playback for the performers and their teachers. Human musicians may compare performances, improvisations of their own, and of all manner of musical repertoire to enhance their abilities, techniques, and understanding through this technology.

When you play back a recording of your own playing, you listen to what you thought you heard and you begin to perceive what you did not hear consciously when you performed; thus, there is interactivity, stimulation of memory, and consciousness. (This was true of the introduction of the alphabet and writing as well in the history of consciousness—technologies support memory.) Humans plus technology equal transhuman activity. We are experiencing a new wave of consciousness because of our relationship with technology.

The first tool of my trade that had a wire to plug in (and trip on) was my Eico tape recorder that I received from my mother for my birthday in 1953. My first impulse was to put the microphone on the windowsill of my San Francisco apartment and record whatever was sounding outside. I learned that the microphone was hearing sounds that I missed while listening during the recording. The challenge of this perception caused me to vow to listen to everything all the time and to remind myself when I was not listening. I have been tripping on listening ever since and minding the reminders. My life and listening were expanded and changed.

The story of my early relationship with the tape recorder is the beginning of my more conscious relationship with technology and the body. Tape recorders were not common in 1953 and had just become available for consumers after their German origin in World War II[2]. My understanding of listening was changed by my experience even though my ears were physically the same. The microphone and tape recorder became extensions of my body and amplified my hearing. The tape recorder became an essential tool in my development as a composer, performer, and improviser. The tape recorder enabled me to more deeply access body consciousness through improvisation. From the moment I recorded my practice sessions, for me or for my students, the immediate feedback improved the speed of error correction for performance. I incorporated improvisation and recording as part of my composing. I notated what I liked from recorded improvisations.

By 1959, I had made my first tape piece to be included on the initial concert of what was to become the San Francisco Tape Music Center. There were no electronic music studios available to me at the time, so my friend Ramón Sender Barayón started a studio in the attic at the San Francisco Conservatory of Music. I made my piece at home using only the tape recorder at seven-and-a-half and three-and-three-quarters ips[3] plus a special feature that allowed me to hand wind the tape in record mode so that I had manual variable speed. I discovered this feature through experimentation, as it was not a documented use of the machine. I was improvising with sounds and with the uses of the recorder. I imagined how an improvised passage recorded at high speed would sound at low speed and visa versa. Thus my real-time improvisation added a new layer that involved projecting future modification and manipulation of the tape recorder as an instrument. Since I had no other electronic equipment, I recorded through cardboard tubes for filters, put the microphone in the bathtub for reverberation and amplified small vibrating objects on an apple box with a contact microphone. The resulting four-channel piece was called *Time Perspectives*. The final sync was done with two stereo tape recorders—there were no four-channel tape recorders at the time. Ramon and I lined up the tape in the long halls of the San Francisco Conservatory to get the starting points.

From the beginning, my work in electronic music proceeded from a performance relationship with sounds and the characteristics of the workings of the tape recorder. For *Time Perspectives,* I improvised long sections of the piece for each channel and avoided cutting and splicing as much as possible. I had improvised a rudimentary home electronic music studio and improvised the music. My later electronic pieces such as *I of IV* and *Bye Bye Butterfly* were entirely improvised in real time in a studio with hardwired equipment that was hardly convenient to move onto a stage. The classical electronic music studio was monolithic! Thus my studio improvisations had to be presented on tape. Throughout the 1960's, I made a lot of music on tape. I also performed live as much as possible. S.F.T.M.C. concerts always included group improvisations with acoustic instruments as well as tape and sometimes a long tape loop.

When I left San Francisco to teach and establish the electronic music program at the University of California, San

Diego, I had a twelve-hour farewell concert in an Embarcadero loft in San Francisco and played all of the tape music that I had made so far. (Morton Feldman attended this concert and later introduced me at a party in New York as "the foremost lady composer in the U.S.A." I appreciated his validation, but had to correct his language, telling him in front of everyone that "a lady", a term used to belittle women in those times, was not the identification of choice.) Until recently, the only music available of mine on record from that period was *I of IV* and *Bye Bye Butterfly*. I still have hours of unrecognized, unreleased electronic music.

The S.F.T.M.C. was moved to Mills College in Oakland from San Francisco in 1966. I served as director of the Tape Music Center at Mills (now the Center for Contemporary Music) from 1966 to 1967. There, I combined my tape techniques with the newly invented Buchla Modular Synthesizer and developed what was to become the Expanded Instrument System (EIS), an improvisational environment that I use today for solo performances and with the Deep Listening Band.

I left Mills for U.C.S.D. in 1967 where I was invited to establish the electronic music program for the graduate students. U.C.S.D. was a great window of opportunity for me. The atmosphere of the department was open for experimentation and the mission was to educate the students to new music and ideas about music. In addition to electronic music courses, I taught The Nature of Music—a large service course that included making tape pieces by cut and splice editing from pre-recorded sounds, group improvisation with found instruments, and graphic scoring.

In 1970, I began composing my *Sonic Meditations* and studying the structure of human consciousness. I formed a women's group that met at my house in Leucadia once a week. We did body and dream work together along with improvisations and *Sonic Meditations*.

Sonic Meditations were explorations on my part concerning how attention is directed in creative work and spontaneous performance. I needed to find a way into how the mind works to make music. Electronic music had expanded me. The electricity in my own body seemed to be flowing differently than before my exposure to electronic sound. However, there were no answers for me other than my own experiences. There were no guidebooks concerning the effects of improvisation and new sounds on the body. I had to find my own way.

I continued to compose, and insisted on performing live electronic music rather than producing pieces in a studio. I had devised a way to use tape delay as a performance tool and extension of my accordion. I think of delay systems as time machines. I play a sound in the present that will come back in the future. When it comes back it is a part of the past. Thus time is expanded to past, present, and future as performance continuum.

Tape delay was cumbersome with large tape decks to lug around when touring. Nevertheless, others and I persisted. I wrote an article in 1969 about the future of delay systems[4]. I had hit some limitations and wished for more flexibility for adjustable timings and modifications of the delayed sounds in real time as I improvised. The built-in limitations of technologies provoke alternative ways to use them, just as the hand winding of tape during recording had provided me with variable speed with my second tape recorder. The distance between the record head and the playback head of a tape recorder had not been intended or engineered for a delay loop but musicians soon discovered the potential and used it.

After I left U.C.S.D., I acquired a couple of Lexicon PCM 42 delay processors in 1983, one for each hand of my accordion (bass and treble). For a time, I enjoyed the performance aspects available with these instruments: modulation, pedal controlled VCO for pitch bending, looping, and feedback. I realized that I wanted numerous delay processors and a way to control them simultaneously and instantaneously during performance. I had challenged myself as a performer by entering the expanded time domain with my EIS to deal not only with what I was playing in the present but with the result in a later time, or times, in counterpoint with the present. Actually, I had begun this work with *Time Perspectives* by integrating recorded passages improvised for later speed modification. Complexity in my improvisations was evolving from a very simple idea, feedback through time delays. It was exciting! Both hands and feet were busy performing.

I experienced a new kind of performance frustration—how could I control multiple performance parameters spontaneously during improvisation when my hands and feet were too busy to access other controls? Interactive software has provided the answer for now. Performance algorithms in Max/MSP[5] provided some relief. I composed algorithms that improvise using material that I generate with my accordion or voice, though the interface—computer keyboard and mouse, pedal board and faders—is still necessary and unsatisfactory.

My body is yearning to participate with the more than eighty-five performance parameters in the interface in an integral way. Once my perception (listening) indicates a response, the parameter change needs to be available spontaneously in the interface. The physical performance motions need to be accomplished smoothly, without breaking attention from the music. Additionally, I need a monitoring system that gives me the ability to hear the spatialized performance from any perspective in the performance space—I need to always be in the field of sound displayed by the performance. What if my ears could detach and fly around the space, merge with any other ears in the audience? I want to listen from the perspective of audience members as well as from my own point-of-source perspective.

Returning to recording, distancing the body and disembodied music: why the intense desire on the part of humans to record? To clone? Why the millennial evolution of technology that increasingly distances the body in music-making, and what is the meaning of disembodied music?

All humans (so far as I know) are confronted with mortality and the desire to overcome mortality. Recording and cloning represent a kind of permanence. (Even so, media impermanence is also a threat.) The headlong thrust in research all over the world to move towards the singularity, or merger, of humans and technology in a posthuman future is a way to overcome the "weakness of the flesh" and overcome impermanence—to delay or eliminate death. What, then, about birth?

In order to resolve my increasing performance frustration—how to access and control more than eighty-five parameters instantaneously—what if the technology was all on board a posthuman body? No wires to trip on—a new world—new frontiers—a new trip—no return. Software must have sentience, intercommunication, and memory; in other words, consciousness. At this point, who is improvising?

MIDWORD

Have you ever stopped, mid-word, and then continued on? Have you ever listened, in seemingly slowed-down time, as each syllable of your voice crumbles into sound, a division continuing without end? Have you ever found yourself on stage performing and then—suddenly—listened as something totally unexpected sounded forth from your body? Have you ever listened—*really* listened—and then, mid-word, or mid-phrase, or mid-life, changed directions?

Pauline Oliveros has a knack of being a catalyst to those surrounding her, for changes of every sort: musical and personal, outward and visible, inner and transformational. One of the most revolutionary aspects of her professional life has been to reject the conventional hierarchical role of the composer.

Rather than asking performers to set aside their creativity in service to hers, she invites them to develop their own musical potential. Rather than asking audiences to be recipients of the creative efforts of others, she invites them to be participants in the process. In Pauline's music there is an elision between the traditionally authoritarian role of the composer and the resulting subservient roles of the performer and the audience. She offers instead a continuum where performers also compose, audiences also perform, and most importantly of all, everyone listens. The energy created by this type of intentional listening is palpable, and it is in this listening that the transformational power of Pauline's compositions becomes most evident.

In *Sounding the Margins,* Pauline Oliveros brings to the foreground the importance of developing the creative potential of all individuals, including those who have been unfortunately—and sometimes deliberately—marginalized. By consciously moving away from structures of power where the composer's creativity is the sole one in evidence, Pauline is able to realize her musical vision while at the same time explicitly encouraging and supporting the development of creative potential in others. As a world-renowned performing composer, she continually provides opportunities for lesser-known artists to join her onstage.

Unparalleled as a collaborative artist, her generosity of spirit defines her teaching as it does her music and her life. In the most literal sense, what I offer as a Midword will be centrally placed within this volume. However, what I have received from Pauline—what she has offered me and the world through her compositions, performances, teaching, and listening—has been centrally placed in my life.

It is fitting that Pauline herself have the last words of this Midword, words that from my own experience I know can change a thought, a musical phrase, and a life: "Deep Listening is listening in every possible way to everything possible to hear no matter what you are doing."

Monique Buzzarté

Harmonic Anatomy: Women in Improvisation

Published in *The Other Side of Nowhere: Jazz, Improvisation, and Communities in Dialogue*
Daniel Fischlin and Ajay Heble, editors
March 30, 2004

In this universe—and perhaps many others—life forms, matter, and energy are constantly interacting to promote flow or movement from one moment to the next. This is improvisation.

In music, theater, dance, and the visual arts, improvisation includes acting from inner intelligence and/or impulse without premeditation from the whole field of available possibilities as well as acting with vocabulary within more prescribed forms.

My early musical education did not include improvisation or any reference to the word. However, at age sixteen, there was an inner improvisation of sounds and music exploding in my mind as I listened to unprompted musical forms taking shape. I heard great whooshing orchestral textures mixing with white noise, pops, whistles and other odd sounds that I would identify later as electronic. I announced that I wanted to be a composer.

By age seventeen, I had begun to engage in jazz improvisation on my accordion with standard tunes such as "Body and Soul," "Deep Purple," "Stardust," etc. I was studying with Bill Hughes—an extraordinary improviser on the accordion who played with Houston jazz groups. I had entered the world of professional music as a soloist—playing standard tunes and improvising over the chord progressions.

Persisting in my desire to be a composer, I would sit at the piano keyboard, searching for the notes running through my mind. I realize now that I was slowly learning to improvise as I fished around the piano keyboard. I learned laboriously to write these notes down.

I was nineteen when I wrote my first piano piece but I found that the keyboard was extremely limiting. Ten years later, I discovered what I wanted to express in the electronic sounds of my first tape pieces.

It had not consciously occurred to me that women were not included in the musical canon that I learned as a performer. Perhaps this was because women had taught me from early childhood.

My mother and my grandmother taught me to read notes but didn't discourage me from playing by ear if I tried it. I do remember striving hard to learn to read music. I was trained to be a performer of other people's music.

My mother, Edith Gutierrez, and grandmother, Pauline V. Gribbin, were dedicated to their piano teaching. Lessons often began early in the morning before school and continued in the afternoon and evening. On Sundays, they played duets and two-piano pieces together with me as a fascinated listener. Edith would practice by herself for hours. I picked up their dedication and devotion early on and tried hard to learn to play as they did on my instrument of choice—the accordion.

Edith tells me that she was unaware of the word improvisation, although she began to improvise while playing piano for dance classes in the 40s. She called it "filling in". My grandmother had learned to play strictly by the notes. However, her husband, my grandfather John M. Gribbin, played only by ear and was always improvising pieces—called "compositions". My grandmother wrote the pieces down for him.

From an early age, I attended numerous concerts of the Houston Symphony and Opera and endless recitals by soloists and chamber groups. Among many touring artists, I was excited to hear Stan Kenton, Spike Jones, and the Israel Philharmonic Orchestra with Leonard Bernstein conducting.

I listened to the radio every week for years to the New York Philharmonic, the NBC orchestra (Toscanini conducting), the Metropolitan Opera, Grand Ole Opry, and Bob Wills and the Texas Playboys. Radio shows with sound effects like *I Love A Mystery* and *Fibber Magee and Molly* fascinated me. Music on the radio had a very large influence on me.

We owned a wire recorder in the 40's—I used it to record myself and music from the radio. I tried to write down what I recorded or to imitate the style on my accordion.

I was thoroughly grounded in many styles of Western music. Exposure to world music came much later. This was the 1940's.

Edith came home one day when I was about thirteen years old and played some "compositions" she had done for a modern dance class at the YWCA. These pieces were oddly dissonant and rhythmical. I also began to notice her "fill ins" when she played the piano at home. There was still no mention of improvisation. Little did I know the profound effect that her cue would have for me. I loved the pieces and still do. Her creativity had jumped out at me.

Gender Challenges

I joined the band in junior high school. Since accordions had no place in the band, I was introduced to the tuba by the female band director. She would be my last female music teacher. The senior high school was a different story. There were already twelve male sousaphone players, so the male band director handed me a French horn to learn to play.

Later, when I became serious about studying, the first sexist remark came from a male horn teacher. "Why do you want to be a horn player? You will only get married and have children." Feelings of betrayal welled up inside. My anger made me feel wary and circumspect with male teachers—there was no recourse for me. I was powerless in the student-teacher relationship to express my feelings directly. I quickly abandoned lessons with that teacher but continued with determination to play.

My first composition class at the University of Houston in 1951 included several women with a male teacher. The teacher seemed respectful of everyone, both male and female. I wrote my first pieces in this class, which were performed along with those of my classmates. So far, my experiences were relatively positive as a woman interested in composition, although the music models presented by the teacher did not help me. Those models were all by men, even though there were women in the class including me.

In 1952, I went on from Houston to San Francisco searching for a composition teacher, reaffirming to myself that I wanted to be a composer and true to what I heard inwardly.

It was in San Francisco that I met with more gender issues from prospective composition teachers—mostly in the form of doubtful remarks about women and composition. To those teachers, women were not candidates for composition lessons.

The composer's workshop at San Francisco State College was populated with men and taught by a man. I joined the workshop. Whenever the instructor considered my music, all twenty or so male students would leave the room. I felt this concerted exodus as another kind of betrayal. However, lack of peer support did not deter me from writing my music. I was determined. This lack of support continued until one day, Terry Riley, Loren Rush, and Stuart Dempster were staying and listening to what I was doing. We began to share our musical interests and became lifelong friends.

The mentor I finally found, Robert Erickson, never made sexist remarks and treated me no differently than his other students. I met Erickson at a Composer's Workshop concert at San Francisco State College in 1954. We admired each other's compositions after that program. His attitude of respect for my work drew me to make an appointment for my first lesson.

I left my first lesson feeling very elated. I discovered that Loren was studying with Erickson, too. Eventually, Terry took lessons as well. We shared our enthusiasm for the excellence of his teaching. In addition to supporting our compositional efforts, Erickson often invited us to his home for family-like occasions. I felt accepted for who I was at the time, even though I was the only woman involved in this circle.

Erickson encouraged all of us to improvise. His prompting was, of course, totally unusual for a person of his academic training in music. He encouraged me to improvise my way through pieces I was composing. His prompting was encouraging and validating and reinforced my way of working.

My first group improvisations were with Terry Riley and Loren Rush in 1957. There were no models; there were no scenes for improvisation as there are today. Gathering three composers of concert music to improvise together was unprecedented.

Terry had to compose a five-minute film score. He didn't have time to write it so we went to Radio KPFA in Berkeley where Loren was working and recorded several five-minute improvisations for Terry to use for the film soundtrack. Terry selected a track and used it very successfully. We were so interested in the results that we decided to meet again and improvise for fun.

We found that it was best to improvise first and talk about it afterward. If we discussed what we were going to do, the improvisation seemed to fall flat. Improvising without discussion seemed to give us an exciting edge and arena for discovery—the world of possibilities remained open.

After my initial improvisations with Terry Riley and Loren Rush, I began to improvise in a similar way with Ramón Sender Barayón—also a student of Erickson. Morton Subotnick joined us in 1960 and we performed many concerts together under the auspices of our San Francisco Tape Music Center. We always included a group acoustic improvisation in our home concerts and tours of tape music.

My early composition was gestural rather than formal. I wrote what I heard. As a composer, I was not interested in the textbook forms presented to me in classes, I was interested in sounds—the interplay and sensual nature of sounds that ran through my mind.

Later, when I began to work with tape music, I found a friendly medium for my musical inclinations and concerns. I could sculpt sound in this medium through improvisation. I improvised almost all of my early electronic music, gleefully avoiding tedious cutting and splicing of tape. Gradually, improvisation, the combination of tape techniques, electronic sound generation, processing, and acoustic instruments became solid and continuing parts of my music-making

By the end of the 60's, my experience with improvisation was almost exclusively solo or with groups of men. My position was unique. I held my own with male musicians though sometimes I felt discomfort. Even though I was included in the groups that I worked with I felt an invisible barrier. As I had noticed early in life, males bond strongly around music and technology and leave women out of their conversations and performances.

Values

Values often emphasized by male musicians and their critics include technique, intelligence, structure, precision, concept, drive and so forth. For example:

> *"Blessed with a seemingly effortless technique, a wittily deconstructive approach to his instrument(s), and a generous intellligence, he never produces work that is less than thoughtful or other than exuberant."*

> *"...draws from a heady bank of extended techniques that both amplify and personalize the range of his horn."*

> *"...a genuine original, a percussionist whose combination of hyperactivity, arhythmical structure and intense precision have played a crucial role in the European free aesthetic."*

Penguin Guide To Jazz[1]

On the other hand, critical remarks in reviews about women improvisers go toward qualities of sound, spirit and feeling—the language softens to emphasize different values:

> *"Ms. Ibarra deftly maneuvered from delicate brushwork to crashing rim shots as the ensemble alternated between soft harmonies and sharp dissonance. Even the cushioned mallets could not dull her insistent inchoate rhythmic patterns."*

David Yaffe, *The New York Times*[2]

> *"Ingrid Jensen is mindful of the tradition in that she swings, plays real pretty AND with fire, but realizes that you don't live up to "the tradition" by playing it safe."*

Mark Keresman, *Jazz Review.com*[3]

"Claire Daly's lips blow sweetly and the jazz comes forth sweet and low! She is a great talent that is hard to define. Her expertise on the baritone saxophone is truly remarkable and without peer, and to be sure, listen to "Swing Low" and discover how well this lady knows her jazz techniques and blends them with her own intimate, personal visions! Claire Daly gives a sensual performance of harmonic phrasing, and the power of that jazz sophistication is evident".

Lee Prosser, *Jazz Review.com*[4]

The reviewers language seems to emphasize other values in operation with women. The distinction between the qualifiers in the language used to review the women are striking. Susie Ibarra is "deft" and "inchoate", Ingrid Jensen is "mindful" and "plays real pretty." There is, indeed, a reference to Clare Daly's skill, but it is doubtful the male reviewer would write that "Gerry Mulligan's lips blow sweetly" (even if they do) or speak of his "intimate personal visions and sensual performance." Both sets of values are present in the improvisations of men and women. Gender construction sets them apart.

What about the women?

It was not until 1969—the threshold of the emerging women's movement of the 70's—that I explored improvisation with other women. I organized the Women's Ensemble in San Diego. The ensemble featured Betty and Shirley Wong (voice), Lin Barron ('cello), Bonnie Barnett (voice), Joan George (bass clarinet), and the late poet Lynn Lonidier ('cello). I realized then that women needed opportunities to express their inner voices. No one in the university environment was going to recognize this need or do anything about it, so I set about inviting the women to work with me. (I was teaching in the music department at the University of California San Diego during those years.)

The group met at my house in Leucadia, California every week for two years, exploring non-verbal time together, mind/body exercises, dreams, journal writing and reading, and improvisation through my *Sonic Meditations*. The Women's

Ensemble was an important step for me in experiencing the energy of working with women in improvisation informed by the concerns that we shared with one another. Occasionally, we performed concerts as well. We were creating a kind of meditational improvisation based in the layering of sounds. We recorded *Music for Expo 70,* which was featured in the Pepsi Pavilion in Expo 70 in Osaka, Japan.

I was making a transition in my own work with the Women's Ensemble. My music was now coming from a deeper inner place. Working with women gave me a kind of permission to be myself that had been covered or hidden in the mostly male musical environment I inhabited where, as a woman, I had to prove myself more intensely. Coping with competitive males at times was daunting. There was no blueprint for me, either.

Improvising with women brings about a feeling of kinship, collaboration, and co-operative listening. The music is about inclusion rather than exclusion. There is less emphasis on technical mastery and more concern for sounds weaving into shared textures. I feel that I have been heard and included in consciousness as a collaborator, rather than regarded as an intrusive competitor.

I resigned my position at the University of California San Diego in 1981 to pursue a freelance career of composition and improvisation in the Northeast. I started my own non-profit organization, the Pauline Oliveros Foundation, that became the platform for my own creative and educational ideas and concepts. I was on my own and worked mostly as a soloist, performing my own music or collaborating with choreographers.

Through the 1980's I continued to develop my freelance work as a soloist and with the Deep Listening Band* with my old friend Stuart Dempster. I concentrated on the development of my electronic processing—the Expanded Instrument System (EIS). EIS grew out of my way of performing my electronic pieces such as *Bye Bye Butterfly* and *I of IV*. I wanted to apply the processing technique to acoustic sounds. EIS is used as an improvisation environment by me as a soloist and by the Deep Listening Band. EIS continues to evolve, with the assistance of Panaiotis in the 1980's and David Gamper today.

In the meantime, I enjoyed my growing consciousness of other women appearing as composers and improvisers.

In 1996, after meeting violinist India Cooke at the John Coltrane Church in San Francisco, I invited her and a vocalist friend of hers, Karolyn van Putten, to improvise with me. After a couple of sessions at home, we performed as a trio in Berkeley at Bean Benders (formerly a popular venue for improvising musicians in the Bay Area). We were invited to come back to Bean Benders the next month and have played together every fall since and produced a recording, *Live at the Meridian*.

Improvising with India and Karolyn was immediately arresting. I felt their responsiveness was uncanny and very musically rewarding. The Circle Trio (as we called ourselves) was the second all-woman group I organized. I was delighted that more women were available to play together with me. The experience made me miss the Women's Ensemble from San Diego, which had dispersed because of graduations and changes.

Dana Reason (piano) and Philip Gelb (shakuhachi) invited me in 1996 to join their improvising duo for a concert at Radio Valencia, an alternative venue for musicians in San Francisco. I was delighted by their skillful, creative performing and listening. We performed again with saxophonist Jon Raskin of the Rova Saxophone Quartet as our guest at the Center for New Music and Audio Technology (CNMAT) in Berkeley and were recorded by David Wessel. The recording was released on Sparkling Beatnik as *The Space Between*. We continue to perform under that name and released another CD with guest artist Barre Phillips on bass. We delight in negotiating the space between our three different tunings—accordion in just intonation, piano in equal temperament and shakuhachi in its unique pentatonic system.

In 1999, drummer Susie Ibarra invited me to perform with her at Tonic in New York—an important venue for new music on the Lower East Side. I suggested the addition of Monique Buzzarté (trombone), Rosi Hertlein (violin/voice), and Kristin Norderval (voice) to form The New Circle Five. We return to Tonic every year and will soon make a recording together in the studio at Deep Listening Space.

Notably, the 90's included more improvisation with women than ever before in my career. Encouraging as this may seem, improvisation groups in the various "scenes" that exist throughout the Western world still seem to consist exclusively of men unless there is a singer or a token woman included, as is the case with most genres in Western music. This can be seen in the make up of most concert programs, festivals, and touring groups now at the beginning of the 21st century. A casual look at newspapers, magazines, internet sites, and media reports will verify this statement

If a music group consisting exclusively of women turns up (as they do from time to time), they may be viewed as an oddity and taken less seriously by audiences, presenters, and critics than male groups. Otherwise, such groups would sustain themselves and proliferate as readily as male groups do and receive more critical attention. Why do presenters not seek out and engage women's groups to make public appearances? There are exceptions, such as New Music America in the 80's, the Guelph Jazz Festival in Canada, and The London Music Collective in the UK, and a few others. Hopefully these examples will proliferate.

Improvisational music (as well as composition) appears to remain the province of men. Perhaps in a field that is already difficult for men, women don't see any future for themselves as improvisers or composers. Women see few if any role models or mentors, few performance opportunities in the field, and relatively no financial support to launch or sustain a career. The socialization of women continues to reinforce the role for them of spectators, supporters, and administrators where men hold forth as participants in the art.

Harmonic Anatomies

Following are introductions to some of the women musicians that I know through our experience improvising together. Their feelings and thoughts about improvising may shed more light on the issues of gender, language, and the crucial nature of improvisation as a process for dialogue across communities.

Anne Bourne is a professional cellist, vocalist, composer, and improviser based in Toronto. I first improvised with Anne between Toronto and New York via PictureTel connection with the Deep Listening Band. (PictureTel is a video monitor with a camera mounted on top. The system can be connected to an Integrated Services Digital Network (ISDN) telephone line for sound and video distance communication.) Anne has extraordinary tone and can carry an ensemble with her voice and rhythms as well as lovely melodic lines with her cello. Anne burst out of her usual reticence with an emotional reaction:

> *"Fred Stone used to lead his band like Miles Davis, calling out rhythms and lines midstream. I used to get mad and freeze every time he'd tell me to "take a solo," so he once reversed the strategy and whispered in my ear "Whatever you do, don't take a solo." This made me mad enough to play, and became the beginning of a long phase of making music out of anger."*
>
> Anne Bourne

Tapping into emotional energy seemed to open the portals for Anne to express her music. I recall how my own anger spurred me to continue playing horn. This is no less true of men, but the "cool" aesthetic tempers how men play. To be cool is to be technically competent. A flash of technique by an instrumentalist is "cool". An outburst of emotion is definitely not cool. Fred Stone called out "rhythms and lines" to the band—Anne could not respond to this language. Fred's psychological twist turned Anne on to a more accessible way for her to improvise.

Monique Buzzarté is a professional trombone player based in New York. Her admirers describe her playing her "butter trombone". Her beautiful tone spreads through an ensemble with great ease and connection.

> *"I have sometimes felt as if I was reaching far into the future or far into the past—time-travelling while performing. This is especially true of several short improvisations on conch. I let go of myself and open to other experiences, and they happen to me, through me, as if I in the Monique-body am a channel for the expression of something else much bigger than myself. I don't know how explicit I want to be here, but certainly they are the strongest experiences I've ever had performing. Great power for healing and great responsibility for others are carried in these sounds."*
>
> Monique Buzzarté

Monique seems to have a natural propensity for a state of consciousness that opens a large space of spirit. The feeling of being a channel for something bigger than oneself is common to practitioners of healing. Her sense of the power of sounds coming through this mode of consciousness and responsibility for others is an important aspect of healing practice and an important function of music.

India Cooke was introduced as "the world's best kept secret" at one of our concerts in San Francisco. India explains that she is a classically trained violinist—that "playing classical music is challenging". She crossed over to playing jazz. "I found that challenging too. However, the most challenging music to perform is free improvisation." Playing with India is like taking the A train to heaven.

> *"I exercise the resources available to me...I channel psychic energy—not exclusively musical energy—I have gathered. Then I put together harmonies and melodies and rhythms and whatever comes out as a result of this combination is the musical statement."*
>
> India Cooke

India's reference to channeling may mean something similar to Monique's channel. Definitely there is an opening of consciousness implied that infuses India's music and affects other players and the audience—a space of spirit that is wider than ordinary consciousness in daily life.

Susie Ibarra plays the drum set like no other—she plays the space as well as the drums, drumming the air with precision and fluidic confidence. Based in New York, Susie has established herself in improvised music as a top professional, supporting and transporting other players.

> *"I always improvised when I was young. I used to always answer a question with a question. I often felt that there was never only one straight answer to a question."*
>
> Susie Ibarra

Susie's metaphor of the question seems to be the root of her way of improvising—especially the concept that there is always more than one straight answer to a question. Her's is an attitude of discovery and freedom to seek alternatives through the analogy of conversation, where rhythms are constantly in flux.

Frances-Marie Uitti is professional cellist and improviser based in Amsterdam and is noted for her use of two and three bows simultaneously. Her ecstatic playing takes you away immediately.

"I've always enjoyed improvising more than reading music. I feel that improvising is more natural for me than reading music. When I was a child, I would much rather play by ear than read. My father played violin and would play my pieces for me. Once my father found out I was copying him rather than reading, he stopped playing for me and I had to learn to read through many a tear. I studied classical music and stopped improvising until I went to Rome in the late 70's and started group improvisation with vocalist Michiko Hirayama and trombonist Giancarlo Schiaffini. Then I started improvising solo again. It was easier for me to push myself into different corners by myself than in a group."

Frances-Marie Uitti

Frances-Marie expresses a common experience for musicians. Playing by ear is discouraged over the ability to read. The two ways could just as easily be integrated from a fairly early age. Frances found her way out of her classical training to her own music. Her solo work seems to come from a very deep inner place that eschews the diversion of performing with others. She seems to need the quiet of her own "corner" to get to her own inner voice, even though she negotiates group improvisations beautifully.

Kristin Norderval is a professional lyric soprano, composer, and improviser. She is classically trained and is based in Norway and in New York. Kristin can hold her own with an orchestra or an industrial soundscape. Her beautiful lyric soprano can sail through any atmosphere and also blend as an instrumentalist in a group.

"Really interesting acoustics usually bring up spontaneous vocal improvisations for me. I'm unable to resist diving into a beautiful acoustic pool, it's so delightful to explore the caverns,

corral and cut of the stone of the space. I've been recording on-site improvisations in various places for the last four years. The sites give me their own input and offer rhythms, pitches and timbres that I wouldn't come up with on my own. Likewise, when I then process portions of those recordings electronically, the material itself calls for responses from me. The acoustic properties of the sites or the objects that I work with might provide drones or microtones or modalities, but the processing might provide different harmonic or rhythmic structures, so there is a merging of various styles that happens automatically. Also, although I'm a classically trained singer, when I'm working over unusual sound landscapes I may borrow from other singing traditions, or imitate sounds that I wouldn't use in a classical context. Some friends hearing my music have described it as urban-tribal."

Kristin Norderval

Kristin's interest in acoustics shows that she is listening. She is responsive to spaces and dialogues with sites. Her consciousness of environment informs her work. She is aware on many levels at once, drawing from the site at hand, vocal flexibility, her memory of styles, and her imaginative interplay with all of these elements.

Dr. Jackie Pickett plays acoustic bass and is equally at home with both oral and written traditions of music performance. Classically trained with a DMA from the University of Wisconsin-Madison, Jackie plays all genres as a freelance professional and devotes herself to teaching inner-city kids. Playing with Jackie is an uplifting experience. Her techniques carry her anywhere in the musical map.

"When the group enters an "out of body" space, it is like you can actually look "up/down/over/under/across" and see the group playing...locking in. There is a similar sensation in cycling up a hill with the proper "spin" in the pedal."

Jackie Pickett

Out of the body from in the body to a state of global consciousness that provides for a witness like overview of the performing—again, an acute awareness of the state of mind and body sensations.

Dana Reason plays the piano, composes, and improvises. She thinks deeply about improvisation and is completing a dissertation for her Ph.D. in improvised music at the University of California, San Diego. Dana explores the coloristic possibilities of the piano on the keyboard and inside the piano with daring and intensity. Her intricate patterns weave an ensemble together.

> *"I was always playing things by ear and really didn't want to read music for a while. I liked making things up, although I thought I was composing, not improvising. I didn't really know the term improvisation. I liked putting the television on and turning down the volume to "make the soundtrack." I also liked putting on the radio and playing along with the songs. I used to try and fool my parents into thinking I was practicing by improvising in the style of Bach, Beethoven, or whatever."*
>
> Dana Reason

Dana found her way to her music by improvising even though she had no word for it. I wonder how often her parents were fooled by her attempts to imitate the style of Bach or Beethoven? Like most of the other women, my mother, and me, self-teaching and "playing by ear" brought about the ability to improvise music directly.

> *"There is something about improvising with women that is like coming home. Almost a tribal feeling compels us to find the musical way to understanding and carries the listeners inside. Our bodies merge with the vibrational complexity of a deep ocean.*
>
> *Improvising with women, the undulating movement between chaos and form is strong and challenging and finally, understanding is expressed lovingly with respect. This I have experienced improvising with both men and women. However, the resonance of harmonic anatomy can move me to the bone marrow."*
>
> Anne Bourne

The unique values, understanding, and expression each woman brings to our improvisations helps me to understand my own evolution as an improviser in a continually expanding collaborative process and language. That process includes sharing space/time, sharing states of consciousness and body consciousness, and elevating the sensuous nature of sound onto a par with technical mastery in making the music. This process is of the body, in the body, and out of the body. The vocabulary of the language includes sounds as well as pitches, the syntax comes through inner and outer dialogue with self, space, and others through weaving and sharing in the moment; the forms arise and shape themselves from the energy of the body—breath, sensations and consciousness through listening and tuning to the presence of others—this is "harmonic anatomy".

> *"Musically speaking, it is a very large language that is constantly growing for me. Sometimes, it is the gift of playing pure music, which seems to be falling right out of the sky. Sometimes it is a gift of communication between people, like a common language that breaks all barriers. Sometimes in life experiences, it is the deciding action that can help keep the motion moving and constant. Sometimes it is a saving grace in situations. And sometimes, it is a random small act that can make you laugh deep inside at life's absurdities. Sometimes it is an act of love."*
>
> Susie Ibarra

Approaches to improvisation vary and evolve with new groupings of performers and dialogues across musical communities. All could benefit greatly from the integration of new feelings, energies, and ideas that come from the language women are developing through improvisation.

> *"My improvisations are primarily tonally coloring an environment/emotion and/or gestural. I don't think about limitations, I think about possibilities, of using my instrument to realize inner hearing."*
>
> Monique Buzzarté

Gender Questions

Equality for women in music does not yet exist as we enter the 21st century. There will be no equality until all musical organizations, all music educators—from schoolteachers through institutions of higher education, all professional musicians, all producers, publishers, agents, managers, critics, audiences, and anyone associated with music recognize the need for all people, regardless of gender or ethnicity, to be included in musical activities of all kinds.

> *"...gender can not really be separated from other issues surrounding the production of music such as racism, sexism, or class. One only needs to open many of the current magazines which discuss improvised music to note the use of an essentialized language to describe women improvisers, the reduction of women to their physical descriptions, the lack of experimental and cutting-edge women performers included in reviews, articles, and books, or the relative exclusion of many women on the handful of festivals which present improvised music. Really, the list can go on. I can only think of a few of the recent books on improvisation that include specific women artists, or include their experiences and voices. There is a lot of work to be done, there are hundreds of women improvisers yet we tend to present or write about only a small number of women—the majority of which tend to be very well established musicians. While this is a positive step, we need to include the growing contributions of the younger generations of women improvisers."*
>
> Dana Reason

Dana's forthcoming dissertation on women improvisers[5] will surely give exposure to many new voices and bring many more issues to the surface for resolution.

> *"Almost all of the professional work that I've done that involves improvisation has been with women, and virtually all of those situations have been both welcoming and inspiring. I haven't worked with very many men professionally in this way. That in itself is a gender issue—it seems integration of groups is hard to come by."*
>
> Kristin Norderval

Integration of musical groups as well as other kinds of groups is a major issue in the world everywhere. Women—no less than men—need invitations to perform, financial reward, and validation for their creativity.

> *"Because of my social and institutional training, I have done pretty well in this business. However, I as a black woman and other black women can hold ourselves back because of our preconceived beliefs of what we think other people think of what we should be or who we should or might be. My experience in the performing arts in jazz as well as classical is that the dominant male culture has a tendency to stereotype women in a curious light. If we are not singers we are not always taken seriously. Playing hot and heavy could be considered a gender-wise personal dysfunction."*
>
> India Cooke

Because of my sexual orientation, men sensed that they could be my friend but not my lover. Perhaps not participating in a stereotypical relationship was a relief for my male friends. If you play your part in a stereotypical role, you lose your original voice. India doesn't do that and neither do I.

> *"I am anti conformist, I am rebellious, and I refuse to accept what I do not believe true. I do not want to be captive of only one repertory. "*
>
> Cathy Berberian

Singers have played a leading role in the development of improvised music, even though their contributions do tend to be minimized in various ways through stereotyping and disparagement of the value of their musicianship—"can't keep time, doesn't sing what's written," and so forth. The great blues women really led the way for the horn players in jazz improvisation with their expressive phrasing and melodic invention. In concert music, Cathy Berberian taught Luciano Berio the sounds that he fashioned into a composition for her. Her own composing and improvising is much less known than the work of her famous husband.

"Improvisation allows me to communicate with others in an honest and direct way. Improvisation teaches me about the importance of being ready to play exactly who, where and what I am about at that moment. When you improvise, you can't stop time and say 'now wait a minute—I wasn't ready for that,' you must be ready for the unexpected and I think that is very much a part of how one thrives in life."

Dana Reason

So what if equality in music is achieved in this century? What difference could it make to you? If you are a father or brother, how would you feel if your daughter or sister was excluded from participating in the creation or performance of music? Would you support such exclusion, knowing that participation in the creation of music is a profoundly gratifying process that can lead to mind expanding development?

"Lots of people talk about how art reflects life. But if jazz is art, how can it reflect life if there are only men playing it?"

Susie Ibarra

The growing improvisation movement around the world is reaching across boundaries. The difference between composed and improvised music—not often well understood by musicians and music educators who have practiced the classical canon—is changing.

"Improvisation draws from a vast amount of experiences...the past, present, and future...instantaneously. The improviser is at once the composer, player and interpreter—it is truly a liberating experience that occurs in the moment...a moment born from the totality of all we are. Written music provides an authority (the composer writes...and you shall play...) relationship between creator and the creation."

Jackie Pickett

The difference between composition and improvisation is drawn succinctly by Jackie's statement—liberation. Liberation from the box that can be formed by over-emphasis on training and technique and a lack of respect for the nature of sound. Improvisation can bridge differences and open new musical pathways.

> *"It is vital for each of us to tap into our own creativity, to consider ourselves as creators, and not simply re-creators of other people's creativity. "*
>
> Monique Buzzarté

It is crucial that all be encouraged to explore their own creative potential. Playing other people's music is a service that can be rewarding as a regenerative experience for the performer as well as the audience.

> *"Improvising allows for responding in the moment instead of "preparing" for something in a future moment. The more I improvise, the more I'm able to bring the spirit of improvisation to notated music as well—I try to sing it in the moment as if I was making it up on the spot, and not as if I know already what will come next."*
>
> Kristin Norderval

Improvised music comes more from the intuitive body and composed music more from the intellect, which is more closely connected to writing. Women may feel more comfortable with the language of the body as a way of composition although there is really no separation. We also need our intuitive bodies to write music and our intellect to improvise music.

> *"Improvising differs from performing written music because, when reading, or even after memorizing a long piece, when you try to internalize and personalize the piece to become authentic expression, you are still taking on, on a physiological level, a preconceived pattern generated from another's soul and body.*
>
> *One of the benefits of a score is that it can distract you from self-consciousness.*

Improvising seems to come from a deeper unconscious part of myself and springs forth unexpected. There are times when the structure and limits of my own personal patterns seem to disintegrate to allow a loud arrival of musical and sensual material previously unknown to myself. Improvising allows me a deeper relationship with the other performers. This is especially apparent when accompanying dance.

Without the grid of a preconceived score between you, one can be open to any new impulse that may emerge from one of you. I merge with a fellow performer and follow their soul walk on an instinctual level. Improvising performers are often surprised, when going beyond craft we find ourselves making choices that lead to simultaneous musical arrival. I am often surprised that being true to myself and singing authentically is exactly the thing that co-creates the strongest and most moving musical event.

The truest voice for myself is the one allowed to be a "composer" in the immediate experience of time and sensation. Being an improvising composer is being a sonic architect to sound lines of geometry allowing for relationship between the invisible and the unknown qualities of life."

Anne Bourne

Anne's unique statement about the composer/improviser dualism twists one's perspective or habitual thought patterns as a good improvisation can do to open new pathways of thought—the problem solving or creative part of the brain/body. For mental and spiritual human development it is important to get beyond the habit of learning patterns to engage in problem solving activity.

"I remember William Parker talking to me about composition and spontaneous composition. I also feel that improvisation is composition in the moment. These two are written and oral languages that, although dealing with a common basis of music, can produce very different things."

Susie Ibarra

I myself was neither supported nor prevented from participating in creative music (composing/improvising). I found my way to creative music through listening to sounds in my imagination and taking a cue from my mother's compositions. I practiced my instrument faithfully every day, though my true interest was to create my own music.

> *"I come out of solo and chamber music background where listening is crucial. I use improvisation as a compositional tool—that's my path. One has to study written music until it comes out of you and becomes yours. What I like about in improvisation is that I surprise myself with sounds and musical ideas that would never happen otherwise. That's the big pleasure for me to have a new idea. The longer I go on with improvisation the more important it is for me."*
>
> Frances-Marie Uitti

Improvisation is an essential tool for my work as a performer and composer. For me, improvisation is a way of life and life is an improvisation. Each day brings new challenges. Each moment has infinite possibilities or choices unless one is committed to some binding schedule or limiting design. However, the moment always offers choices, even if you are committed to going to work or to a class or to catching a plane. Flux forces us to improvise. Flexibility helps us to cope with the changes that we encounter whether in daily life or in music.

> *"I find improvising offers me far more musical challenges than playing notated music. Being able to play anything and any time in any way, the basics of the improvisational palette, demands a far greater level of preparation from me than anything else I've ever done musically."*
>
> Monique Buzzarté

Improvising truly in the moment can be a breathtaking musical challenge that gives enormously to the performer and consequently to the audience. The gift is the expression of the human spirit carried in the music that emerges momentarily and synergistically with all consciousness. Such a shared experience can be empowering to all involved and is the basis for growth and change.

In conclusion, the words of improviser LaDonna Smith provide an excellent summation:

> *"Music improvisation is, for me, a powerful resource of transformation in the moment. It is a divining tool, a centering technique, and a celebration outlet. It is a direct line for the expression of our inner forces, spirituality, and emotions. It is an indicator of both personal and universal disturbance or beauty, the blooming and expression of the psyche.*
>
> *In the purifying flame of the moment, the gift of music that comes through our voices and hands, speaks to us directly from our own souls. In listening and responding, pulsing with the beat of my own heart, and the rhythms of the world, singing from the source, channeling unselfconsciously, comes the elixir, the equilibrium, and the expression of my own sanctuary. It is an activity that I return to, over and over, as a vehicle for connection of my Spirit with the Great Mystery and Cosmic Creator. As an improviser, I am thankful to be a listener and a player in the direct flow of the Universe."*
>
> LaDonna Smith

For a major part of my career, I was without peer relationships with women. It is gratifying to find them now, creating music as the bridge to dialogues with diverse musical communities of men and women. Improvisation is an excellent portal for creative women musicians to communicate with others and express themselves musically in this century. All people need an egalitarian atmosphere for all means of creating music, whether composed or improvised. The power of music used in this way could bring about significant changes to benefit everyone—equality, collaboration, and cooperation.

Coda: The Moment of Empowerment

By DeJuana McCary,
whose experience resonates with all women.

In our environment today, there are many ways that people, particularly women, feel the sense of little or no power in their lives. This may be a result of childhood, marriage, or just their own inner voices telling them that they do not have the right to do or be this or that. I have discovered a new way to walk through the dense entanglement of vines that appear to bind me to a previous way of thinking. This tool is the gift of being in the moment—or ***improvisation.***

As a girl growing up in Mississippi, I was taught that children are to be seen and not heard. This taught me early on not to have a voice. This training continued as I was traumatized in school for not being like everyone else. I was slower physically and did not wear the latest styles and did not know how to socialize very well. I had this ever-present thought that no one would ever want to hear anything I had to say. One of the things I loved to do was sing. Even that was a source of pain, however. I participated in a small Southern Baptist church and was constantly taunted by a group of boys and even the person who led the choir. He had given me the nickname "Gorilla", commenting that I looked like a monkey and sounded like one too before laughing. As an adolescent, these ideas took root in my being like a kudzu vine, unwilling to let my true spirit and essence of being come forth.

From that path, I entered marriage and chose what was familiar to me. A person who had to control me, tell me that I could not do anything right, and refuse to let me voice my opinions. I entered deep wells of depression—constantly wanting and wishing for some waters of renewal.

Years passed and I continued to exist. I was not living. I was maintaining. I had survived only by being on medication and having psychotherapy. If I had a dollar for every time the therapist told me "you have options", then I would be a millionaire. It took me around eight years to really know that I did have options. Then I began to make some better choices in my life. I chose to get out of my marriage and begin a journey of discovery and exploration of new ideas and new ways.

I stumbled into a community of artists and then into a smaller community of improvising musicians. My spirit felt like a feather floating in the wind, instead of one confined and pressured to be something it was not. It did not take me long to realize that even though I could not "read" music, the community not only allowed me to have a voice, they actually encouraged and celebrated it. Amazing, the joy and new life that rose up in me like a geyser, springing up from the very core of the earth. The old shackles of having to be a certain way have slowly fallen off and new wings of being in the moment as I am, without judgment, internally and externally, have risen up like the phoenix from the ashes.

As the gift of improvisation enters society, and the life of women, I believe that paradigms will shift. Those who have never experienced power in their being can know and discover this and have a voice to speak for themselves without hesitation or reserve. So the next time you hand a woman a rattle, a drum, or a tambourine, or just invite her to make a sound, remember that you are enabling her to make choices and changes in her life by learning to be in the moment. To be *who* she really is, instead of *what* someone else has demanded that she be. May the spirit of freedom embraced by the art of improvisation change the world to be a world not of confinement, but a world of choices.

THE ACCORDION (& THE OUTSIDER)

Published in the webzine *The Squid's Ear*
April 26, 2004

Calling all accordions! If there is an accordion in your attic, basement or closet why not get it out and let it breathe with you? Accordions are good friends and get lonely sitting around unused! They want to be played just like any other good instrument.

Get the accordion out of its isolation, put it on and just depress the air button. Let the air go through as you pull and push the bellows in a smooth arc and just listen to the air. This is the breath of the instrument. Let your own breath join with the accordion.

After this breathing duet, gently depress a button or a key (just one or the other at first) and listen to the tone—join the breathing.

Here is a piece that I wrote for myself to explore breathing with the accordion:

Horse Sings From Cloud
For solo or ensemble

Hold a tone until you no longer desire to change it.

When you no longer desire to change the tone then change it.

I have played the accordion for more than sixty years. I consider my accordion to be an amplification of my breath. The ancestor of the accordion, the 4,000-year-old Chinese *sheng* (mouth organ), is breath-driven with a mouthpiece attached to a gourd resonator with free metal reeds vibrating inside of vertical bamboo pipes fixed into the gourd. There are finger holes in the gourd for changing pitches. The fingers pick up vibration from the gourd. The *sheng* is a beautifully integrated instrument for breath and touch.

The accordion (invented in 1840 in Vienna) with its keyboard, buttons and bellows, remove the reeds from direct human breath, but it is still a wind instrument with air-driven free reeds. The keys, when pressed, open valves that let the bellows blow air through the reeds to cause them to vibrate. I synchronize my breath with the air in the bellows as the reeds come to life and sound.

Playing the accordion has influenced my interest in breath-oriented music—that is, pieces that are shaped by breath-like rhythms that flow organically as illustrated by *Horse Sings From Cloud*.

The instrument also lends itself very well to sharp articulations or accents so that dance rhythms and polyrhythms found in conjunto and tango are natural to the accordion as well

I started learning accordion when I was nine years old. I was fascinated when my piano-playing mother brought one home to learn in order to increase her earning power. Accordion was very popular in the 1940's. There were very large accordion schools in Houston Texas, where I was born in 1932. I quickly learned the basics of music with melody with bass and chord accompaniment. I soon could play many tunes, especially World War II songs like "Coming in on a Wing and a Prayer" or "White Cliffs of Dover" and many others.

A very significant experience for me in my first year of study was performing in the rodeo in the Houston Coliseum in a 100-piece accordion band. The overall sound of the band remains with me today. The sound was powerful and resonated throughout the Coliseum. That was the first experience that turned my attention to the timbre of the instrument and of many instruments sounding together simultaneously.

The accordion is rich in overtones. Subtly varying key/button and air pressures brings out different overtone structures for each pitch. The use of registers to open and close ranks of reeds increases the richness of possibilities. Unison reed sets tuned a few cents apart cause even more commotion with the overtones and beat frequencies.

After about a year of instruction from a rather limited teacher, I began to lose interest. I needed more stimulation and challenge. In 1945 my new teacher returned from serving in the Army. Dr. Willard (Bill) Palmer rekindled the fire of passion for the accordion and challenged me in many new ways. I began to progress again.

According to the *Austin Chronicle* column *Mr. Smarty Pants Knows*, "Professor Willard Palmer is credited with having the longest continuous master's degree program in accordion ever (it was at the University of Houston). Palmer also appeared on the television show, "America's Funniest Videos" playing the "Beer Barrel Polka" on the accordion. It fell apart in the middle of the song."

My teacher showed two sides with his accordion playing: the serious musician seeking to elevate the accordion into the classical canon and the commercial comedic musician seeking to make some money to support his family. Eventually, Bill took up the harpsichord, got a PhD in musicology and became an expert on baroque and classical ornamentation. He edited Bach and Mozart for Alfred Publications and wrote the Palmer-Hughes accordion method books with his former student and partner Bill Hughes. These books were formulated while I was studying with him and have served thousands of students through the years.

I entered the University of Houston as an accordion major in Palmer's program. During that time, I learned to play baroque and classical solo pieces and also participated in an accordion quartet that played Haydn string quartets. Sometimes, I filled in for the lack of string players in the University orchestra. I also played popular music, folk and jazz to earn a living. I began teaching accordion privately when I was fifteen years old.

One special thing Palmer taught me was to listen for difference tones, a third pitch which is the difference between two frequencies sounding simultaneously on the accordion. Difference tones fascinated me and later became the basis of my early electronic music *I of IV* (1966), which was released in 1968 by Odyssey and Bye *Bye Butterfly* (1965), which was released in 1975 by Arch Records (Arch 1750). These have been reissued on CD along with other titles that are just now being released after thirty years on the shelf.

My awareness of timbre increased as I joined my high school concert band as a French horn player. No accordions were allowed in traditional musical ensembles. The accordion is an outsider instrument invented after the Baroque and Classical periods so there is no repertoire except for transcriptions from the Western classical canon. I tried to imitate the timbres I perceived in band and orchestra with my accordion. I could do this through air pressure and touch.

My interest in composition increased with Palmer's encouragement. I left the University of Houston to seek a composition mentor after three years of study and went to San Francisco. There, I met and studied with the composer Robert Erickson. I realized that composition was my path. Performing took second place for a while as I plunged into writing music and making electronic music.

In the 1960's, I helped to found the San Francisco Tape Music Center[1] with Ramón Sender Barayón and Morton Subotnick. We made our taped electronic music there and also created a concert series. Soon, we were creating many pieces that involved performers with tape or live electronics. Additionally, we engaged in group improvisation.

I began to improvise with my accordion and to perform again. Ramon wrote a solo accordion piece with tape accompaniment for me called *Desert Ambulance*. I wrote *Duo for Accordion and Bandoneon with Possible Mynah Bird Obbligato* for David Tudor and me. *Desert Ambulance* had about twenty-five performances with visuals by light artist Anthony Martin.

David and I performed the "See-saw" version of the *Duo* with the see-saw conceived and constructed by Elizabeth Harris. She also constructed a mobile suspended above the center of the see saw for Ahmed the mynah bird and created choreography for the movement of the see-saw. The see-saw went up and down, clockwise and counterclockwise and had seats that spun around as well. The varieties of motion effectively distributed the sounds of our instruments spatially. Anthony Martin created a light score for the *Duo* as well.

The *Duo* had only two performances until it was revived in the late 80's for a show in San Francisco. I performed the piece with Gordon Mumma without the mynah bird (much to my chagrin) and without the light score. The *Duo* seems to have a long life in memory as people continue to mention it to me after almost forty years since the premiere performances. Toru

Takemitsu, Toshi Ichiyanagi, Kuni Haru Akiyama and John Cage were in the audience.

One highlight of the San Francisco Tape Music Center performances was the premiere of Terry Riley's *In C* for instruments at our 321 Divisadero concert hall. Terry had intended In C as a piece for his friends to play together. I played accordion, Mort played clarinet, Terry played flute. Steve Reich played as well. None of us could keep together so the piano pulse was added. All of us felt that Terry had created something very special even though we didn't play the piece very well. Alfred Frankenstein of the San Francisco Chronicle hailed *In C* as a 20th-century masterpiece. From the perspective of almost forty years and innumerable performances later, Frankenstein was right! I played in many of those performances with my accordion through the years. I would like to hear it with a 100-piece accordion band—what a sound that would make!

When I left my teaching position at the University of California, San Diego, I was considered a composer of electronic music rather than a performer. I kept my hand in with an improvisation ensemble I organized outside of the University

Leaving a full professorship with tenure in 1981 was a leap of faith. I moved from San Diego to upstate New York to live in back of Zen Mountain Center in Mt. Tremper. I lived in an A-frame in a meadow that looked at the mountain. There was no running water and just enough electricity to run my first computer, which I bought in 1983. I sent out a postcard with a picture of me playing the accordion noting that I was available for concerts, lectures, workshops and consultations.

It was important for me to assert my identity as an accordion player at the time. For me the accordion is a symbol of the outsider. Accordion music is associated with the working class and had no place in the establishment musical organizations representing the Western musical canon. As a composer I also felt like an outsider. I realized that to earn a living outside of the university I would have to perform. I embraced my old friend the accordion.

I played many solo concerts in the meditative style of *Horse Sings From Cloud*. My first solo album was *Pauline Oliveros: Accordion and Voice*, which was released by Lovely Music in 1983 and included the pieces *Horse Sings From Cloud* and *Rattlesnake Mountain*. I also began to play duos and trios with other musicians including Stuart Dempster (trombone), Malcolm

Goldstein (violin), Guy Klucevscek (accordion), Fritz Hauser (drum set), and Karl Berger (vibraphone).

In 1967, I wrote a piece called simply *Accordion* and played it using a tape delay system. I had worked extensively with tape delay to create my electronic music since 1960. In 1982, I returned to this delay concept with my accordion using two Lexicon PCM42 delay processors—one for each hand. The digital delays allowed me to process the accordion more flexibly than the tape delays. I could layer, modulate, and bend the pitch of the delayed sound with foot pedals. This was the beginning of what I have continually elaborated as the Expanded Instrument System (EIS).

I recorded *The Roots of the Moment* in Switzerland for hatArt as the first example of my solo work with EIS. Panaiotis worked with me on this recording, assisting the distribution and mixing of delays and reverberation. Two years later, I recorded *Crone Music* for Lovely Music.

In 1984, I recorded a solo for an album called *Vor der Flüt* (released by Eigelstein in 1985) in a cistern in Cologne Germany. The reverberation time of the cistern was 45 seconds. I treated the cistern as a huge delay processor even though all of the sound was acoustic. Later, in 1988, Stuart Dempster invited me to play with him in the cistern at Ft. Worden in Washington state. The reverberation time was also 45 seconds. Panaiotis joined us and we recorded what became the *Deep Listening* CD (released by New Albion). This was the beginning of the Deep Listening Band and many more recordings including one in a cave. Currently, I use an Apple G4 laptop running Max/MSP to create the delays with modulation, looping, layering and spatialization in a multi-channel sound system.

My accordion playing informed my electronic music and my electronic music informed my accordion playing. This relationship continues today as I perform acoustically. Time after time, people tell me after concerts that they didn't know the accordion could sound like that. This is because I don't play like an accordion player. I have found my own voice and send it through the instrument. I am not replicating a tradition of accordion playing but inventing a new one. I enjoy each opportunity to play—solo or with others. There is always the challenge to sound authentically.

The accordion is younger than the city where I now live, Kingston, New York (founded 1661). Since it's invention in

Vienna, it is now played on all continents throughout the world. The accordion is a messenger. With its ancestry to the Chinese *sheng,* the East and West meet and a 4,000-year-old idea—the free reed—carries music to people in a community throughout the planet.

LISTENING FOR THE CHANGES: 21ST-CENTURY CHALLENGES

Presented to the Society for Electro-Acoustic Music in the United States (SEAMUS)
November 20, 2004

Congratulations to SEAMUS for twenty years of sustained activity and support for the electro-acoustic music community. I am honored and grateful to be among the recipients of your Lifetime Achievement Awards. I only wish that SEAMUS could have existed when I needed such an organization forty years ago! Then, in the early 60's, my colleagues and I at the San Francisco Tape Music Center struggled to create our electronic music with a variety of World War II surplus test equipment with very little support at the beginning of our efforts.

It is amazing to reflect on the acculturation of electronic instruments over the fifty years of my career, which began with me using a tape recorder, microphones, and a few signal generators to now using computers that can convincingly simulate, edit, and modify any sound.

Also amazing is the difference in cultural attitude concerning these instruments. At the end of the 50's, electro-acoustic music was unfamiliar to most professional musicians and audiences. Now, all kinds of electronic music and electronically-produced music pervades our world. A certain divide still exists, though, between those who cling to traditional acoustic music and have no tolerance for electronics, and those that are interested in innovation and electronic music.

The future holds numerous challenges for SEAMUS. This digital divide may widen. Technology is changing more rapidly than ever before and by extension, music-making is changing with the gradual hybridization of humans and machines.

Recording technology has already enhanced musicianship by providing immediate feedback from rehearsals and performances, heightening our musical perception. Through technological enhancement (chip implants and nanobots), musicians may someday develop the following abilities:

- The ability to recognize and identify instantaneously any frequency or combination of frequencies in any tuning, timbre, tempo, rhythm, style, or space,
- The ability to produce any frequency or sound in any tuning, timing, timbre, dynamic, and articulation within the limits of the selected instruments or voices used. Maybe the musician will be able to morph from any instrument to any other instrument or voice at will.
- The ability to recognize, identify and remember any music—its parts as well as the whole—no matter the complexity.
- The ability to perceive and comprehend inter-dimensional spatiality.
- The ability to understand the relational wisdom that comprehends the nature of musical energy—its form, parts, and underlying spirituality—as the music develops in performance.
- The ability to perceive and comprehend the spiritual connection and interdependence of all beings and all creation as the basis and privilege of music making.
- The ability to create community and healing through music-making.
- The ability to sound and perceive the far reaches of the universe, just as whales sound and perceive the vastness of the oceans. This could set the stage for inter-dimensional galactic improvisations with yet unknown beings.

Music may be needed as never before as a benevolent force as computing power continues to accelerate. Machines will continue to speak and sing back to us in more and more complex and intelligent ways as the acceleration continues.

SEAMUS may be challenged theoretically and philosophically as the intelligence of machines continues to increase and boundaries between humans and machines become blurred. It will be exciting (to say the least) to hear the new music and the discussion of problems and techniques in the discourse, dialogue, and publications of future SEAMUS conferences as the organization surfs the waves of change in the 21st century.

SPACE FOR LISTENING AND LISTENING TO SPACE: A MUSICIAN'S WAY OF "LOOKING"

Abstract submitted to architecture I music I acoustics
Toronto, Ontario
June 8-10, 2006

The mission of the Deep Listening Band is to seek out, listen to, and interact with unusual spaces in order to make music. Space is an integral part of sound. One cannot exist without the other. We explore natural, constructed, imaginary, and virtual spaces to savor and enjoy their salient acoustical characteristics. This work is done with ears, voices, instruments, technology, shared experiences, and perceptions. Performance space is ordinarily held as a stationary paradigm in performance practice, but qualitative changes occur with our instruments and voices throughout the exploration process.

Listening to space changes space and changing space changes listening.

Music and spaces combine in symbiotic relationships that can create very limited or very powerful interweaving expressions of the arts. The effectiveness of any space for performance is related to the listening abilities of composers, performers, audiences, designers, and architects. A good deal of looking often happens without conscious listening among all participants. It is our task to bring listening to consciousness and consciousness to listening.

Deep Listening Band has performed in caves, cisterns, cathedrals, concert halls, and a great variety of unusual spaces including virtual cyberspaces. We always begin with a listening meditation before we sound the space. Listening creates new shapes and feelings.

The Expanded Instrument System (EIS) is a tool for creating and using virtual spaces within acoustical spaces. It allows for the creation of spatial movements in a performance space that are analogous to harmonic progressions; spatiality is a dynamic parameter of music.

EIS can virtually change a performance space, making it sound like the inside of a teacup, a cathedral, or a closet. It can change dynamically, resembling many different spaces during the course of a performance, and also can allow for endless combinations of spaces to be perceived simultaneously (i.e. several musicians performing from separate spaces, or one member of the band sounding from a space inside the larger performance space, etc.). Spatial characteristics such as shape, volume, and reverberation may continually change and progress at varying rates during a performance.

Sounding the Borders

Presented at the conference Visiones Sonoras
Universidad Nacional Autónoma de México, Mexico City
September 22, 2006

"An analysis of the history of technology shows that technological change is exponential, contrary to the common-sense "intuitive linear" view. So we won't experience 100 years of progress in the 21st century—it will be more like 20,000 years of progress (at today's rate). The "returns," such as chip speed and cost-effectiveness, also increase exponentially. There's even exponential growth in the rate of exponential growth. Within a few decades, machine intelligence will surpass human intelligence, leading to The Singularity—technological change so rapid and profound it represents a rupture in the fabric of human history. The implications include the merger of biological and nonbiological intelligence, immortal software-based humans, and ultra-high levels of intelligence that expand outward in the universe at the speed of light."

Ray Kurzweil, from *The Law of Accelerating Returns*[1]

Let us review a slower, more familiar process:

When a sperm from my father succeeded in uniting with an egg from my mother, that sperm crossed a pre-human border.

How many other primordial borders were established and crossed by countless subatomic particles through the millennia to slowly become these forms, sperm and egg?

How did the processes that fuse sperm and egg first occur?

Was it an accident of evolutionary improvisation that accelerated our species out of the expanding primordial soup?

How did the wondrous reciprocal union of sperm and egg spawn the embryo that became me—a human being?

"Fertilization is the process whereby two sex cells (gametes) fuse together to create a new individual with genetic potentials derived from both parents. Fertilization accomplishes two separate ends: sex (the combining of genes derived from the two parents) and reproduction (the creation of new organisms). Thus, the first function of fertilization is to transmit genes from parent to offspring, and the second is to initiate in the egg cytoplasm those reactions that permit development to proceed.

Although the details of fertilization vary from species to species, conception generally consists of four major events:

1. Contact and recognition between sperm and egg. In most cases, this ensures that the sperm and egg are of the same species.

2. Regulation of sperm entry into the egg. Only one sperm can ultimately fertilize the egg. This is usually accomplished by allowing only one sperm to enter the egg and inhibiting any others from entering.

3. Fusion of the genetic material of sperm and egg.

4. Activation of egg metabolism to start development."

Scott F. Gilbert, from *Developmental Biology*[2]

I wonder how the collision of sperm and egg sounded.

Was it peaceful or violent?

a crystalline phononic tinkling?

a *whoosh*?

a gentle *mmmmmmmmmm*?

What if we could listen in on these natural processes at the subatomic level? What would we hear?

How many borders were created, crossed, and sounded by the developing embryo to evolve into the fetus?

When I finally left the comfort of my mother's womb, where I listened to her heartbeat and the biological sounds of her body, I entered the world and emitted my first sound—a cry.

The first cry seems to be an experience universal to all human beings. Birth is leaving one world, entering another, and sounding at the border between mother and new life.

How would it be to remember that sensation of air rushing into newborn lungs and out through untested vocal cords to enable the first cry? How, as an infant, did I sense and hear this border-sounding activity?

Can you auralize with your memory and inner listening the quality and mystery of your first sound?

The word "border" is ambiguous as it can be a noun such as a line that divides two areas geographical, physical, political, theoretical, or virtual, or it can be a verb. One can speak of bordering along the edges of two different regions, systems or thoughts. A garden can be bordered by a line of trees.

A border can be a decorative enclosure indicating a space for some kind of use or action. In my cultural understanding, a place-mat at a table indicates a space for dining. Eating is also a universal experience for humans, though the spatial indication for dining may differ considerably from culture to culture. Also, each culture has differing preferences, customs and rules for the way to eat, what to eat, and when to eat.

Thus when we cross borders, we may feel either the need to impose our own cultural preferences or to change our behavior to be more appropriate for the culture we are amidst.

We have a hundred years of recordings of music from most parts of the world informing and challenging our musical preferences, customs, rules, instrumentation and venues.

What are our musical customs and where did they originate? The earliest forms of sounding may lead us to universals that have been shaped into the diversity of musical forms that we enjoy today. Though music-making is universal, the forms of music are relative to their diverse cultures.

* * *

Some Musical Universals

Hand clapping

Foot stamping

Body slapping

Nonverbal emotional sounds

Vocal toning or singing

The universal basics of music-making come from the body.

* * *

The rise of technology in ancient music-making led to the creation of instruments like bone flutes, plant seed rattles, reeds, log drums, and conch shell trumpets. These instruments are an extension of human body vibrations to instrumental bodies. The body may be connected to the instrument by the mouth, hands, or feet, and it may also resonate with the sounds of the instrument, blurring (but not eliminating) the border between the human and technology. All instruments, like other technologies (i.e. the bulldozer, computer, or automobile), are extensions of the human body, distancing it from the direct expression of sound, but enabling forms of music beyond what are possible with the basic universals alone.

Recognizing or going back to the bodily basics of sounding may enable us to participate more fully in intercultural, interspecific, and technological musical encounters.

How, for example, is your musical instrument related to your own body?

My instrument, the accordion, has free reeds (vocal cords) that vibrate in a box (torso) with air blown from the bellows (lungs). My fingers on the keyboard choose the valves that release the air through selected reeds. The muscles of my left forearm control the bellows and shape the sounds.

When I began to make electronic music in the 60's, I had the realization that electronic instruments are more an extension of my nervous system than of my muscular system. More recently, I have been working with a representation or extension of my intellect by using the computer with my accordion. The computer keyboard and mouse have been stubborn customs officers at the crossing of this border. In my current research, I am working with a neuroscientist to find new interface possibilities in order to make the computer instrument a more natural extension of my body.

* * *

The global network of creative musicians that we enjoy today at a conference such as Visiones Sonoras is truly exciting and nourishing.

Each compositional or improvisational style at this conference observes, approaches, creates, or crosses many borders. A heightened awareness of sound, silence, and sounding that does not judge, analyze, or criticize can help us to reconcile differences, fertilize, and fuse new musical forms (which may lack the womblike comfort of familiarity) across these many different borders.

What will be our newborn cry?

Some questions to consider:

How do you know you are approaching a musical border?

When have you crossed a musical border without knowing it?

When have you imposed or made musical borders?

Do musical scores represent actions that are taken inside borders?

How were such borders established and by whom?

Is improvisation a way to open the borders?

The technological advance that began many millennia ago continues to accelerate, evolve, and define new borders, such that today we are faced with the prospect of the merging of humans and computers. As mentioned before, all instruments and machines have always been an extension of the human body. The merging of humans and computers may mean the birth of a new life form with mental and physical characteristics far beyond present day human capabilities. Will the human body eventually become an extension of a machine, as Kurzweil described?

Clearly, we are already reliant on machines and computers to do work that the human body is insufficient to do. So perhaps today, we are willingly or unwillingly a part of another birthing process.

These theories and thoughts are widely condemned out of fear, but it is important to go beyond fear to consider the implications of these future possibilities.

What kind of music will we experience in this post-human era?

How will it function?

What will be its function?

How will it evolve?

Is it already evolving?

As we are on our way to this era, what changes are taking place now as an indication of the post-human musician?

Will post-humans perform with humans? Surely their performance abilities will surpass human abilities—will there be a new creative fusion of forms?

What will "feel good" music be for post-humans?

Will they dance and sing?

Will they go into trance?

Will they find altered states of post-human consciousness?

* * *

I have worked for many years on what I call the Expanded Instrument System (EIS). Development of this electro-acoustic system began with magnetic tape delay in 1960 and has since crossed the analog/digital technological border, so that physical and algorithmic inputs control entirely digital processing of sound.

The System accepts (through microphones or direct input) any type of human or animal acoustic sounds as well as electronic signals and either passes the input directly to the analog output (speakers) or to digital processors (software). This software can create multiple voices through delays, modulations, reverberation, and other modifiable processes. Parameters such as the ratio of dry to wet signal, phase relationships, spatial sound distribution, and others affect these processes.

In the present evolution of EIS, I control more than 85 of these parameters with faders, pedals, and switches. I have "controller greed" and always want more! Obviously, I don't have enough appendages to control every parameter simultaneously while performing with an acoustic instrument. I need many more hands and feet. To compensate for this lack of appendages, I use algorithms to control some parameters. These algorithms learn from my behavior and intelligently emulate the ways I control the System, but without the physical limitation of a finite number of appendages.

I fully expect EIS to become more and more intelligent and self-determining so that someday, it will be able to make music that no human could dream of making. When that future border is crossed—when EIS is not merely an extension of my being, but half of a reciprocal merger of human and computer—my music will be a new birth cry from and for post-humanity.

IMPROVISATION IN THE SONOSPHERE

From *Contemporary Music Review*, Volume 25, No. 5
October 2006

The sonosphere[1] is the sonorous or sonic envelope of the Earth that is comprised of two irrevocably interwoven layers, the biospheric[2] layer and the technospheric[3] layer.

Humans sense the sonosphere according to the bandwidth, resonant frequencies, and mechanics of the ear, skin, bones, meridians, fluids, and other organs and tissues of the body, which are coupled to the Earth and its many layers—from the core out to the magnetic fields. All cells and molecules of the Earth and body vibrate, and these vibrations are transmitted through this complex network to the auditory cortex and nervous system, where they become sound.

Technospheric advances have moved us out of purely biospheric amphitheaters and led to the construction of concert halls that focus, amplify, and enhance our perception of musical sounds while shutting out "noise" and interference from the biosphere and unwanted noises of the technosphere. I appreciate beautiful concert halls, especially those that are free of fan and ventilator sounds, electrical hums, and other technospheric noises, but I also enjoy performing in indoor or outdoor spaces where the sounds of the biosphere and technosphere are present. Some of the most beautiful sounds in the world are produced in the biosphere by the cries of creatures such as the loon, coyote, spring peepers, tree frogs, and cicadas. From the technosphere, we have the beauty of carefully crafted acoustic signal sounds such as train whistles, foghorns, and bells—sounds that were once integral parts of our communities. I have noticed, listened to, and grown with the changing sounds of both layers of the sonosphere through my lifetime.

My personal approach to improvisation is centered in the sonosphere. I listen to everything that I can possibly perceive in order to tune to and flow with the sonosphere. I listen inclusively so that virtually any sound (with some exceptions) can be acknowledged and incorporated as part of my piece, regardless of its origin. I call it Pauline's orchestration.

* * *

Recently, I performed solo with my accordion and Expanded Instrument System (EIS)[4] at the East-West Center in Vancouver, BC. About 45 minutes into the improvisation, with EIS projecting delays of my accordion sound around the beautiful and resonant wooden space of the Center, two fire engines raced by, their wailing sirens joining the reverberation.

After the concert, three different people independently asked me, "How did you get the fire engines to go by on time?"

* * *

During another solo accordion performance (this time without EIS) at an Anglican Church in Ontario during the 1997 Guelph Jazz Festival, I had a similarly remarkable experience.

I arrived in Guelph on September 6, one day after the passing of Mother Teresa and the day of the funeral of Princess Diana. Millions of people worldwide (including me) were watching Diana's funeral on television. It was the largest media event in history; more brain waves were sharing a single experience than ever before.

Inspired by this phenomenon, I suggested to the audience at the concert that night that we take an exploratory musical journey into the spirits of these two great women in acknowledgment of their great humanitarian works. As I spoke, the stained glass windows of the church lit up with a flash of lightning and we heard a low rumble of thunder. A storm was beginning.

I listened to the thunder as I performed. I heard the storm gather momentum and saw the windows continue to flash with lightning. I laughed and felt that God's percussion and lighting were accompanying me.

There were two tremendous thunderclaps right over the church and my head at the peak of my solo. They were the loudest thunderclaps that I had ever heard and they cut through the furious rat-a-tat of the rain on the roof.

After about an hour, I ended my duet with the biosphere. As I finished, the storm faded away.

The next day, someone handed me a newspaper clipping that noted that not one, but two tornadoes had blown through Guelph during my performance. Could those two tornadoes have been the spirits of Princess Diana and Mother Teresa resonating through the sonosphere?

A review of the Guelph Jazz Festival concert noted the storm as well as the music.

PAULINE OLIVEROS IN THE ARMS OF REYNOLS: A COLLABORATION

Leonardo Electronic Almanac Volume 15
January 2007

On a visit to Buenos Aires in 1992, I was invited to do a week-long seminar on my practice of Deep Listening[1]. Among the varied group of people in the seminar were a couple of intense and punkish looking young men – Alan Courtis and Roberto Conlazo. They seemed somewhat skeptical and a bit defiant with their questions and comments.

I was not sure that they were getting my drift. However, they were there every day and participated in all of the exercises and discussions.

Little did I know that this was the start of a collaboration which has since produced three recordings, a couple of concerts, and continues to this day.

I performed a solo accordion concert after the seminar in the Biblioteca National. What a lovely concert hall! Every sound is crystal clear in dynamic range from the faintest pianissimo to the very loudest – a very delicious space for a soloist.

To my surprise, Alan and Roberto were sitting in the front row seats right under my nose as I performed, their facial expressions open and surprised. They were making a pirate recording of the concert.

At a farewell party in an artist's loft, Alan, Roberto, and a few others of their group showed up to play a serenade for me. They had all brought brass instruments and none of them knew how to play them. They improvised an outrageous serenade for me that was wonderful, hilarious, and full of soul. Later, Alan asked me if it was possible to learn about new music in a University. I left Buenos Aires with good feelings about Roberto and Alan and all of the good people I met during my seminar.

A year or so later, Alan showed up in New York and greeted me at a concert at The Kitchen.

Shortly thereafter, I had an email from Alan asking permission to re-mix the pirate recording that he had made of my Buenos Aires concert. I replied that it would be fine with me and thus the collaboration was born.

I knew by now that Alan and Roberto called their music group Reynols. They took the name from the actor Burt Reynolds but had dropped the D.

Reynols started e-mailing proposals to title the CD production of their remixed version of my concert. First they wanted to call it *Deep Heavy Metal Listening* or *Heavy Deep Listening Metal*—Alan and Roberto are accomplished electric guitar players. Finally they hit upon a title: *Pauline Oliveros in the Arms of Reynols*. I accepted with delight.

The first edition of 100 CD's included individual hand-painted covers, a cassette version, and a tiny bag of colored sand to represent the grittiness of the music. Cream Gardens of Amsterdam produced the second release of the CD with Roberto's drawings[2].

Reynols is a remarkable group in many ways that has produced a hundred recordings of their work. Two noticable recordings are *Blank Tapes*[3] — a production made from found blank cassette tapes—and the *Ten Thousand Chickens Symphony*[4].

The voice heard on *Pauline Oliveros in the Arms of Reynols* belongs to Miguel Tomasin, their percussionist and poet. Miguel has Down's syndrome. Alan and Roberto consider him to be their teacher — they pay close attention to what he says. His sayings are poetic and full of invented words. Alan and Roberto work with other physically challenged people as therapists with their music. Because Miguel cannot travel with them on their numerous tours, they include him with recordings during their live shows.

Our second project was hatched because of my interest in distance performance. I started working with remote locations in 1990 when I participated as an interviewee from the Verbum Gallery in San Diego with my interviewers Morton Subotnick and David Rosenboom in Santa Monica at the Electronic Café, run by Kit Galloway and Sheri Rabinowitz. The medium was video telephone. The video updated every five seconds as a new still image. This was a fun medium to play with. There is a lot one can do in five seconds to change the way things look. Kit and Sheri started the Electronic Café with a benchmark piece–*Hole in Space*[5].

Hole in Space was a Public Communication Sculpture. On a November evening in 1980, the unsuspecting public walking past the Lincoln Center for the Performing Arts in New York City, and The Broadway department store located in the open-air shopping center in Century City, Los Angeles, had a surprising encounter with each other. Suddenly head-to-toe, life-sized, television images of the people on the opposite coast appeared. They could now see, hear, and speak with each other as if encountering each other on the same sidewalk. No signs, sponsor logos, or credits were posted, no explanation at all was offered, no self-view video monitors to distract from the phenomena of this life-size encounter. *Hole in Space* suddenly severed the distance between both cities and created an outrageous pedestrian intersection. There was the evening of discovery, followed by the evening of intentional word-of-mouth rendezvous, followed by a mass migration of families and trans-continental loved ones, some of which had not seen each other for over 20 years.

In 1991, before I met Reynols, I celebrated 40 years of composing with a six-city video telephone broadcast[6]. I invited friends from the cities where I had lived and worked to perform something to help me celebrate. I performed with friends from my living room at home in Kingston, New York. There were 20 minute performances from the Experimental Media Foundation in New York, my mother reading from our letters from a studio in Houston, Texas, friends and former colleagues at the University of California San Diego, friends at the home of Joe Catalano and Wendy Burch in Oakland, California, and others at the Electronic Café in Santa Monica with Kit and Sheri.

We could all see and hear one another. Each broadcast was unique. At the end, we performed a six-city audio and video improvisation. The loudest signal would grab the line so everyone took heed to give and make space for others to sound and be seen and not just dominate this interactive improvisation. Each image was a surprise. All the video documentation from the six cities still awaits editing.

Later I worked with PictureTel, a video monitor with a camera mounted on top and connected for transmission to ISDN high-speed telephone circuits, for several distance productions with the Deep Listening Band. From The Kitchen we once played a concert with a group in Toronto and we also played with a group in Paris. The audiences in both places got to talk to one another after the concert. This way we created some more 'holes in space'. At another time, the band was distributed with one member each in Seattle, Chicago and New York. Each of us performed with the other two members of the band on screen and with our own audiences present.

Around 1996, I began to improvise with others over the internet. I appreciated the latency of the medium (about eight seconds between Boston and California, for example) since I work with delays as the basis of my Expanded Instrument System (EIS).

I decided to invite Reynols to improvise with me between Buenos Aires and New York. Reynols was very excited and thought they could arrange to do it. They made many arrangements for a space and PR and were including Miguel Tomasin. I kept cautioning them about the necessary protocols with the ISP for the ports to be open. They kept assuring me that all would be well. On our end we were set to go on the day of our netcast at The Thing, a digital arts center in New York. Our streaming on to the Internet was working but there was no connection with Buenos Aires. We recorded our work and so did Reynols. However the actual netcast did not happen because of the technical problems in Buenos Aires.

Our second project—*NetCast*—is a mix of the two recordings we made simultaneously during our phantom netcast. I am currently borrowing and mixing tracks from *NetCast* into a film score that I am making with Vicky Funari on the Maquiladores, the factories of Tijuana, Mexico. Those tracks will later be further remixed by the Nortek Collective of Tijuana.

Reynols arrived in New York on tour in 2000. They took part in my *Lunar Opera* at Lincoln Center Out of Doors—a very large production with 250 performers involving all the outdoor spaces at Lincoln Center. During this visit, we played our first live concert together in upstate New York at a local venue resulting in a third recording mixed by Reynols, *The Minexcio Connection: Live! At The Rosendale Café* produced on vinyl by Roaratorio[7]. The manager of the Rosendale Café, Mark Morgenstern presents many wonderful musicians every weekend and throughout the year. He told me after the concert that Alan and Roberto were the most spiritual musicians he had ever experienced at his café. He was very impressed with them.

During their stay in Kingston, New York, Reynols also performed a duo concert at Deep Listening Space, the facility for the Deep Listening Institute, a non-profit organization that I founded in 1985. Additionally, Reynols conducted a workshop with 20 children from the Kingston Children's Home. We watched as the initially reticent and despondent orphans were gradually drawn into making sounds. By the end of the hour, they were unmistakably making music together and taking delight in the process that Alan and Roberto had set in motion with them. This is the magic of Reynols and their deep commitment to making music and helping others.

Last year, Reynols announced that there would be no more of Reynols. Many, including myself, were shocked at this announcement since the group has done so much and established a true musical presence and statement.

Their answer is "we will go on but want to take a break from this particular name and form so we can begin again." I look forward to beginning again with them.

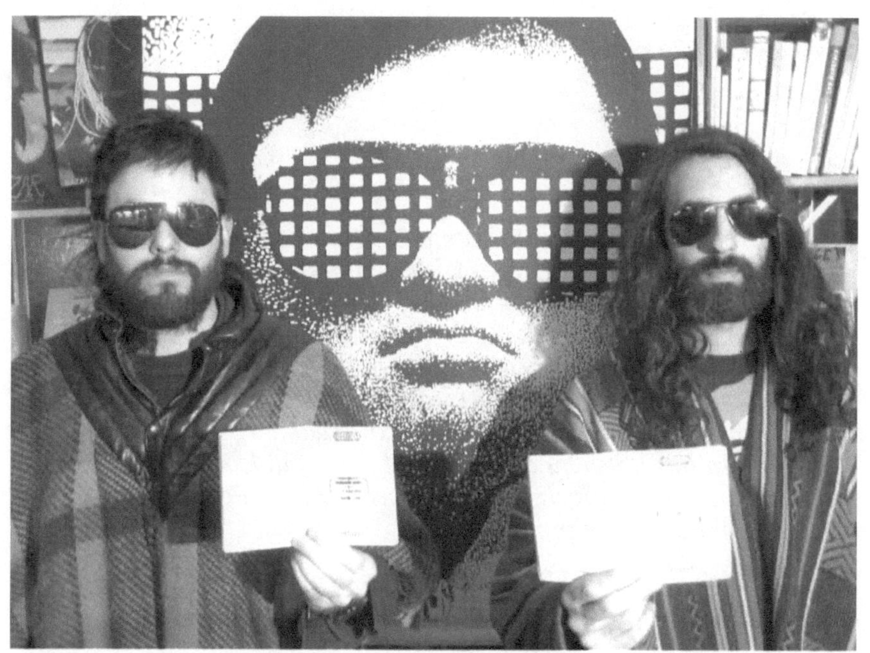

Reynols (l-r: Roberto Conlazo, Miguel Tomasin, and Alan Courtis)

THE ADAPTIVE USE INSTRUMENTS PROJECT

Interview with Pauline Oliveros and Zevin Polzin
by Andrew Pask (Cycling '74)
December 7, 2007
www.cycling74.com

Recently I bumped into composer and performer Pauline Oliveros (PO) in San Diego. We got to talking about one of her current projects, the Adaptive Use Musical Instruments for the Physically Challenged. This project introduces software designed to be used in therapy sessions to give children with limited motor skills the opportunity to participate in music, and offer them an outlet for musical expression. I arranged for a follow-up interview by email so that we could learn more about what this project involves. Joining us is Zevin Polzin (ZP), the technical lead in the project.

How did the Adaptive Use project get off the ground?

PO: I have a longtime friend, Leaf Miller, who is a drummer and certified occupational therapist. We talked for years about how to use technology to help children with severely limited volitional movement to play in her drum class at REHAB Programs North Road School (now Abilities First, Inc.). I finally secured a small grant from the Malcolm S. Morse Foundation to begin.

In January 2007, I assembled a team together with Don Millard, director of the Academy of Electronic Media at Rensselaer Polytechnic Institute, RPI student researchers, and the staff of Deep Listening Institute, Ltd. (a non profit arts organization that I founded in 1985).

I asked Leaf for three students with the least volitional movement to begin the project. These students are confined to wheelchairs, cannot speak, and have some controllable head movement. Our team did a site visit to assess the situation and the technology in use at the school. It was clear that we could do something not only to help the students but to also help the therapists.

How did you go about creating the software interfaces for the kids in the first place?

PO: Zane Van Duzen, an undergraduate at the time, came to the next session with a camera tracker programmed in Max/MSP/Jitter on his MacBook Pro. Most of this patch is based on the cv.jit library developed by International Academy of Media Arts & Sciences and Jean-Marc Pelletier.

Van Duzen's prototype showed the student's image on the computer screen with a marker placed on their virtual nose to move within the object zone. With very little lateral head movement crossing a line the student could trigger a digital switch programmed arbitrarily with a snare drum sound. The object zone is of course adjustable.

Additionally, the patch had a virtual keyboard programmed with a blues scale. The keyboard could also be played with lateral head movement. The Max patch was an immediate success and allowed the three children to improvise melodies. They made music for the very first time in their lives. Needless to say, to experience that moment with each child was very moving. Everyone present was changed by those moments.

Questions and comments from the therapists helped us to advance our work together. What colors to use for the interface, positioning of the camera, attack time of samples in relationship to movement, resolution, length of sessions, these are all important details. There is new information in every session.

Why motion tracking?

ZP: We've really been focused on motion tracking for the time being, because it means that there are no moving parts or things to attach to the kids. Their movement ranges can vary day-today depending on a number of factors, so the software can be programmed to accommodate that.

Most existing tools presuppose a full range of movement, or more complicated gestures than these children are capable of. The real meat of this project is amplifying very small, limited movements into real musical expression. The only gestures these kids have made previously to communicate are all binary—yes/no answers, or using physical switches to turn music on or off. Opening up a whole gradient of movement is new to them and is something we're in the middle of exploring.

Tell us about the kinds of things which have happened in sessions.

PO: Early on, we upgraded the patch so that 4 different drum sounds could be triggered with slight side to side up and down head movements. With this increase in possibilities we had a breakthrough. Leaf played a drum pattern for A, a 16-year-old and then pointed to her to play. A answered with a pattern of her own using the 4 sounds. She improvised! Everyone in the room cheered. Without any prompting at all A understood on her own that she could move quickly to any of the 4 sounds by staying in the center of the quadrant pictured on the computer screen.

In the next session, Leaf brought in some students from the drum class. They would play and listen for A. She played! We really felt like we were getting somewhere.

In the most recent session with A, we hooked up larger speakers so that her sounds had as much power and volume as the live drums. In this session A initiated patterns for the others to answer. This improvisation generated a great deal of excitement among all the students and therapists.

G, an 11-year-old played the virtual keyboard for the first time for an hour and did not want to leave the session. In a later session his mother came in the door and was stunned to hear her son playing music. G's mother was overcome and could not speak. When she came back another time she was able to participate. She told me that they are a musical family. G's sisters play flute and clarinet. She was excited and remarked that G was not in his high tone (stiffness) during instruction. We noticed that the students were more and more relaxed for subsequent sessions. G's mother was very helpful during the rest of the session.

B, a 9-year-old, was often distracted by seeing himself on the computer screen. We learned to remove the picture and leave just the marker as a bright orange spot. Though B's response time was slower than the other two B could also trigger drum sounds and play the virtual keyboard.

How are these musical activities contributing to the kids' overall therapy?

PO: As I suspected, opening a creative, empowering portal for these children has initiated the beginning of potential for others with more mobility at the school to improvise and create their own music as well.

We are still in formative stages of the work. It is definitely improvisational and very creative for all concerned. The important thing is that the three students that we selected to work with have all been successful in making music of their own. It is quite easy to see how affected they are with their musical results. There are holistic and therapeutic side effects as well. We want to increase their possibilities for choice with improvisation as an empowerment for them.

Honing their physical movements with musical feedback gives the students greater ability to learn and interact in their environments and more precise control. My RPI colleague Curtis Bahn is very adept at translating physical motions into musical phrases using sensors and Max programming. Curtis is one of our technical advisors and is joining the Adaptive Use project. His interest in computer interfaces for the physically challenged is a great asset to this project and its future evolution.

How is the project developing and how do you see its future? Do you have any plans to open source it or make it available for others to use?

ZP: We're interested in moving away from grids and using relative movement. This will enable us to track more subtle movements and create more sophisticated sounds.

We're working to make the patch more modular and "open source" so other people can participate in the development. However, the underlying patch will never be entirely "open source"—not for commercial reasons but because a large part of the project is developing a methodology with the therapists which greatly influences the design.

The sound-making algorithms themselves are modular and open source, and we hope to provide guidelines on how to program "modules" for this project in the future.

PO: Nan Jia, an engineering student from RPI has created a robot drummer that plays a miniature drum set. We connected it to the camera tracker so the children could play it. The robot drummer is an important direction for this project as my ideal plan is to make it possible for these students to play real instruments with robotic interfaces.

For the future we want to have an Adaptive Use wiki and invite the participation of others to develop the high potential of this project and to meet the needs of millions of people who would benefit greatly emotionally and spiritually from making music.

Cycling '74 would like to thank Pauline and Zevin and all the staff on the Adaptive Use project for making this interview possible.

FROM TELEPHONE TO HIGH-SPEED INTERNET: A BRIEF HISTORY OF MY TELE-MUSICAL PERFORMANCES

Presented to the International Society for Improvised Music
Telematic Music Panel
Lutkin Hall, Northwestern University
December 14, 2007

Why would anyone care to perform music between distant locations? If you are on the East coast and the musician you want to perform with is on the West coast, then there is a reason. If it is possible to do such a thing then there is even more reason. As telematic technology improves, there will eventually be no reason not to make music over any distance, and making music together makes friends.

Successful attempts at tele-transmissions have occured since the 1860's, which led to the advent of the telephone as a key means of communication today. But even before before such technologies existed, transmitting sounds over distances has been important to humans and animals for many various purposes. Mammals communicate sonically to warn others of predators and as a means of self-defense, birds sound out their territory with their song, and insect species make a plethora of sounds to attract mates and ensure the survival of their species. Resonator pillows helped to warn ancient sleeping Chinese armies of approaching attacks from others during times of war. Whistling is a form of communication in the Alps and other mountainous regions where the landscape helps signals reverberate and travel for long distances. The language of talking drums can be heard throughout African forests and plains over distances that the human voice cannot travel. All of these are analog varieties of distance communications and precursors to telecommunications.

The telephone has been developed and refined primarily for voice communication. Music transmitted over phone lines is subject to compression and equalization that degrades its sound quality. The telephone signal is confined to a narrow bandwidth that attenuates typical voice frequencies and suppresses high and low frequency noise. Nevertheless, musicians can and do play together over telephone lines and—more recently—over high-speed internet.

My first large-scale music transmission was a six-city celebration of 40 years of composing in November 1991. A video telephone bridge was organized by Joe Catalano[1] to connect Kingston, NY, New York City, Houston, TX, San Diego, CA, Los Angeles, CA, and Oakland, CA. I invited my friends to perform whatever they would like in order to help me celebrate this marker in my composing career. The musicians gathered in each city performed their own 20-minute broadcast prior to a massive six-city improvisation. Since the telephone line would pick up on the loudest signal and suppress the others, the improvisation was based on musical sensitivity and give and take—there is a message in the medium. The video feed consisted of a still image that was updated every 5 seconds. This latency provided for surprising changes in sequences of images.

The next telecommunications technology used for musical performance was the PictureTel System 4000, which utilized the Integrated Services Digital Network (ISDN). With this system, the audio quality was improved over standard telephone audio and the video, now a moving image, had only a slight delay that created impressionistic onscreen "pixel trails". Using this technology, Deep Listening Band performed *Through the Distance* as a distributed trio in 1996. David Gamper was at the Kitchen in New York City, Stuart Dempster at the Speakeasy Café in Seattle, WA, I at Northwestern University in Evanston, IL, and audiences in all three locations[2]. Each of us had two screens that showed the other two members of the band.

Live internet transmissions became possible in the late 1990's. In 1998, The Rocking Horse Trio—Maggi Payne (flute), Brenda Hutchinson (long tube), and me—performed *Loose Ends/Connections*[3] with Helen Thorington, Jesse Gilbert, Zeena Parkins, Scott Rosenberg, and others, transmitting via the internet between New York, California, and Massachusetts. The composite audio from all three locations was streamed over the Web. These early internet transmissions had an 8-second latency, which, naturally, became a structural element of our improvisation—another message in the medium.

iChat AV for Macintosh, developed in 2003, afforded many fruitful improvisations with distant partners. Latency with this software depended on bandwidth and traffic but was often around 1/2 second with a slightly longer video delay. Using iChat AV, I performed *40 Days and 40 Nights*[4] by True Rosaschi (an accordion duet with sound track) from New York with Raimondas Sviackevicius, who was performing to a sell-out crowd at the 2005 Jauna Muzika Festival in Vilnius, Lithuania.

Scot Gresham-Lancaster and I performed *AB_Time*[5], a three-way video and sound transmission with dancers and musicians at Mills College in Oakland, CA, Skalken Dance Company Studio in Marseille, France, and iEAR Studios at Rensselaer Polytechnic Institute in Troy, NY. All could see and hear one another via iChat AV. Additionally, in Marseille, the video artist Patrick LaFonte arranged projections so that the audience experienced the live dancers on screen with the distant performers simultaneously, creating illusions that blurred distinctions of place and time. This project demonstrated the vast potential for multimedia art in virtual spaces.

Stuart Dempster and I gave a concert celebrating 50 years of musical friendship in October 2005 for audiences at Mills College[6]. He performed from DXARTS at the University of Washington in Seattle and I from iEAR Studios. Our images appeared side by side on a large screen in the Mills College Concert Hall. On stage, two dancers, under the direction of choreographer June Watanabe, improvised with our images on the screen. Occasionally, their images were projected on screen as well, joining the virtual (but live) spatial interplay of our networked improvisation. Remarks from the audience underscored how "intimate" this performance was, even though we were not physically in the same room.

In 2006, with my colleague Jonas Braasch, Assistant Professor of Architectural Acoustics at RPI, weekly transmissions were initiated with Chris Chafe, director of the Center for Computer Research in Music and Acoustics (CCRMA) at Stanford University. For the first time, we experienced low-latency CD-quality audio transmission and began a long term improvisation collaboration with musicians from Stanford using JackTrip[7], an open-source software developed by Chris Chafe. In the summer of 2007, we began using UltraVideo Conferencing software (developed by Jeremy Cooperstock at McGill University) for DVD-quality video[8].

We presented our work at the June 2007 International Conference on Audio Display (ICAD)[9] at McGill University in Montreal with musicians at RPI in Troy, NY, KAIC Institute in Seoul Korea and Stanford University in Palo Alto, CA. Visual artist Bart Woodstrup added video treatments for this performance. Later, in August 2007, we presented our work at the Siggraph[10] international conference at the California Institute for Telecommunications and Information Technology Auditorium at University of California, San Diego.

The most recent transmission involved UCSD, CCRMA and iEAR on Nov 16, 2007 in a concert prepared with a total of 44 musicians participating in a three-site improvisation guided by sound painting by Sarah Weaver and Mark Dresser.

The question asked at the beginning of this paper "Why would anyone care to perform music between distant locations?" has larger implications. It is heartening to think that I can connect with my many friends throughout the world and strengthen our relationship with global culture. The ability to link with partners around the globe with less and less latency is an exciting development. After 18 years of engagement with telematic music performance, I look forward to the continued evolution of the medium. Musicians are leading the way to a new, nonviolent development in global communications.

IMPROVISING WITH SPACES

Proceedings of the 13th International Conference on Auditory Display
Montreal, Quebec
June 26-29, 2007

This paper explores qualitative changes that occur in voices and instruments in relationships with changing spaces ordinarily held in a stationary paradigm of performance practice, spatial transformations and the effect on sounds in multi-channel speaker systems. Digital technology allows one to compose and improvise with acoustical characteristics and change the apparent space during a musical performance. Sounds can move in space and space can morph and change affecting the sounds. Space is an integral part of sound. One cannot exist without the other. Varieties of sounds and spaces combine in symbiotic relationships that range from very limited to very powerful for the interweaving expressions of the music, architectures and audiences.

This brief non-technical paper references the practice of Deep Listening[1], improvisation[2], the Expanded Instrument System (EIS)[3], acoustics as a parameter of music[4], and discusses selected recorded examples with differing acoustical characteristics for the music.

Varieties of music and acoustical spaces combine in symbiotic relationships that range from very limited to very powerful for the interweaving expressions of musical art, architectures and audiences. The effectiveness of any space for musical performance is related to intention, architectural acoustics, and to the listening abilities of composers, performers, audiences, technicians, designers and architects.

A good deal of looking often happens without conscious listening among all participants. A worthy goal for the composer and performer is to bring both inclusive and exclusive listening to consciousness and consciousness to listening. Dedicating attention to sound and sounding in consonance with the acoustical space best achieves this goal.

Deep Listening is a multi-dimensional practice created with the intention of heightening awareness of sound and sounding to connect profoundly with sensations, feelings, memories, and dreams. The ultimate intention is the expansion of the consciousness of listening.

For architects the look of the space may take precedence over acoustics. For the audience looking at performers may take attention away from listening. Internal visual imagery triggered by sound may also divide the attention of the listener, distracting from a fuller consciousness of sound.

The desirable integration of looking and listening during which the two modes – visual and auditory – are approximately equal and mutually supportive comes with conscious practice.

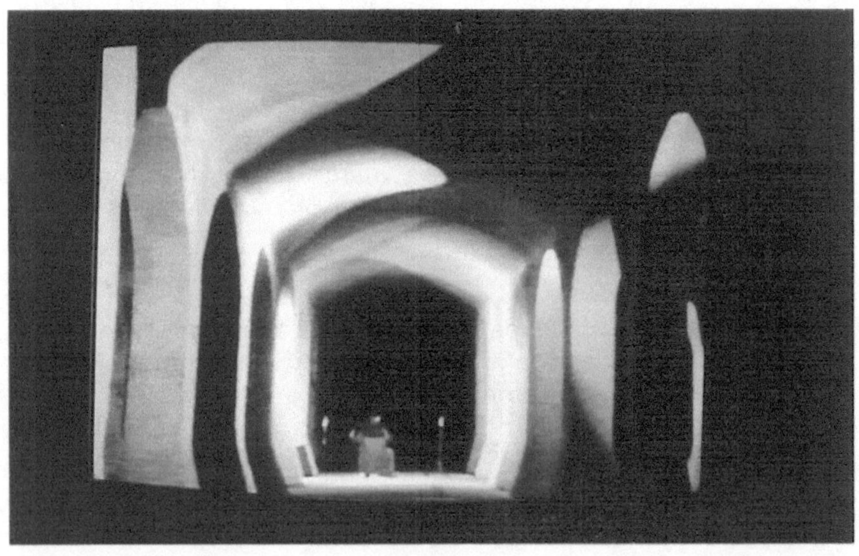

The cistern for water supply for the city of Köln emptied for repair and used for recording **Vor der Flüt**, *Eigelstein Musik Productions, West Germany (1984)*

Listening with eyes closed in order to heighten and develop auditory attention is especially recommended. This is also true for performers if they are not reading music or trying deliberately to draw attention to themselves.

If a performer is modeling listening the audience is likely to sense or feel the listening and be inspired to listen as well.

As soloist and member of the Deep Listening Band[5] (founded by the author in 1988 with Stuart Dempster and Panaiotis) the shared mission is to seek out, listen to and interact with unusual spaces in order to make music. The band, through the practice of Deep Listening, explores natural, constructed, imaginary and virtual spaces with the purpose of savoring their acoustical characteristics. These characteristics in our improvisations are a musical parameter, just like melody, rhythm, harmony, or timbre.

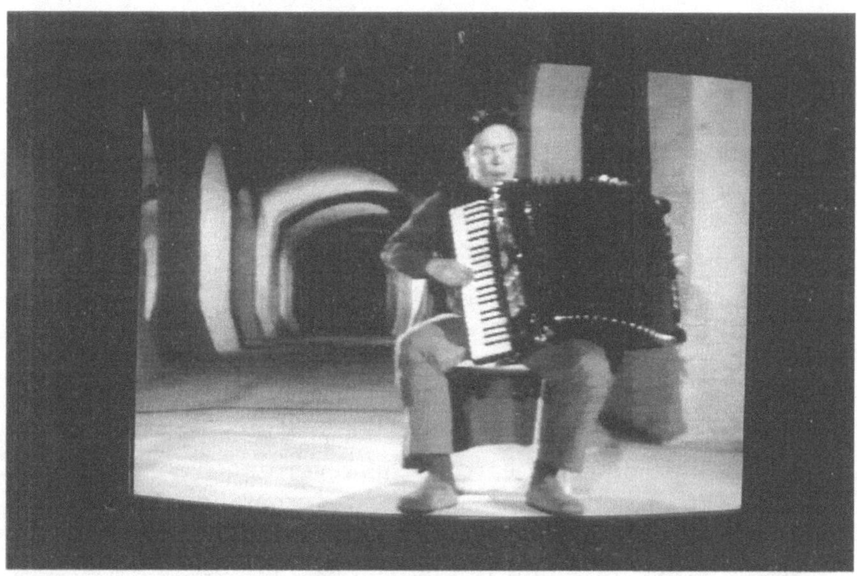

The author recording in the Köln cistern for **Vor der Flüt**

The relationship of spatial acoustics and the acoustics of musical instruments is a complex matter that needs more attention and investigation by all concerned. The band with ears, voices, instruments, technology and multi-channel systems as well as shared experiences and perceptions achieves acoustical explorations. Instruments and voices are transformed in varying spaces by this process. A space is also transformed by sounding it. The natural acoustics of musical instruments and electronics are also transformed.

Deep Listening Band has performed in caves, cisterns, cathedrals, concert halls, and a great variety of adapted spaces including cyberspaces. The beginning of rehearsals involves a listening meditation before sounding the space. Listening brings about new possibilities and feelings.

Listening to space changes space. Changing space changes listening. This phenomenon is termed "the listening effect"[6]. An understanding of this effect pervades all Deep Listening Band improvisations. Thus the stage is set for the power of listening to guide the music. This practice is extended to audiences by Deep Listening workshops offered prior to concerts.

* * *

Following are examples intended for comparison of the qualities of acoustic characteristics of musical environments and how sounds are affected by these characteristics. Each example involves a duet or ensemble improvised with the space as musical partner as well as being the container of sound.

The first example is the first track from *Deep Listening*[7] (1988), entitled *Lear,* a signature recording of the Deep Listening Band. The music was improvised without pre-planning and recorded in a large cistern[8]. The unique acoustical characteristics of the reverberant cistern transform the instruments.

The instruments heard in this recording were trombone, didjeridu, accordion and voice. The reverberation time of this underground cistern is 45 seconds. The difference between the direct and reflected sound in this venue is almost impossible to discern. Layering, phasing and standing waves emphasizing and de-emphasizing harmonics and partials transform the more recognizable sounds of the instruments. The experience of performing in the cistern was like being inside a hall of audio mirrors. The cistern itself was performing.

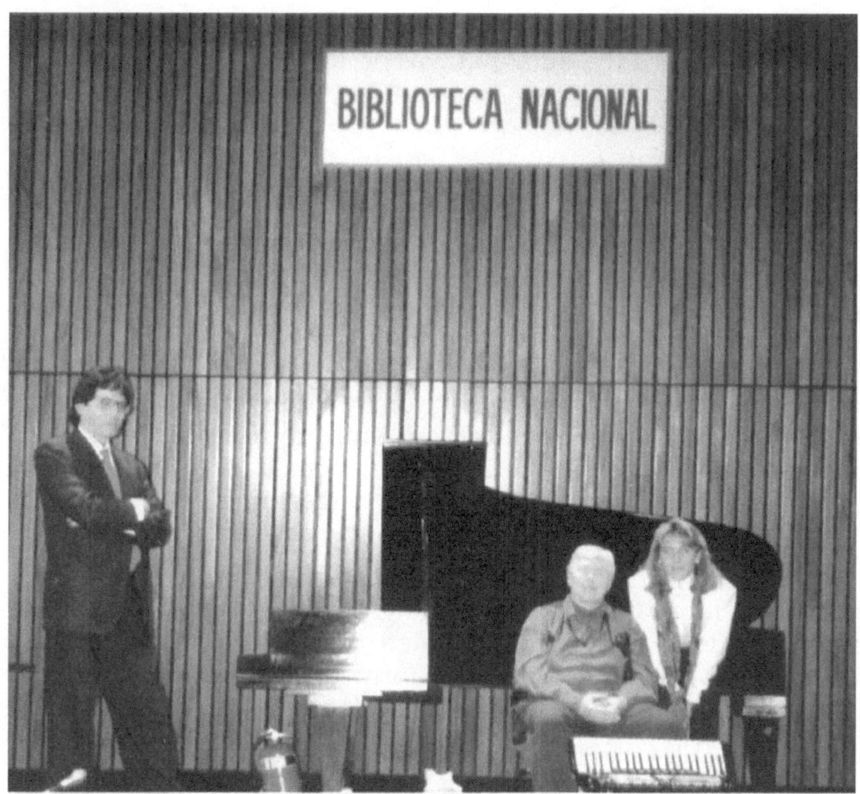

The author after performing at the Biblioteca Nacional (Photo by Alan Courtis)

Quite opposite to the experience of playing in such a reverberant space was a singular experience of performing solo accordion in the Biblioteca National[9] in Buenos Aires, Argentina. The hall was extremely quiet. The sound of the accordion and its acoustics could be heard directly – there was a near perfect coupling of instrument and hall. The softest sound made could be heard anywhere in the hall—one of the most unusual performance experiences ever. The richness of the sounds of the instrument had no interference from reverberation and seemed exceedingly pure and new in that remarkable space.

St. George and the Dragon[10] (1991), an accordion solo recorded in the chapel of the Pomfret School in Connecticut, is an interaction with the chapel's acoustics, including a noisy squirrel who joined the music! As requested, the room microphones were aimed at the acoustic reflections from the walls and mixed with the direct mics from inside the accordion in order to record the duet that was performed with the space.

* * *

The notion of duet playing with space occurred in 1960 while experimenting with reel-to-reel tape recorders. The short time delay between record head and playback head could be used to create reverberation depending on the amplitude of the delayed sound. This tape delay[11] effect could be extended by passing the stereo tape from the supply reel from recorder one to the take up reel of recorder two. Sounds from both tracks could be routed using a patch bay from the second machine back to the first in a variety of configurations, short and longer time delays and out to multiple speakers (mixers were not yet available).

Though the recorded results were in stereo there were virtually four channels sounding. Sound sources for the improvisations were heterodyned oscillators. The iterated sounds were layered and transformed by phasing from the returning sounds in the tape delay system.

I of IV[12] (1966) is an example improvised in real time that uses the tape delay system described above.

Applied to the accordion or any other acoustic instrument or voice the Expanded Instrument System (EIS) (pronounced "ice"). is a tool for creating and using virtual spaces[13] within acoustical spaces. EIS has developed from hardware tape delay systems to software over the past 40 years.

Crone Music[14] (1989) is music created with solo accordion and Expanded Instrument System (EIS) still in an analog version. There is the illusion of one space morphing to another.

Qualitative change occurs in voices and instruments in relationships with changing spaces that ordinarily are held in a stationary acoustic paradigm.

Digital technology makes it possible to go further. A virtual space may sound like the inside of a teacup, a cathedral, or a closet. More than one space may be perceived simultaneously—several sounds may be perceived in separate spaces—a single sound could seem to be sounding from a space inside some other space and endless other creative configurations.

I OF IV – 1966

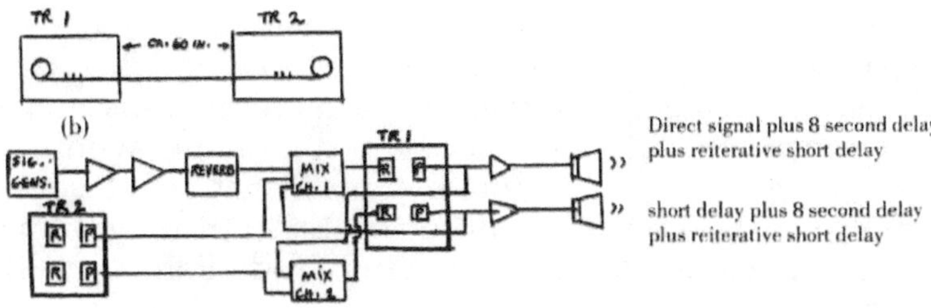

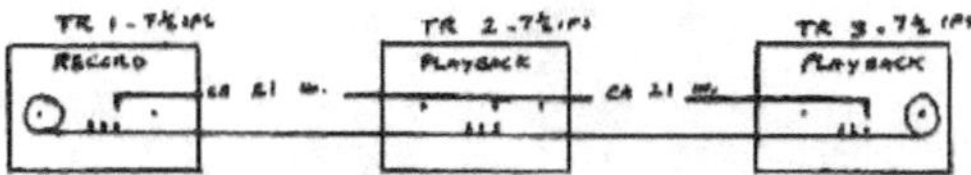

3″ delay from TR 2-Ch. 1.

6″ delay from TR 3-Ch. 1.

short delay from playback head plus 3″ lag from TR 2-Ch. 1. and 6″ lag from TR 3-Ch. 2. plus cross-coupled reiteration loop from TR 1, Ch. 2.

short delay from playback head plus 3″ from TR 2-Ch. 2 and 6″ lag from TR 3-Ch. 2 plus cross-coupled reiteration loop from TR 1-Ch. 1.

3″ delay from TR 2-Ch. 2.

6″ delay from TR 3-Ch. 2.

I of IV *schematics from* **Tape Delay Techniques for Electronic Music Composers** *(1969) in* **Software for People** *by the author.*

Such progressions may move with continually changing characteristics such as shape, volume and reverberation time and parameters incorporating a range of spatial motion from very slow to very fast.

Moving Spaces[15] (2006) was created with four different sounds—wood blocks, percussed conch shell trumpet, thunder tube and serrated wood scraping shell. The four sounds apparently sound in many different spaces and transform in many ways during the course of the piece. Sounds move and spaces move in differing speeds and volume within a 5.1 surround system. The continual transformation of sounds is accomplished by improvisation using EIS. EIS programmed in Max/MSP includes Vector Based Amplitude Panning (VBAP)[16] and Monoverb[17].

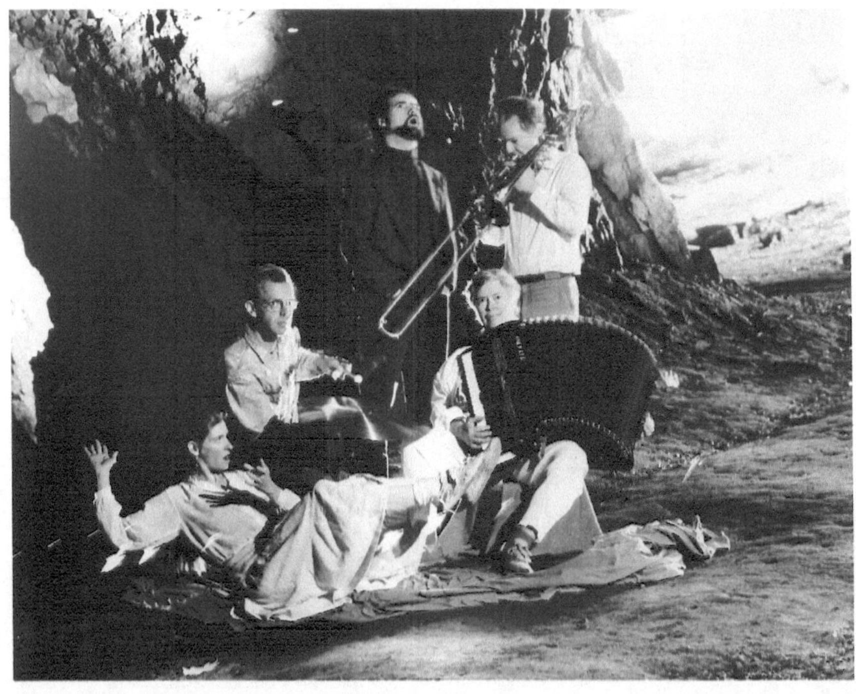

Deep Listening Band recording* Trogolodyte's Delight *in the Tarpaper Cave at Williams Lake Hotel, Rosendale NY. 1991.

The album *Trogolodyte's Delight*[18] (1990) was performed first as a concert in the Tarpaper Cave in Rosendale, New York, The Deep Listening Band (Pauline Oliveros, Stuart Dempster, Panaiotis) with guests Fritz Hauser, percussionist and Julie Lyon Balliette, vocalist explored the sound properties of this man-made limestone cave by moving to different locations inside the cave. The audience relocated for each piece. Each part of this large cave had unique acoustical characteristics including the beautiful water drops. The longest reverberation time was 9 minutes. After the concert we returned to the cave to record. Among the pieces *Cannery Row* used a variety of sizes of tin cans placed strategically under the water drops to play with the acoustics in another way.

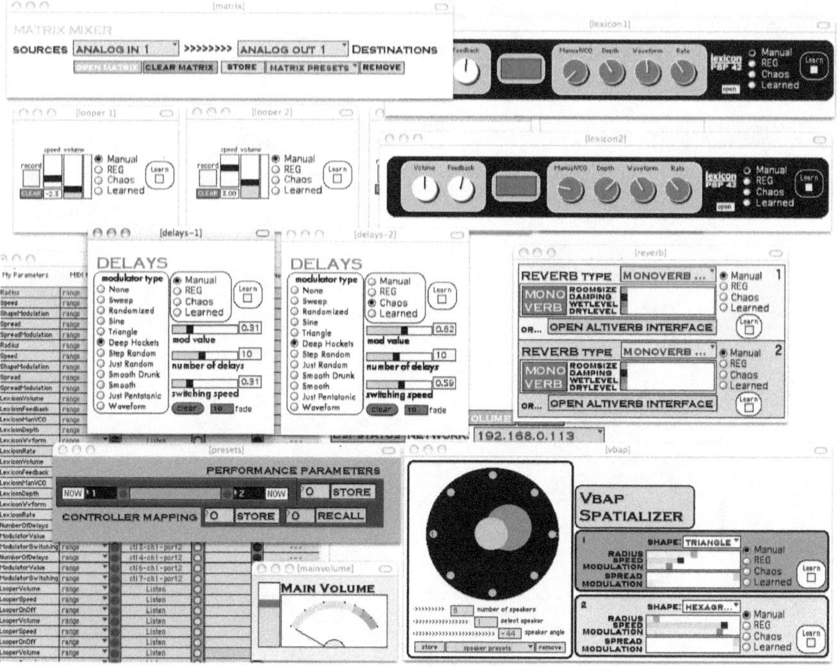

Graphical User Interface for the Expanded Instrument System (EIS)

* * *

In each recorded example discussed in this paper, the unique characteristics of the environment shape and flavor the sounds of the music heard whether acoustic or electronic. The paradigm of one type of acoustic or environment for a specific performance space or for sounds is challenged in the piece *Moving Spaces,* which was first presented at meeting of the Acoustical Society of

America in Providence, RI, June 8, 2006 during a special session of 5.1 surround performances.

Acoustical characteristics that may be performed as an active and changing musical parameter makes it possible for a single sound to have a multi-dimensional existence—or many contexts—during a performance. This understanding of alternate ways of listening to foreground and background offers new possibilities for improvisers, composers, audiences and architects.

Deep Listening Convergence: Report

Presented at the Guelph Jazz Festival Colloqium
University of Guelph, Ontario, Canada
September 5, 2007

The Deep Listening Convergence took place as a virtual residency for forty-five musicians from January 15 to June 10, 2007. All of the musicians were familiar with Deep Listening[1]. Using Skype[2], a VoIP application, the musicians were invited to form new ensembles in a kind of musical "dating game" to prepare for a private concert and three public concerts that took place June 7, 8, 9, and 10 in Troy, Hudson and High Falls, NY.

Musicians from Switzerland, Canada, and the United States participated in Skype jams, discussions, rehearsals, and creations of improvisational pieces. The majority of the musicians were holders of Deep Listening Certificates[3] from 1998–2006 and the rest were artist associates and staff members of the Deep Listening Institute, Ltd. Some musicians were already acquainted and others were not. Many new relationships were formed.

The Deep Listening Convergence project was conceived and named by DLI staff member and certificate holder Vonn New, a drummer/composer/improviser and administrator. The project was made possible by a grant of $65,000 from the New York State Music Fund[4]. Governor Eliot Spitzer (then attorney general of New York State) made available a pool of money gained from suits against record companies that used payola to get their music on the radio. All $150 million gained from these suits was designated for non-profit organizations to use for alternative music.

Pauline Oliveros served as artistic director for the project and Scot Gresham-Lancaster[5] served as technical director. DLI staff member Lisa Barnard handled administration.

Gresham-Lancaster and Oliveros have collaborated for many years on many projects and since 2002 have worked on low- and high-tech telematic[6] music transmissions using public internet and the private Internet2/CANARIE[7] network. In 2005, they began to utilize iChat AV[8] for three-way transmissions between iEAR Studios[9] at Rensselaer Polytechnic Institute in Troy, NY, Mills College[10] in Oakland, CA, and Skalen Dance Company[11] in Marseille, France. Oliveros worked with her RPI ensemble Tintinnabulate[12] in transmissions with Arizona State University in Tempe, AZ, and Wesleyan University in Middletown, CT via iChat AV and with California State University at Hayward and the Society for Arts and Technology in Montreal, QC via Internet2/CANARIE. Subsequently, Tintinnabulate performs in a weekly transmission with the research group SoundWire[13] from the Center for Computer Research in Music and Acoustics, Stanford University with eight-channel CD-quality audio and DVD-quality video.

iChat AV is a Macintosh application so Skype was selected for the Deep Listening Convergence project because it works cross-platform for both Mac and PC. Additionally, although telephone transmission is readily available with speakerphones, it would be costly to mount such a project using land-lines. With Skype, there was no charge.

Most of the forty-five musicians were familiar with computers but not all were familiar with Skype and the other applications (discussed below) that were used with the project. Technical director Gresham-Lancaster created online tutorials and FAQs[14] for the most technically challenged participants. All forty-five musicians participated in the virtual residency for at least one ensemble piece. Others were more or less present for many sessions and pieces. Skype sessions were recorded with Ecamm Call Recorder[15] or Pamela[16] and uploaded to the social networking service imeem[17], which hosts profiles, sound files, and video files. The files are public but the group is private so that no one outside of the group could post files. All communications for the Deep Listening Convergence were posted in the project-management software Basecamp[18] so that they could be archived and read at anytime. Messages could be sent to the whole group or only to selected members of the group.

The virtual residency began with a low-tech jam hosted by trombonist/composer Monique Buzzarté. A time for the event was posted and up to ten participants at a time could join the audio conference on Skype. As these jams continued, others began to make appointments with one another until there were a number of ensembles in the works.

It was apparent that feedback could be a problem unless the participants wore headphones. To skirt this problem, DLI purchased twenty remaindered Sony speakerphones[19] and gave them to participants. The quality was good and the need for headphones was eliminated for some. Additionally, more than one participant could play on the same connection if they happened to be in the same room. The rehearsal jams were more or less successful depending on the stability of the connection. All participants had high-speed connections with cable or DSL but not all were always stable. There were dropouts and lost connections. However, such was not the norm and the virtual residency proceeded very well.

Latency is inherent in low-tech transmissions. Latency on Skype varied from 32 to 84 ms, which is not necessarily greater or lesser than some concert halls. The musicians took latency into consideration as part of the aesthetic of the music they created.

During the residency, four curators were appointed—one for each concert—with the help of communications producer Anne Bourne. The curators requested concert proposals, which were limited to one per participant. Before the Convergence on June 5 began, there was more than enough material for the concerts and each of the four programs curated was completely different. Altogether, twenty-five diverse pieces were created with unique ensembles to play each one.

All of the pieces were rehearsed during the virtual residency as there would only be time for sound checks at the venues. All technical arrangements were organized for each venue by the technical director and DLI staff and volunteers. All of the technical needs were communicated via Basecamp, email, or Skype chat. Administration and provision for accommodations and venue at the beautiful Lifebridge Sanctuary[20] was made by the DLI staff. The majority of the musicians who came from Switzerland, Canada and outside of New York state stayed at the Sanctuary. Meals and transportation to the concert venues were provided.

Each concert was documented with audio, video, and photographs. A feature article—*Meditative Music Mines the Depths of Listening* by Joseph Dalton[21] appeared in the *Times Union* in Albany, NY.

The musicians and audiences were very happy with the concerts and performed very well. The concerts were the proof of the concept that a virtual residency could work.

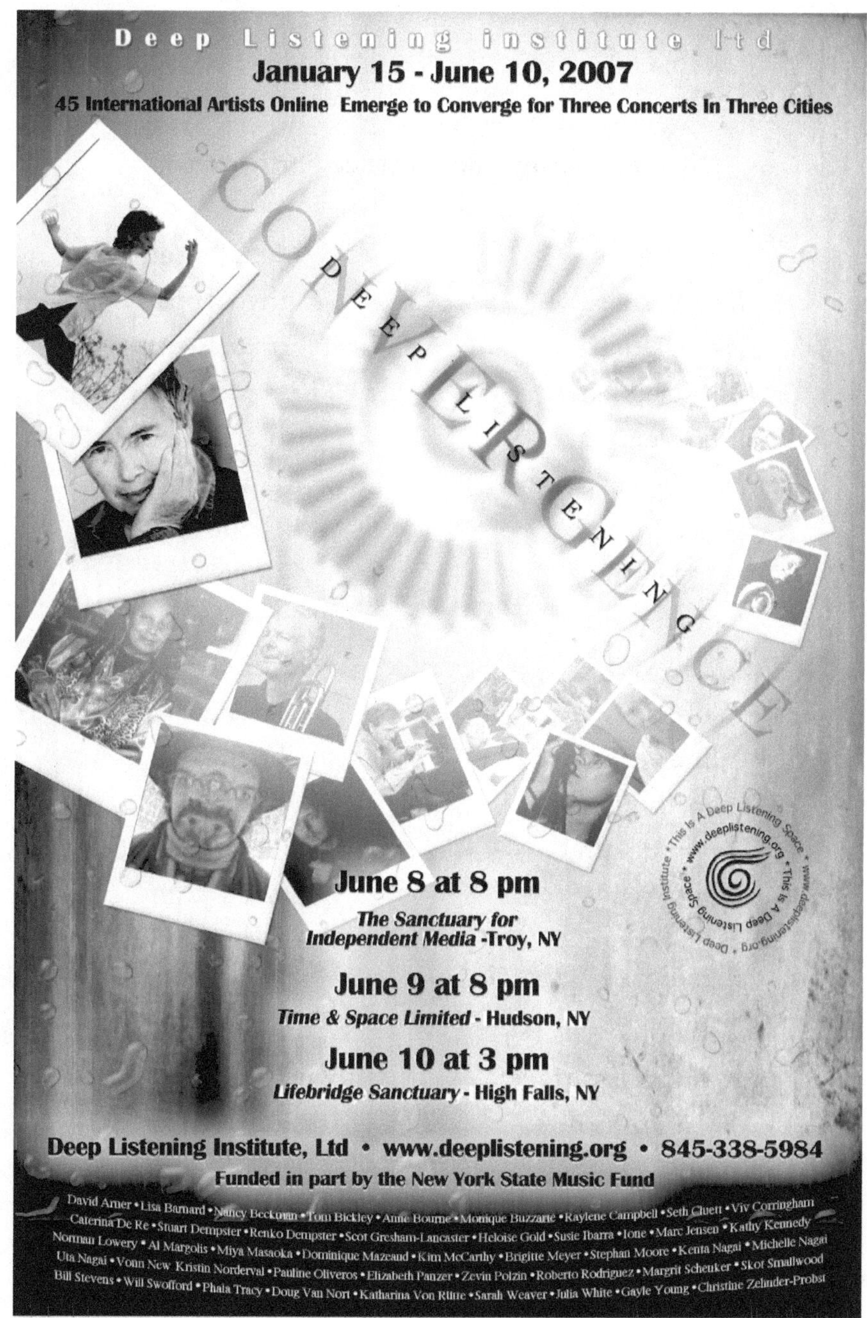
Deep Listening institute ltd
January 15 - June 10, 2007
45 International Artists Online Emerge to Converge for Three Concerts In Three Cities
CONVERGENCE
DEEP LISTENING
June 8 at 8 pm
The Sanctuary for Independent Media -Troy, NY
June 9 at 8 pm
Time & Space Limited - Hudson, NY
June 10 at 3 pm
Lifebridge Sanctuary - High Falls, NY
This Is A Deep Listening Space • www.deeplistening.org • Deep Listening Institute
Deep Listening Institute, Ltd • www.deeplistening.org • 845-338-5984
Funded in part by the New York State Music Fund
David Arner • Lisa Barnard • Nancy Beckman • Tom Bickley • Anne Bourne • Monique Buzzarte • Raylene Campbell • Seth Cluett • Viv Corringham
Caterina De Re • Stuart Dempster • Renko Dempster • Scot Gresham-Lancaster • Heloise Gold • Susie Ibarra • Ione • Marc Jensen • Kathy Kennedy
Norman Lowery • Al Margolis • Miya Masaoka • Dominique Mazeaud • Kim McCarthy • Brigitte Meyer • Stephan Moore • Kenta Nagai • Michelle Nagai
Uta Nagai • Vonn New Kristin Norderval • Pauline Oliveros • Elizabeth Panzer • Zevin Polzin • Roberto Rodriguez • Margrit Schenker • Skot Smallwood
Bill Stevens • Will Swofford • Phala Tracy • Doug Van Nort • Katharina Von Rütte • Sarah Weaver • Julia White • Gayle Young • Christine Zehnder-Probst

Deep Listening Convergence Participants

David Arner
Lisa Barnard
Seth Cluett
Stuart Dempster
Renko Dempster
Heloise Gold
Susie Ibarra
Al Margolis
Stephan Moore
Ikue Mori
Vonn New
Pauline Oliveros
Elizabeth Panzer
Zevin Polzin
Sarah Weaver
Tom Bickley
Nancy Beckman
Anne Bourne
Monique Buzzarté
Will Swofford
Raylene Campbell
Viv Corringham
Caterina De Re
Scot Greshman-Lancaster
Marc Jensen
Kathy Kennedy
Norman Lowrey
Kim McCarthy
Brigitte Meyer
Kenta Nagai
Michelle Nagai
Uta Nagai
Kristin Norderval
Margrit Schenker
Scott Smallwood
Bill Stevens
Phala Tracy
Doug Van Nort
Stacy Denton
Katharina von Rütte
Julia White
Gayle Young
Christine Zehnder-Probst
Andrew Kaluzynski
Filip Gilissen
Susie Ibarra
Roberto Rodriguez
Dominique Mazeaud

Glyka

by Gayle Young (Toronto, Canada)
and Katharina von Rütte (Basel, Switzerland)

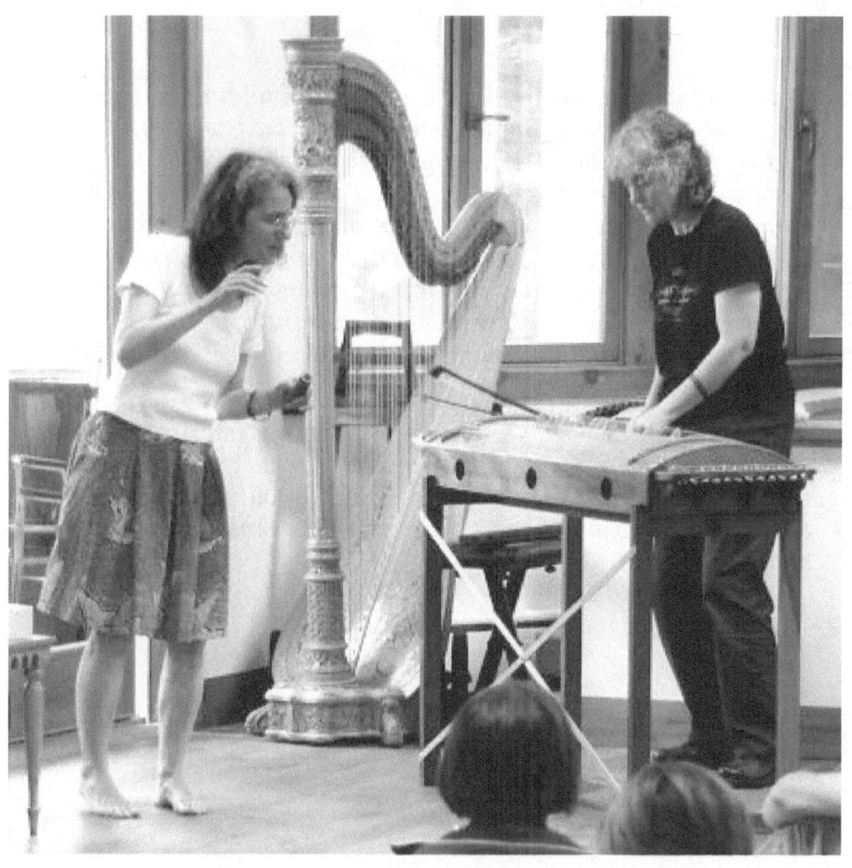

Young and von Rütte met for the first time in a Skype jam. They continued to improvise together and formed a duo. The piece they performed, *Glyka,* used von Rütte's voice and the amaranth and columbine, instruments invented by Young which utilize just intonation.

"I've found that the on-line playing is building a musical connection in spite of the technical issues. Last weekend I was part of a larger group that included two people I've played with quite a lot but don't know very well at the in-person level. I found that I was tending to play in response to those two players with a stronger sense of what sounds would work out well, and a few sub-duos developed within the context of the larger group. This indicates to me that there has been some musical familiarization taking place, that these sessions have had similar results as playing in person.

Our far-flung community of listening improvisers has found a new way of connecting and we are all very excited for this new dimension of communication. We will be able to work together in new ways with improvising, composing, teaching and publishing."

Gayle Young

Threads of Peace

by Julia White (Canada)
for large ensemble

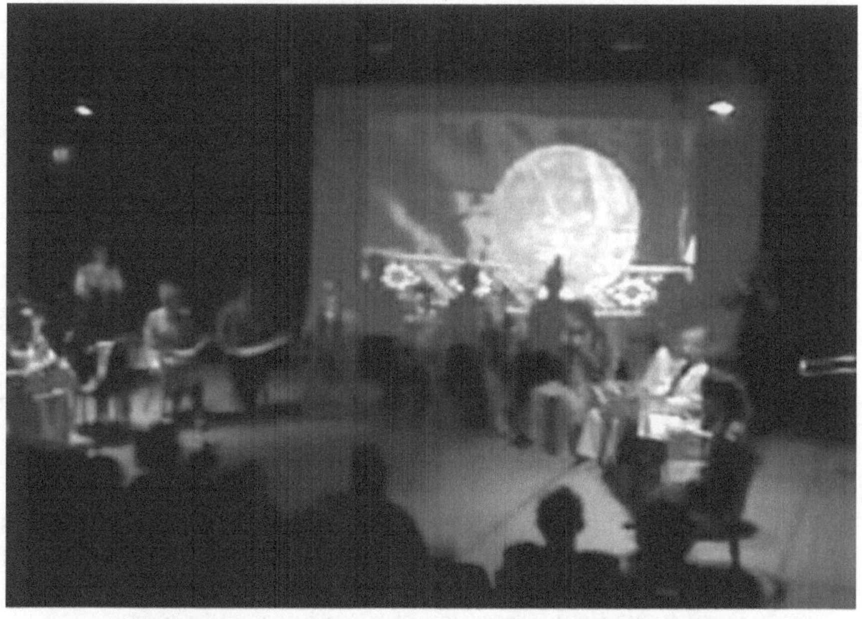

White invited everyone to contribute "pieces of peace"—handwritten or online, fragments of dreams or stories from life that have the theme of peace – and scanned these writings and images, transferred them to fabric, and sewed the panels together in one long piece to be scrolled, projected, and read as a score for improvisation.

"I feel the technique of global listening became essential when, for example, we rehearsed Julia White's Threads of Peace with 9 women. It expanded the consciousness of my imagination to locate each woman to sing with her. I looked at images of Julia's textile piece on-line, and saw her interpretation of my grandfather's WW2 British Army Issue silk scarf that said in 17 Asian languages 'Hello I am not your enemy.' and 'Please may I have a bowl of rice'. I began to hear explosive moments of Skype distortion that evoked in me the imagined sounds of war. This interspersed with the women's singing voices and a shakuhachi calling to each other. I also found the latency effect an effective vocal processing delay sound. My performance listening techniques are not seeming changed yet but their usefulness is confirmed in a real way with this technology, much the way a sound that comes from outside a room's sound sources confirms the intersection of room tones and the voices of other listening souls."

Anne Bourne

DLC-GO

by Doug Van Nort (Montreal, Canada)
and the DLC Genetic Orchestra
for laptops and voices

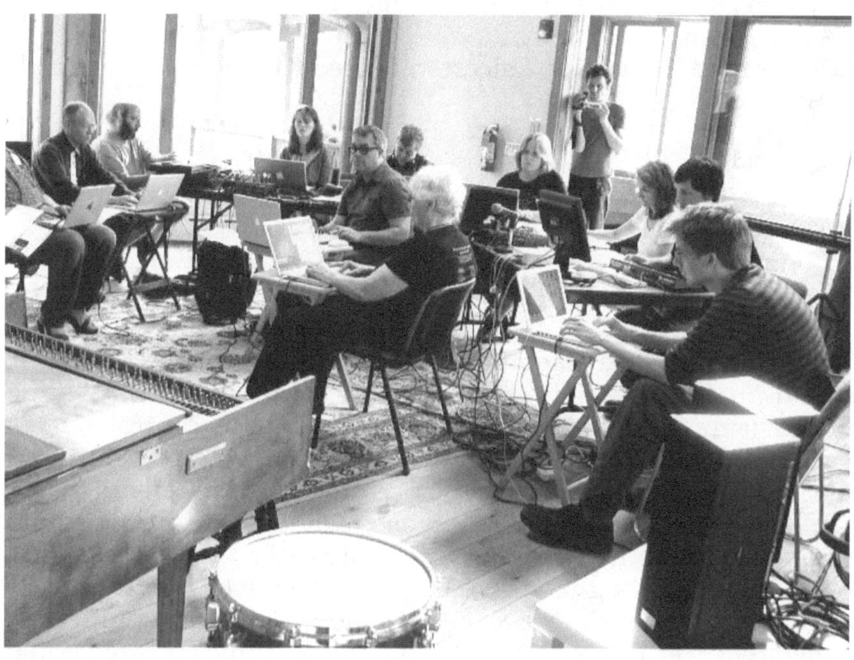

Performers were invited to upload files of their own creation of less than 1 minute each to create a "gene pool" for *DLC-GO*. Each file was rated on a scale of 1-10. From the surviving files, performers could choose files to "mutate" by splitting them, processing their halves, recombining them with other halves and returning them to the gene pool. After several mutations and additions to the gene pool, the surviving files were used for live group improvisation.

The Expanded Instrument System: An Introduction and Brief History

Keynote address given at the colloquium
Music, Technology, Innovation
De Montfort University, Leicester, United Kingdom
November 2007

The Expanded Instrument System (EIS) is an evolving electronic sound-processing environment. EIS is dedicated to providing improvising musicians individual performance control over a variety of parameters that can transform their acoustic input during live performance. EIS has always been intended for acoustic instruments and voices even though electronic sound sources can also be used as well as pre-recorded sources. Until recently, digital signal processing worked well for electronic sound but less well for acoustic sounds; acoustic sounds are generally far more complex than electronically generated sounds.

Performers each have their own setup that includes their own microphones, control devices, and a computer with sound card and audio interface. The computer provides the digital signal processing—variable delays, ambiance, and modulation—and translates and displays control information for this processing from MIDI controllers, foot pedals, and switches. The musicians and their instruments are the sources of all the sounds, which are picked up by the microphones and subjected to pitch, time, and spatial ambiance transformation and manipulation by EIS.

EIS has undergone continual development since 1965 — forty-two years—from tape delay to computers. This is a long trajectory and history through acoustic, analog, and digital means. Software for the recent versions of EIS has been programmed over the last twenty years by Panaiotis, David Gamper, Stephan Moore, Jonathan Marcus, Olivia Robinson, Jesse Stiles, and Zevin Polzin.

The EIS began with the delay that is produced between the record and playback heads on reel-to-reel tape machines. The early development of EIS with reel-to-reel tape machines is described in my article "Tape Delay Techniques for Electronic Music Composers" written in 1969[1]. This article describes and illustrates the configurations of multiple tape machines with the heads connected by stringing tape from the supply reel of one machine to the take up reel of another machine. Today, these delay processes are emulated and elaborated in Max/MSP[2] software.

The premise of the EIS back in 1965 was to challenge myself as an improvising performer. I felt that I could handle more musical information than I was able to perform without the extension of electronic feedback. I began experimenting as I performed with delayed sound fed back to audiences and to me from the outputs of tape machines to loudspeakers. It was important to me that all the sound that I made be live, rather than pre-recorded. This was because a much more nuanced performance could be realized if none of the sources were pre-recorded.

I noticed that layering in time could change the timbre of the original acoustic sound input. I enjoyed the sensations of my acoustic sounds transforming before my ears as the sounds came back to me. I learned that timing was important in introducing new input and that I could disguise the entry points depending on timing and attack so that richly changing timbres could emerge from the delays.

Through the years, I understood the Expanded Instrument System as a kind of "time machine" that produces temporal expansion. Present, past, and future occur simultaneously with transformations. What I play in the present comes back in the future while I am still playing; it is transformed and becomes a part of the past. This situation keeps you busy listening.

This notion of a time machine is not unlike canonical forms, such as the inventions and fugues of J.S. Bach and the repetitions of motives and sequences in the classical forms of Haydn, Mozart, and Beethoven. The phenomenon of echo has perennially inspired musicians throughout history, even into the 20th century when popular musicians and producers began realizing the expressive potential of echo and reverberation. Many of the songs and soundtracks wonderfully described in *Echo and Reverb in Popular Music: Fabricating Space in Popular Music Recording 1900 to 1960*[3] by Peter Doyle influenced me directly. I was particularly impressed by songs like "Riders in the Sky" sung by Vaughn Monroe, "Steel Guitar Rag" by Bob Wills and His Texas Playboys, "How High the Moon" by Les Paul and Mary Ford, "Juke" by Little Walter, and many other selections that I heard on the radio and jukebox as a teenager. It was the sound of the spaces differentiated by echo and reverberation within the songs that captured me.

Canons produced by the EIS can be disguised by the modulations that cause variations in the returns of sound input and also by the variety of spaces created by the multiple and varying delay times. These canons can be (but are not necessarily) pitch canons – they can be time and timbre canons, as well. The EIS is both a time and space machine. The EIS' imperative (and improvisation imperative) is to listen and respond: spatial relationships and progressions are as important as the traditional parameters of music (melody, harmony, rhythm, timbre).

Timbre particularly is affected by space. I discuss this effect in my article "Acoustic and Virtual Space as a Dynamic Parameter of Music," written in 1995:

> *"Virtual acoustics—a perceptual phenomenon—is created with electronic processing within an actual physical space. Simulated walls or reflective surfaces may cause a listener to perceive differences in room size and the tone quality of a musical instrument."*[4]

These virtual acoustics are also part of the expansion of EIS. Virtual acoustics gives the improvising performer new possibilities.

> *"With the advent of signal processors and sophisticated sound systems, it is possible to tamper with the container of music in imaginative ways. The walls of a virtual acoustic space created electronically can expand or contract, assume new angles or*

virtual surfaces. The resulting resonances and reflections changing continuously during the course of a performance create spatial progressions much as one would create chord progressions or timbre transformations (changing the tone quality of an instrument while performing a single pitch). The audience and performers can experience sensations of moving in space as well as sounds moving through space. They can also experience the relationship of moving in space in relation to sounds moving in the same space and while the space itself is changing. Such audio illusions or virtual acoustics can function as a new parameter of music much as timbre became new in klangfarbenmelodie (tone color melody)—where the notes of a melody are distributed to different instruments successively as in the music of Arnold Schoenberg (who coined the term) and Anton Webern."[5]

The EIS is also fun! Acoustic input from an instrument or voice now can be processed with up to 40 variable delays, modulated with fluctuating waveforms, layered, and spatialized. Sounds may be diffused in four, six or eight channels. More outputs could be programmed for sixteen, thirty-two, sixty-four, and beyond. The current version, programmed in Max/MSP, undergoes continual revision due to new performer demands and is already a long way from the limited tape delay system of the beginnings of EIS. Time delays range from milliseconds to one minute or more depending on CPU power.

However, the EIS is never finished and there is always more to explore.

Even though the original concept of echo is very simple, the applications of digital signal processing and routing result in endless variations and possibilities.

The current revision of the patch also includes some intelligent controls for the innumerable parameters involved. These controllers can learn from experience. The controls can be set to run from a chaos generator or from a random event generator as well. The result is like having several partners controlling dozens of knobs, faders, and switches—more than could be manipulated by a single performer. There is a need for a smart metacontroller that understands from experience how to direct all of the subcontrollers and switches with intelligent guesses.

The EIS consists of modules that can be configured in the interface window. Any number of the modules can be used, depending on the performer's preference. Modules can be switched on with the window launcher and dragged to any position. The current list of modules includes the following:

- Window launcher
- Performance clock
- Master volume control
- Matrix Mixer
- Matrix
- Control Mapping Interface
- Performance parameters
- Looper [1-4]
- Delays [1-2] (includes modulation functions and 20 delays each)
- Reverb [1-2]
- VBAP [1-2] (includes geometric spatialization patterns)

Screenshots of the Current Version of EIS

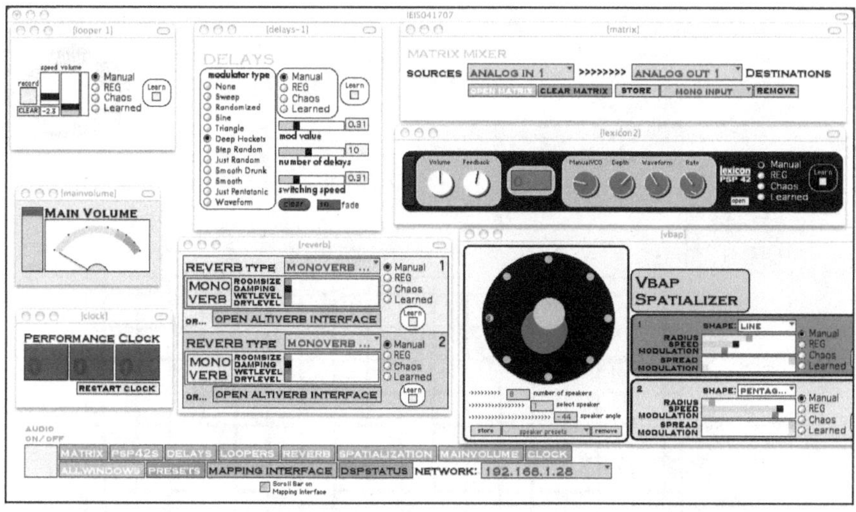

Figure 1—A selected configuration of EIS modules including looper 1, delay 1, matrix mixer, Lexicon 1, main volume, performance clock, reverb, VBAP and window launcher is shown. Other modules could be selected, moved around in the window, or removed as desired.

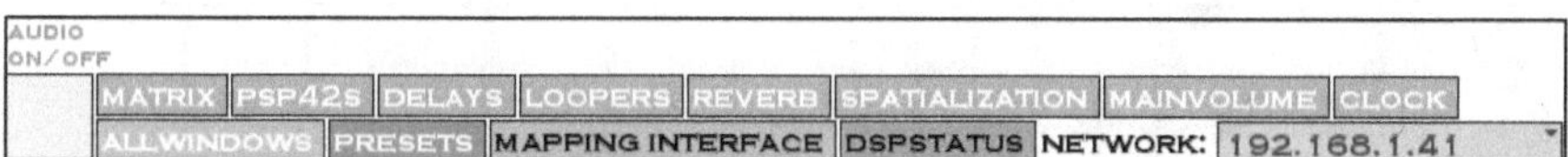

Figure 2—EIS Window Launcher: Each module of EIS may be opened separately or together. Module configurations may be saved by the patcher in Max and reopened later.

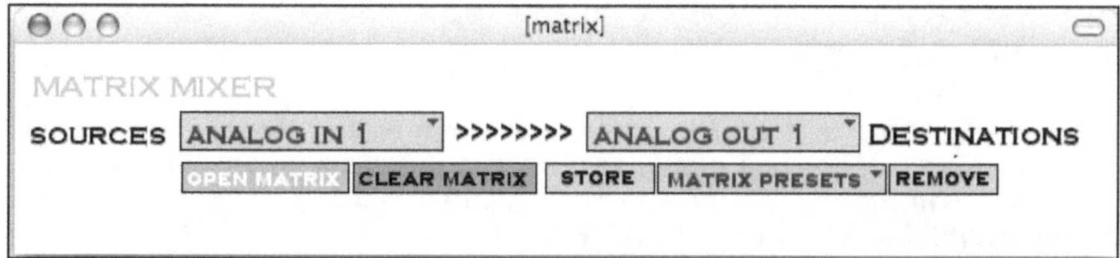

Figure 3—Matrix Mixer: Any input can be connected to any output. Matrix configurations may be stored and recalled as presets. Presets can be recalled in performance or removed. The matrix window can be cleared at any time.

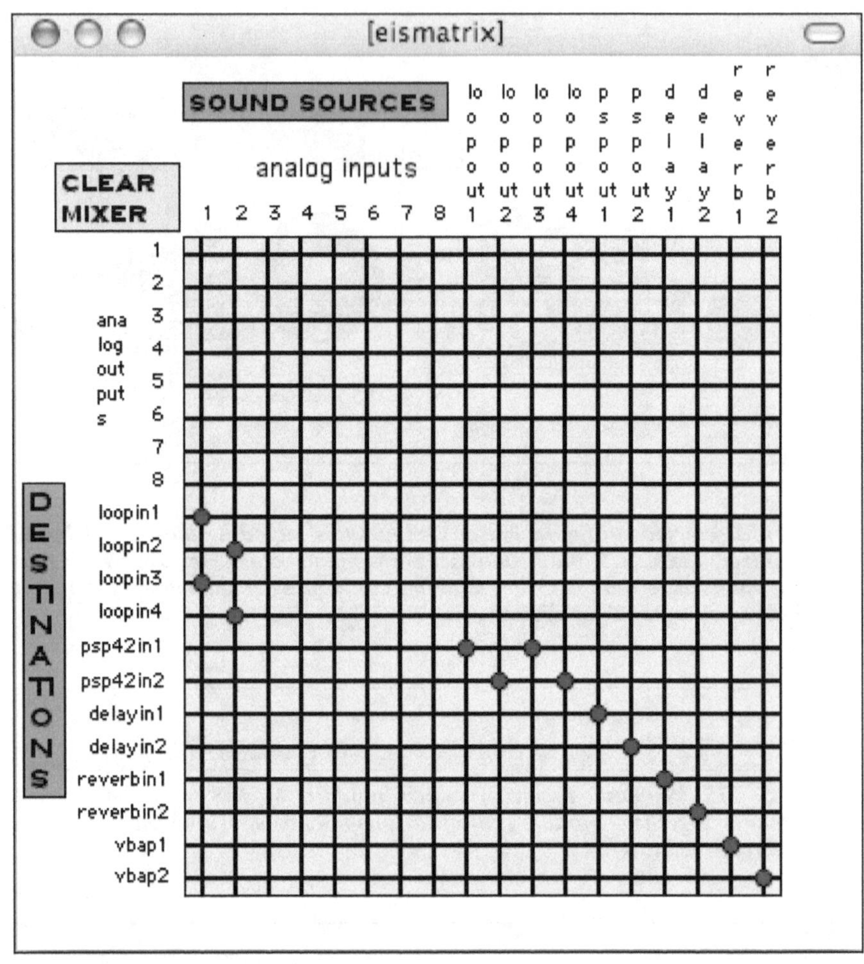

Figure 4—EIS Matrix: A configuration of the open matrix shows analog inputs 1 and 2 going to loopers 1 and 2, loopers 1 and 2 going to Lexicons 1 and 2, Lexicons 1 and 2 going to delays 1 and 2, delays 1 and 2 going to reverbs 1 and 2, and reverbs 1 and 2 going to VBAP 1 and 2.

[control_mapping_interface]

1Radius	range	ctl58-ch1-port0	---
1Speed	range	ctl59-ch1-port0	---
1ShapeModulation	range	ctl60-ch1-port0	---
1Spread	range	Listen	---
1SpreadModulation	range	ctl28-ch1-port0	---
2Radius	range	ctl44-ch1-port0	---
2Speed	range	ctl45-ch1-port0	---
2ShapeModulation	range	ctl46-ch1-port0	---
2Spread	range	Listen	---
2SpreadModulation	range	ctl28-ch1-port0	---
1LexiconVolume	range	ctl53-ch1-port0	---
1LexiconFeedback	range	ctl54-ch1-port0	---
1LexiconManVCO	range	ctl0-ch1-port2	---
1LexiconDepth	range	ctl55-ch1-port0	---
1LexiconWvform	range	ctl56-ch1-port0	---
1LexiconRate	range	ctl57-ch1-port0	---
2LexiconVolume	range	ctl39-ch1-port0	---
2LexiconFeedback	range	ctl40-ch1-port0	---
2LexiconManVCO	range	ctl1-ch1-port2	---
2LexiconDepth	range	ctl41-ch1-port0	---
2LexiconWvform	range	ctl42-ch1-port0	---
2LexiconRate	range	ctl43-ch1-port0	---
1NumberOfDelays	range	ctl8-ch1-port0	---
1ModulatorValue	range	ctl9-ch1-port0	---
1ModulatorSwitching	range	ctl10-ch1-port0	---
2NumberOfDelays	range	ctl12-ch1-port0	---
2ModulatorValue	range	ctl13-ch1-port0	---
2ModulatorSwitching	range	ctl14-ch1-port0	---
1LooperVolume	range	ctl10-ch2-port0	---
1LooperSpeed	range	ctl10-ch1-port0	---
1LooperOnOff	range	ctl19-ch1-port0	---
2LooperVolume	range	ctl10-ch4-port0	---
2LooperSpeed	range	ctl10-ch3-port0	---
2LooperOnOff	range	ctl20-ch1-port0	---
3LooperVolume	range	ctl10-ch6-port0	---

Figure 5—Control Mapping Interface: MIDI controllers may be mapped to any modules. Upon launch, EIS detects any MIDI controllers that are connected to the audio interface as well as users connected through an ethernet connection. MIDI mapping may also be passed to another performer on a different system through this IP ethernet connection. A remote performer on the local network may vary the amount of control of another system module.

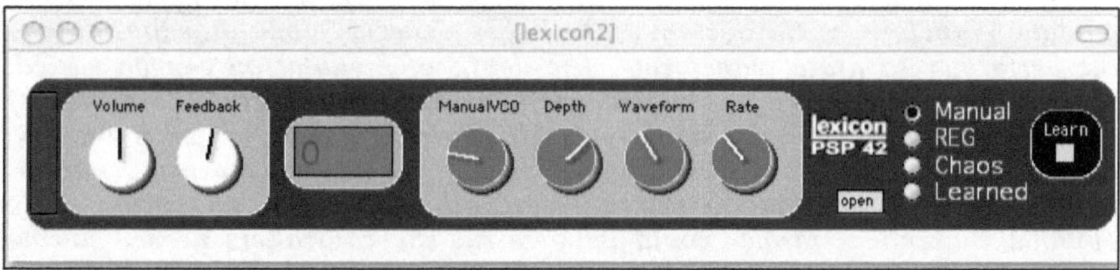

Figure 6 – Lexicon PSP42 VST: Simulation of the original Lexicon PCM42[6] digital delay processor used from 1983 in earlier versions of EIS. Volume, feedback, delay time (0-10"), manual VCO, depth, waveform and rate are controllable and can be mapped to any MIDI controller.

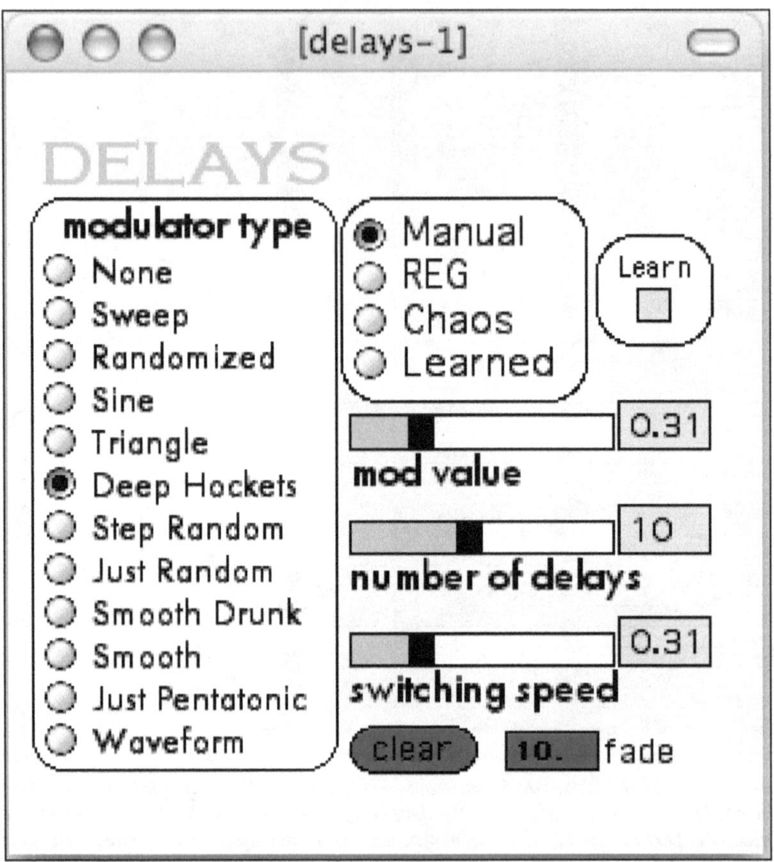

Figure 7—Delays (1 of 2): There are up to 20 variable time delays on each module that can be modulated with a variety of waveforms. The list includes sweep, sine, triangle, etc., and can be seen under "Modulator Type:" on the module. Waveform at the bottom of the list is a special modulator that allows the performer to draw waveforms. The depth of modulation can be varied. Modulation type can be randomized or switched off entirely. The degree of shift in randomization can be varied. All controls can be varied manually, with a random event generator, chaos generator, or through learned behavior. Although MIDI mapping to external controllers could be an option, it is obvious that no performer could manage all the controllers needed during performance. Thus algorithmic control is the best option for these delay modules.

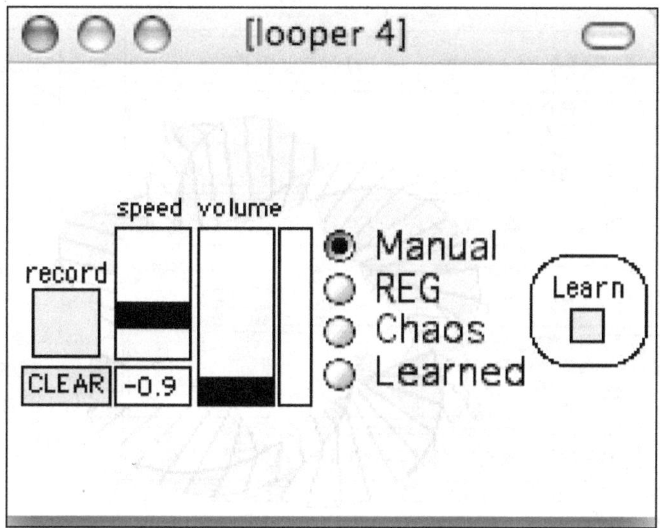

Figure 8—Looper (1 of 4): Analog input can be recorded or input from any other module (including other loopers). The speed control allows the input to increase pitch with + values and play backward with – values. Both speed and volume can be varied manually or algorithmically with a random event generator, chaos generator or with learned behavior.

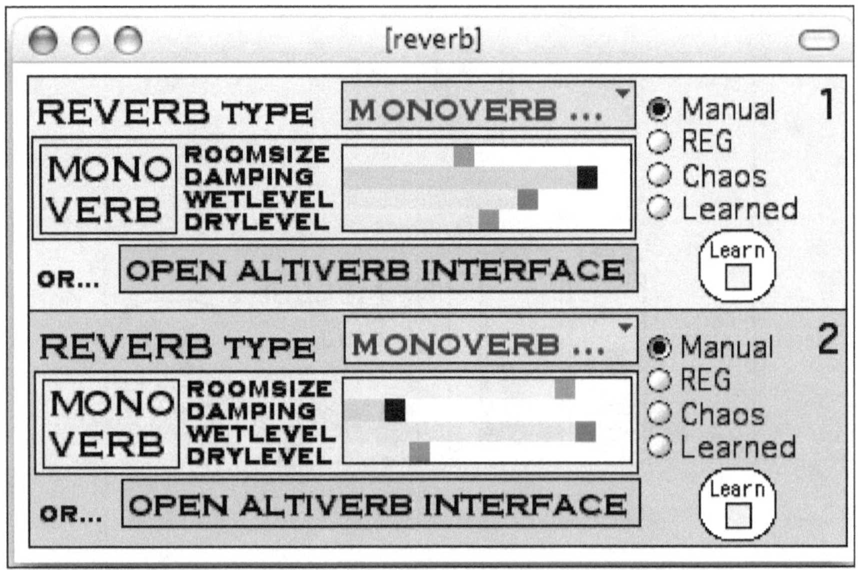

Figure 9—Reverb: Any module or analog input may be mapped to either reverb 1 or 2 or both in parallel or series. All four Monoverb[7] variables – room size, damping, wet level, and dry level—may be controlled manually or with a random event generator (REG), chaos generator, or learned behavior. Monoverb[7] works well within limited CPU power. With sufficient CPU power, Altiverb[8] may be used for richer reverberation choices using impulse/responses as another option.

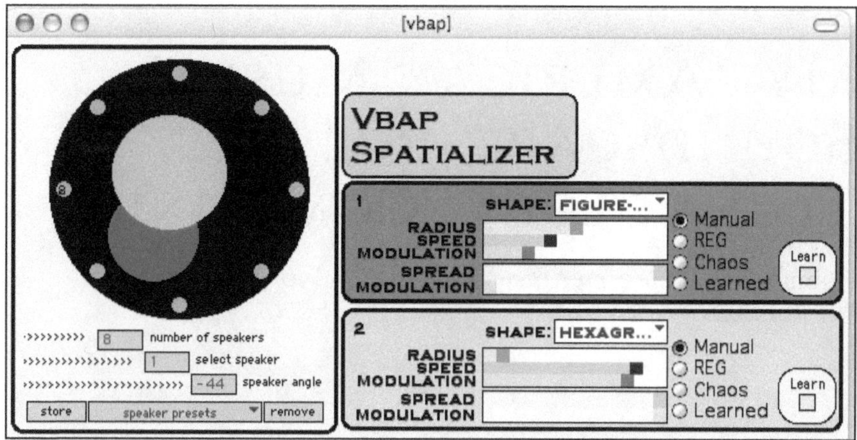

Figure 10—VBAP: Vector Based Amplitude Panning uses objects developed by Ville Pulkki[9]. Configuration of speakers is accomplished on the left side of the VBAP module. The functions available are: number of speakers, select speakers, speaker angle, store, presets and remove. The large circle containing smaller blue and pink moving circles indicates the positions of the speakers and the paths of the two sound sources in the speaker field.

On the right side of the VBAP, the Spatializer module shapes provide patterns of movement through the sound field. Available shapes are listed in the pull-down menu and include ten geometric patterns plus a recordable pattern that can be drawn by the performer, stored, and recalled.

Five variable functions can affect the path of the sound sources and amplitude. These functions are radius, speed, modulation (modulation affects radius and speed), spread, and modulation (modulation affects the size of the sound source in the speaker field). The functions can be controlled manually or by the REG, Chaos or Learn controllers.

The default VBAP configuration uses eight speakers evenly spaced in a circle. Speakers can be arranged in any circular position. Minimum speakers are four.

* * *

EIS runs on Mac OS X 10.2 or higher using 1.25 GHz processor or faster with 512 MB RAM or more. EIS is available as a stand-alone application or as a patch for Max/MSP. The patch version of EIS requires Max/MSP 4.5.3. For more information, see http://www.deeplistening.org/site/EIS. EIS is a project of the Deep Listening Institute, Ltd.

My "American Music": Soundscape, Politics, Technology, Community

Pubished in *American Music,* Volume 25, No. 4
Winter 2007

Is there any point in talking about something called "American music"? Is the idea relevant anymore? Is there Canadian music? Is there Swiss music? We know that nowadays all musical threads are weaving together. "Our" music is becoming assimilated into many worlds of music[1], and because of evolving communication systems, that will happen more and more.

As with the old idea of the American melting pot, we now have a world melting pot. Yet, although a fusion of cultures is happening in all the arts, music may be foremost in this process. Musicians may be the vanguard of fusion because of one hundred years of dissemination through broadcasts and recordings. Now, in the projects and work of the Deep Listening Institute, Ltd.[2] (described below) we are part of this fusion. As time goes on, we who promote Deep Listening will be reaching out further to all continents to try to bring more people into working together across borders.[3]

Some might watch the news and see the world actually dividing more with increasing barriers to communication and guarded boundaries. But that depends on one's perspective. Government perspective is one thing, but people perspective is another. Corporations seem to want to take over the world.

Franchise operations always threaten to drive small businesses out of neighborhoods and change the character of those neighborhoods. Worldwide empires level values: food, for example, accelerates into speedily served hamburgers and French fries without the niceties of fine service, beautiful settings, and time for conversation. Then there is the exponential climb of the world of technology (about which I will say more later).

There's something fundamentally American about resisting categorization. (I certainly resist and refuse it.) Always looking for "the next best thing" seems hard-wired into our character. "America" was born of exploration and westward frontiers. And of course that is exactly what I've been doing all these years: exploring. I began by listening to my home environment as a child and remembering the sounds. Later I was exploring my inner world and experiencing the sensation of music with Sonic Meditation[4]. I was exploring consciousness—a word that for years was not admissible in the scientific community. Consciousness had no location, could not be measured, and was considered an epiphenomenon. Now consciousness is a crucial part of scientific study[5]. When I was beginning my study of consciousness in relation to music in 1970, a conference on consciousness was held at University of California, San Diego (UCSD)[6]. I attended because of my own research. I was looking for scientific evidence of various states of consciousness. This conference brought out a lot of ideas, concepts, and studies that were beginning to take place and which paralleled the development of my work with Sonic Meditation. Of course I had no credence in the scientific community. However, I did have then—and still have—thoughts and ideas shaped by my own experiments and experiences in working with consciousness or attentional strategies and patterns. Perhaps I may now be getting closer to some recognition of my research in this marginal dance between categories that I have been doing for almost forty years.

Soundscape

Certainly my childhood in Texas opened into a "wonderland" of natural sound. There were large rural areas, which I relished early on. I had a recent reconnection with these memories: I was in Houston in April 2007 to receive the Resounding Vision

Award from Nameless Sound[7] (a spin-off organization from the Deep Listening Institute, Ltd.). The reception was at the Art Guys' studio[8], which is right in the old neighborhood that I lived in as a child—not a neighborhood, really, but literally a farm area. All of the farmland is pretty much gone now, but the studio's location is very much like what I knew about and experienced as a child, with a pecan orchard, pine woods, and berry patches. In those days, what you could hear in terms of the natural world was just amazing: very, very dense sound that varied according to the time of day or night, because the lowland of Houston was a natural habitat filled with numerous varieties of insects and birds. The sounds are still present in a few places that are not paved over. But the natural sound is diminishing and masked by technological noise. The asphalt and cement have covered over so much of it. The frogs, for example, have just about disappeared in the inner city in Houston. The seventeen-year cicadas cannot emerge from their underground gestation through cement and asphalt. The great choruses I would hear of birds and insects are not there anymore in force[9]. Even so, the soundscape remains very powerful in my own memories.

In 1970, when I created *Sonic Meditations*, I worked with a group of students at UCSD, taking them outside for practice as often as I could. I took them out to Joshua Tree National Monument for a weekend where we—a group of about twenty—practiced Sonic Meditations in the high desert. The landscape of Joshua Tree is very spectacular and unusual: huge boulders and the Joshua trees themselves growing naturally in very beautiful and unusual forms. Working in such an environment with Sonic Meditations had a profound impact on all of us. Practicing this way has been an important thread going through my work since 1970—always seeking natural environments in which to perform. This means taking performance out of the concert hall paradigm. The concert hall, of course, has a profound effect on music because of the constructive core of the music. But its basic trait is enclosed space. Sound from the outside world is shut out intentionally for exclusive focus on the music being performed. In contrast, my paradigm is to perform in open space and include everything that is sounding.

America, of course, is a country with many beautiful places to go. (I take the song "America the Beautiful" seriously and still love it.) I've been to the desert and also to the woods. For their first ten years the Deep Listening retreats were at Rose

Mountain, 8,000 feet up in the Sangre de Cristo Mountains in New Mexico[10]. Participants all felt very affected by being in such a place with very little impact from development. Rose Mountain was a wonderfully natural place. The only unnatural sounds to be heard were jet planes flying over once in a while and perhaps the intermittent sound of the water pump. We were in a place that used solar energy and rainwater, and the quiet of that technology was wonderful for listening practice[11].

Nowadays a lot of young people go out with recorders into natural environments. They seem very interested in what they can record and then use in their music. It's as if they are trying to recreate that which has been lost; they get very interested in those sounds because they are really beautiful. And natural sounds are also full-range sounds, whereas a lot of electronic sound is not. Car radios or small speaker systems are very focused and localized sources of sound bounded by a narrow audio range. However when you go out into nature, sound is all around you and that immersion brings back a lot of something that's missing. So many composer/performers are now avid collectors of natural sounds.

Of course, an analog or digital recording is only a documentation, a representation of sound and music. No recording as yet can be the same as the real thing in all its dimensions. All recordings require us to fill in what is not there. Just as any score is just a representation of what is intended, one has to understand what the performance practice is in order to really play the score. The performance practice of this wonderland of sound in which I grew up is Deep Listening, of which my brief definition is this: experiencing an expanded awareness of sound, silence, and sounding. Experiencing is the key word. All performance practice has to be experienced to be understood.

Politics

In the late 1960's some of my musical colleagues were trying to adopt a scientific approach to their music and to align themselves with the scientific method. The resulting music was complex and intellectual and brought about a kind of separation from the body. Their disembodied music required exclusive focus to understand. People could not—and cannot—experience it in their body. While many composers were taking this extreme intellectual approach, which I think came from its relationship to the scientific paradigm, I went in the opposite direction. This does not mean that my music has no intellectual component or that I am anti-intellectual. Ideas drive our consciousness, our development and evolution. We must have a continually developing intellect. That is why I admire almost all music, including intellectual music. However for me there must be a balance between exclusionary activity and inclusive activity, a balance of body/mind.

In 1970 when I began to create my *Sonic Meditations*, I was really departing from the avant-garde paradigm of the time and creating my own way, my own path. My colleagues, I think, were very puzzled by what I was doing, because I had been brought to UCSD in 1967 to start the graduate program in electronic music, which I did. By 1970, though, I was beginning to change my ways of listening and responding. It wasn't that I abandoned electronic music or anything else that was progressive. I have always used technology—as all musicians use technology, whether it's musical instruments or computers; they're all a part of "technology."

In my changing perspective on my musical activities I was reacting, in a way, to the death of a student who immolated himself on the plaza at UCSD in a Vietnam War protest. Like many others, I also practically witnessed the assassination of Robert Kennedy on television. These up-close and personal experiences—not to mention the more distant My Lai Massacre—moved me to change[12].

Those were very disturbing times. So I began to center myself with the work I was doing with sonic meditation, feeling that people needed connections, interconnections, rather than separation in order to play together well for one thing (as musicians), but also to be together well as human beings on a planet that is shared by all. I could understand at that point whether people were listening inclusively or exclusively. Focusing hard on something sometimes makes you lose track of where you are because you are so focused. This experience happens often. And I am sure everyone has experienced someone not listening to them. I began to understand that many people felt that they were not being heard (something especially true today, both locally and globally). I recognized that being heard is a step toward being understood. Being understood is a step toward being healed. Understanding is a step toward building community.

I am trying to facilitate inward experience because people have to feel in their bodies what they have to do in order to create change. I don't think one can create change just with words. One has to have a full body response that has total presence and impact. That does not mean that words are not effective. They are; words are powerful. Without engagement of the body, though, words are literally disembodied and become more and more abstract. And the world is not necessarily an abstraction, especially for someone who gets hit with a roadside bomb.

I teach at Rensselaer now, the oldest technological school in the country, established in 1824. Rensselaer president Shirley Ann Jackson has given us this motto: "Why not change the world?" so all of us on the faculty have that thought on our backburners: "Why not change the world?" But are Americans changing the world in a good way? That too depends on one's perspective. I don't think the change that was brought through attacking Iraq was very productive. The result is horrible, completely horrible. The government administration seems to be totally insensitive to this horror of death and destruction. I was very much against the Iraq War even before it started, because I am against war in any case: war is an unsupportable tantrum.

Before the Iraq War began, I was talking to a broker about an investment. The young woman who was working for the brokerage said something about going to war. I said, "Well I'm against war. I don't want to have anything to do with war. I have no interest in investment that supports that direction whatever." She then got a strange look on her face, her eyes turned inward, and it was almost as if she wasn't there. She said, "But war is good for business." I said, "What about the people that will be killed?" and she said, "Oh well, there won't be that many." It was obviously her corporate training saying these words, not her real self. She was too separated from her own feelings.

There is a certain meanness of spirit in corporate culture because of the exclusionary thinking and the goal-oriented straight-line work that they do, the "black box" approach where the corporation is surrounded and protected from any outsiders banging on the box. There is ruthless heartlessness in terms of achieving their goals, their profits, their bottom line. It is unconscionable. And the heartlessness of the present war for me is simply mind-boggling.

Technology

America is noted for its technology, a key element of being American. "Yankee know-how" it was called: inventions, engineering, all of that is part of being in America and being an American. Now we see how technology is impacting the world. Some of it is very unfortunate—like the war in Iraq (and all the other wars). Some of it is harder to gauge. This "know-how" works both ways.

Railroads, for example, had a great impact on the sense of time[13] and that had a huge impact on music. Traveling on a rail and not deviating from it, traveling through time rather than wandering away. But coming back, taking side trips, detours, following your nose—that's the freedom of being free of tracks. The "tracks" became part of our institutions. Tracks are built into the educational system, including the teaching of music. So the impact of the railroad is, I think, very strong. Are you on the right track? The pull of nature is still there but it's more and more difficult to follow it, to be part of nature.

The train was very much a part of my growing up because that was a principal mode of transportation before airlines. Flying is somewhat different. It's point to point, like the railroad, but faster. So it has become one of many impactful accelerations. When I first began to fly from, say, Houston to San Francisco, that was unusual. But in my twenty-nine years in California, flying has become almost as ordinary as taking a bus. Other musicians and I began to have mobility that we never experienced before, now being able to play in New York, for example, then again quickly in Los Angeles. A lot happened with that kind of change. Think of the flying conductors: Seiji Ozawa in Boston and then in Japan[14].

Flying also changes one's perspective of the landscape—very, very different from traveling through it by railroad. I had the experience of flying to Japan in 2005 for a performance. We took a flight with one overhead television monitor and individual monitors at the seat with the camera pointing down at the landscape. We flew over the arctic and Siberia—just amazing, incredible. The scene was dreamlike, because we were looking down and seeing all the patterns in the snow and ice. My partner, Ione, wrote a poem about this experience on the way and performed it at our concert in Kanazawa, right after we arrived. That's how fast art can happen: on the way and drawing on the experience of the landscape.

So inevitably technology distances us from the landscape but also gives us a perspective of the landscape that we could not have had otherwise. Much has happened to extend and expand what we can sense. Expansion of senses will continue to happen. We are in the process of merging with technology as we have been doing for a long time. I have a pair of glasses on right now—technology. To put on a pair of headphones and walk around and listen (more technology) has the effect of expanding your listening. I remember the first time that I appeared on television (in 1950 in Houston) with a dance band that I was playing in. Of course I never had a television set until much later.

Since then television has changed America and the rest of the world. And television continues to change the world. The next thing, of course, is the internet, which is changing the world faster that anything else. The rise of technology never stops. It is in a straight line from the beginning of history[15] and now the rise is in an exponential leap of development. At the same time the human condition keeps going up and down. We have crisis and crash, but never a straight line, as there is with technology.

Community

Being able to commune means being heard; there's listening going on. I began to incorporate this idea into my *Sonic Meditations,* which are really about the direction of attention and the directing of attention to sound or to silence or to sounding with the understanding of when to listen exclusively and when to listen inclusively and how to balance between those two forms of listening. Certainly this has to happen in an ensemble, in ensemble playing. First of all you have to focus on your part and your instrument. But if you are so focused on your part or instrument that you don't understand the interrelationship or interconnectedness of how your part and instrument is working in the ensemble, you'll find it not very easy to play in a group.

Each time I composed a new *Sonic Meditation* during those couple of years in 1971 and '72, I began to play with those ideas or realities of direction of attention. That is what I've been doing all these years, working with the forms of attention, deepening my own experience and understanding of how attention leads to the heightened awareness or expansion of mind I am after. Attentive listening is the core of how to create community, whether it is an ensemble of musicians or a neighborhood watch.

This brings me to the experiences leading up to the Deep Listening Convergence[16], a project of the Deep Listening Institute, Ltd., completed in June 2007. During our seventeen years of doing Deep Listening retreats for one week each summer, we created a community. Several hundred people had been to the retreats—though as of now (2007) only about thirty-two of them have completed the three-year Deep Listening certification program[17]. In 1995 we started an e-list called DEEPL[18] because people would return to their part of the world and then want to be in touch with retreat activities and the people they had met. The DEEPL e-list helps to do that. DEEPL became a very powerful community ground—a community commons, where everything from births to deaths takes place. If somebody has a problem, the community gathers around.

We sadly experienced two deaths of Deep Listeners who had been to the retreat, for example, and the community rallied around. The first one died of a brain tumor. What happened during the nine months between his diagnosis and his death was very well documented on the DEEPL and remains in the archives. The experience and support during this process was quite powerful. I am still in touch with his widow and I know that DEEPL really helped her through this grievous loss. Then right away we had another community member with a brain tumor. Both of these men died at home with their partners and Deep Listeners they knew in the area, who were there for them both actually and virtually. That is community. All were deeply interested and supportive as these tragedies unfolded on DEEPL.

Of course there are also the joyous events, births, the children who are already acquainted with everybody (because it is fun to be included). At the 2007 Convergence we had a sixteen-month old baby among us. He was present throughout and participating in joyful wonderful ways. His mother had composed a piece for the retreat last summer (2006), a piece called *Voice Mommy*[19]. The baby had just been born and so the mother could not attend the retreat. So she sent a piece she had composed for us to do. Here is how it worked: everyone at the retreat was asked to secretly choose a "voice mommy" and all during the week to follow the voice of that person, listen for it, and listen for all its subtle characteristics. On the last day of the retreat she instructed us all to get into a cuddle-huddle, then begin very softly to start sounding, to identify our "voice mommy" from the sounding huddle, then to make our way to that person and let him or her know. *Voice Mommy* was hilarious, wonderful, and touching—a very impressive thing to do. This year the mother was here at the Convergence with her baby (and, of course, everybody knows who the baby is today). That's the kind of community we have built.

In the Convergence we brought together the thirty-two certificate holders as well as a few artists who had been associated either through our recording label or through concerts over the years. Including our certificate holders we had forty-five musicians. Although we were in touch with many other participants, we limited the attendance to certificate holders the first two days in order to answer the central question: "What is your relationship to your certificate?" Through this meeting we wanted to open up ways for them to take responsibility and help to develop this network, this new community.

We convened in the Lifebridge Sanctuary[20] in High Falls, New York—a very, very beautiful place. We had a day of discussing what the certificate program is and how it could evolve. Also, we had prepared material, the forty-five of us, working together on the internet using Skype[21], a telephonic (VoIP) system that can host up to ten people in a web-based audio conference free of charge. One of our ideas was to use this technology to form new ensembles, something like a little dating game: you move around, meet different people you didn't know, and play with them. This activity spawns a lot of ideas, a lot of pieces, and a lot of improvisation.

To be sure, many people were skeptical of the communication system and frustrated with it from time to time because it was not perfect. But the truth is, we would not have time to rehearse the large number of pieces (25) that were created and that we performed. The premise was this: each person rehearsed his or her piece online and got it ready, then when they came to the Deep Listening Convergence they had a little bit of time to check it. That's it. So the concerts were the rehearsals and the rehearsals were the concerts and the people involved had all this training in the retreats that enabled them to make things work. Given the way we had organized all of this, they played the pieces a little differently, of course. There was a wonderful kind of connection they were able to make, first with themselves and then whomever they were performing with—and the audience too, of course.

Four concerts were produced at the Convergence. We began with a private concert at the Lifebridge. The night after Lifebridge, we played in Troy at the Sanctuary for Independent Media, then in Hudson the next night at Timespace Ltd., and then back to the Lifebridge Sanctuary for the final concert in the afternoon. Each concert was totally different—different pieces, different groupings of people performing together. The last audience was the largest, forty or fifty people or so. (In upstate New York it is very tough to get people out to concerts. For us there was maybe a local audience of twenty or so. And of course the group itself is also an audience: not everybody was playing in every piece, but they were listening to everything. So it looked like we had more audience than we did!) We have great documentation of all those performances. We had audio, video, and photo documentation, while several people were writing up the experiences as well.

Overall, I must say that I'm very, very happy about this Convergence. It was generally a very wonderful experience. For a week people came together at the Lifebridge Sanctuary and in the performances and found not only incredible excitement but the wonder of connecting and reconnecting with people they had not met before except over Skype and other technologies. That energy continued throughout the whole week. There were no negative vibes of any kind. Having experienced it, I don't see it as a culminating event. I see it as the beginning and an initiation of a new level of what we are accomplishing with the Deep Listening Institute, Ltd.

Skype technology allows a person to actually see and hear someone, Skype video as well as audio. It is point to point only; video conferences with several people are not possible. If it is just one to one, both can see and hear one another. (For multiple people it remains audio only.) In any case the development of the technology supported the idea and realization of the Deep Listening Convergence. People can choose to be in touch with each other in a more intimate way, using technology. This kind of technology will continue to improve.

We use Skype because it works cross platform (i.e., it works on PC and on Mac). There's also iChat AV, which allows four-way video conferences (Mac only; it doesn't work on PCs, so we didn't use it for the Convergence). We have assembled a lot of technologies—usable applications. One, for example, allows recording all the rehearsals. Another allows recording both sides of a Skype conversation or conference. We can then upload them to the web with an application called imeem[22]. Most of the Convergence rehearsals were posted so people could go to the web and listen to them afterwards, or if someone was just curious about what people were doing, he or she could go and listen, too. With iMeem, a person can also post a profile, add music, or whatever; it accumulates information about each person. So the community is developing with all of these new applications. The time has come where we can extend the community much more than we have in the past and go faster as we keep things moving. We're pretty excited about this and everyone contributes ideas on how to go forward.

This is community building in a different way. The old way is to get people together in a neighborhood and over a long period of time a community emerges. We built our community of Deep Listeners in both the old and this new way. It took seventeen years, and the process accelerates as the technological connections accelerate. Still, understand that we always want to get to the level of being in physical proximity. We're not trying to say that there's a substitute for that. Our Puritan heritage and its denial of the body is very much part of the problem we face with technology. The truth is: we are born into the world, we are very sensual, we need touch, we need to dance, we need to sing. We need all those things and more. But at some point controlling leaders realized that the best way to control people and have them do their bidding was to make people fearful of their bodies. Forbidding anything that is joyful and wonderful brings control over people. Such mean-spirited people use sensual oppression as a tool.

At the same time, though, we are saying that there is a way of facilitating physical contact in such a way that a lot of the rituals of meeting are not necessary. Those rituals can be off-putting for people who are shy and not forthcoming. The right technologies can accelerate the whole process: people come out of cyberspace into physical reality. And, of course, it then becomes fascinating to see how people once known only through technology can now really interact in physical space. This is a whole new dimension.

Epilogue

What is America becoming? That's a very fuzzy question these days. America has certainly changed in my lifetime. Looking over my seventy-five years—three quarters of a century (more than two-thirds of that making music)—many things have changed. Certain values, for example. I remember that in my childhood we saved string, rubber bands, paper bags, boxes, and different kinds of containers—all because we didn't have throw-away packages. A cigar box in my childhood was a really interesting and savable item. (I still have some cigar boxes in a closet in Houston at my mother's house. When I look at them I think about how they've been devalued.) I remember my sorrow as a child when throwaway packaging came into use. As time went on, more and more appeared, creating tons of garbage. The packaging industry has had a forceful impact on the landscape by promulgating "throwaway" stuff—even throwaway cameras! That has clearly devalued our relationship to things. There are times when it's very hard for me to throw things away. Because I was brought up during the depression, it seems extraordinarily wasteful and hurtful to the environment to do away with so much. So that remains a big issue for me.

I also remember the arrival of plastic and how it didn't feel good like wood and metal, especially silverware. Now I think nothing about using plastic cutlery and eating utensils (or paper plates from time to time). But I always have a strange feeling about it. That feeling is always there because I recall the beauty of a fine place setting at a dinner table and the care and the time that it would take to make it. I can hardly understand, for example, how my mother and my grandmother did what they did as I was growing up, preparing all those dinners and other meals, not to mention having our clothes presentable, and all the rest. Now it is a completely different thing: one is often eating in the car on the way to the next meeting or to elsewhere. Those, too, are big changes.

What I'm lamenting in the culture generally is possibly happening in music as well. That could be positive and it could be negative. Some music is literally trash and you throw it away. There is commercial music, occasional music, music for a particular occasion that you don't use again. And then there are the establishment organizations of symphony and operas and chamber music. They may play a piece once and then throw it away or at least never play it again. We have to deal with that. The music was not necessarily intended to be throwaway music, but it gets thrown away.

To be sure, we have to live with impermanence because nothing is forever, even though we'd like to think so. Here is another story. I brought my grandfather's cello back with me from Houston a few weeks ago. It has been in the family for over one hundred years. The cello was given to my grandfather, who was an attorney, in payment for his services by an Englishman who had come through town in his horse and buggy and needed an attorney. He gave the cello as payment because he didn't have cash. So my grandfather learned to play the cello. He played with friends in a chamber group in Houston, a group that eventually started the Houston Symphony. That cello was part of our family heritage and yet had actually been sitting in the house, almost never being played. For a time my mother wanted to sell it because she thought it might be worth something monetarily. But it turned out that both of us are pretty attached to it.

One of our cellists from Switzerland did not want to bring her instrument over for the Convergence because of possible damage by airline baggage handling. We were looking for a cello for her and I decided to bring my grandfather's cello. I brought the cello on the Sunday before the Convergence was to begin, took the bow out of the case, and discovered that half the hair was hanging off. I found two wonderful people in Woodstock, one of whom corrected the bow while the other reglued some open seams on the cello and reset the sound post. I wondered why the bow had eroded like that. The bow maker told me that mites had probably eaten the bowstrings, and also had eaten the glue from the cello body's seams. The damage was repaired and the cello served very well in the Convergence.

I am going to hang on to that cello as a Deep Listening Institute resource for our traveling cellists. We are going to preserve the cello a little longer. Even so, that preservation is part of a larger battle: all our media, the tapes and videos and so forth, even the online files, are all subject to drastic deterioration even though they are thought to be more permanent media. There is a continuing struggle to keep our archive from deteriorating. Existence is impermanent. And of course I struggle with that—although there are some futurists who would like to overcome that impermanence as well.

What, then, of my work do I hope will last? Well, what I'm most interested in is not specific pieces surviving, but the understanding of Deep Listening and of the practices and process that will lead to individual and collective creativity. That is what I would like to hand on. People in many parts of the world are working with ideas that came out of my initial work with *Sonic Meditations* and making the ideas their own. Many composers have incorporated at least some of Sonic Meditations into their work. I have had several hundred people at the retreats but also thousands in workshops that I have given all over the world. I have taught Deep Listening at Rensselaer since 2001—that means about fifty students per year, most of whom are in science and technology and engineering. I also taught for six or seven years at Mills, which I continue to do by telepresence with Skype or iChat AV. (They see me, I see them. See and hear and do.) I've taught Deep Listening at many institutions: UCSD, of course, Agnes Scott College, Oberlin College, University of Wisconsin at Madison, Northwestern University, to name a few. The Society for American Music made me an honorary member several years ago; I presented a talk and workshops on Deep Listening at their conference. There are many musicologists who study and write about my work as well. There have been three or four Ph.D. dissertations about my work in Deep Listening.

Now that we have Google, I have a Google alert for "Deep Listening;" every time those words are used, I get an online alert about it. When I started Google alerts, I would get one alert only once in a while. Now I get them every day. Deep Listening is a meme that has entered our language. Musicians are using it, politicians are using it, religious leaders, spiritual leaders, business leaders. I see it used in all of these contexts, so I know that I have made an impact. People may not know where *Deep Listening* came from. I coined the term in 1988 for the recording Deep Listening, released in 1989 by New Albion[23]. Thich Nhat Hanh started using Deep Listening for the fifth precept in Buddhism in 1991. Deep Listening is traveling around the world and I am very happy about that. The more deep listeners we have, the better the chance of having a peaceful society.

Deep Listening is part of a personal, and now communal, quest for peace. Right now I am wearing a Deep Listening

Convergence t-shirt. The logo on the t-shirt: is "Deep Listening: a gesture of sonic peace." Will peace win in the end? Well, either people will move in that direction and stop the violence in their own hearts and minds, or else we will all die and then it will be very peaceful ("rest in peace," you know). Dying will happen to all of us at some point. Impermanence still rules. However we should think about this question: what is your relationship to peace? Do you want to live in peace or do you want to live in violence? Which would you choose? One of the things we want to do according to my partner and co–Deep Listening teacher Ione is "make peace more exciting than violence." That is the process we are attempting.

Still, we have to thrive amidst a corporate culture. We were able to do the Deep Listening Convergence by using money from a grant that we received from the New York State Music Fund[24] 2007. The money for that fund was obtained by the attorney general of New York State. Eliot Spitzer (now the governor), who sued record companies who were using payola to get their music on the radio. He won his suit, got a judgment of several million dollars, and designated all of that money to go to nonprofit organizations for alternative music. Deep Listening Institute, Ltd., applied and received a grant of $65,000 to use for the Deep Listening Convergence. So Spitzer's action was a kind of wonderful justice that enabled our project. As our master of ceremonies who introduced the concerts said, "Thanks to Governor Spitzer and a bunch of crooks in the music industry."

What we learned from this experience is how we can shake the money tree and get the so-called crooks out of their positions of power. They do affect music. Payola is one of the ways corporate record companies use to get their mindless and narrowly similar kinds of music on the radio. They also buy the radio stations. The radio listeners have no other options unless they tune to listener-sponsored stations. The co-opting of commercial radio is also like that of commercial television with shows like *American Idol* or similar corporate-sponsored programs and venues. Allow me to go a little deeper into this: the idea is that if you keep people stupid, then you can manipulate them more toward buying what you want them to buy. So I think the work we are doing is subversive. And I intend to continue doing it as much as I can. (You have to thank those crooks!)

Yes, I'm an American, although I'm not very happy with the government of our country and I don't recognize the

America that I knew in the government that is currently in power. But we probably are in an evolutionary cycle. There will be a change, of course, though I don't know when or where. For now the bad guys are holding on to their power. But if Spitzer's gesture of suing those record companies could happen, then who knows? If we can take out the ones that are using their power improperly, we will see a big change.

In the long term, I think we can evolve and expand our consciousness through changing our habit patterns, changing our habitual responses. Because if we are scared and do not move through the boundaries or open up new territory like the pioneers, we lose our chance for living in enjoyment and pleasure rather than living in terror and separation.

As I close, I have to challenge one more contemporary American trait. The scientific and technological world in which we live has developed into a kind of absolute certitude: nothing is admitted into the scientific paradigm unless it has been proved among the scientific community. The American Medical Association, for instance, sanctions medical procedures and medicine. At the same time, plenty of people are now saying (as I do in music), "Hey, there's something more to be included in this work." There is the American resistance toward the so-called craziness of alternative medicine, or of inventors, or of artists, all the outsiders who can't bang the door down to get the kind of recognition they often deserve. Of course, there are the crazies who do not deserve recognition. How are you going to tell which is which? Well, the crazies have a role, too. They are the disturbers of the outmoded conventions of our society. This is a dance that's going on all the time in America.

Forty years after I began my study of it, consciousness has now become a very serious object of study in the scientific community. The definition of consciousness, of course, must keep changing because no one (including myself) can pin it down very well. So all of our work is evolutionary and improvisatory. I may seem to be stumbling around trying to articulate something that is important to me because my perception of it keeps changing and I don't know exactly how to express it. But that is really the way most important things are.

Am I hopeful for America? Well, I was able to do what I did with the Deep Listening Convergence because I am in America. That is hopeful. I would not necessarily have been able to do the project elsewhere. Because I am an American I can do what I have to do. Right here. I want to keep freedom alive and happening at least in my own heart and mind with the hope that others can do that too.

LINEAR.NONLINEAR

$$l + nl = i$$

Where ***l*** is linear, ***nl*** is nonlinear, and ***i*** is integration.

$$l - nl = d$$

Where ***l*** is linear, ***nl*** is nonlinear, and ***d*** is disintegration.

$$nl - l = nl$$

linear

adj.

1. Having or being a response or output that is directly proportional to the input.

2. Of, relating to, or based or depending on sequential development. <*linear* thinking> <a *linear* narrative>

nonlinear

adj.

1. (*math.*) Not depictible as a straight line; not changing by a constant amount for each unit of item, distance, or other independent variable. Opposite of linear.

2. (*math.*) Containing variables of greater than the first degree; - of an equation. Opposite of linear

3. (*physics*) Represented by equations containing variables of greater than the first degree; of physical processes or relationships. Opposite of linear.

THE NATURE OF LISTENING

Presented to the fellows-in-residence at the Camargo Foundation
Cassis, France
February 2008

What is the nature of listening?

There is primary or initiatory listening as one enters the world for the first time. What a rush that must be as the ears unplug and air rushes in! Primary listening gives us relationship to place and continues to unfold through one's lifetime—literally and figuratively—with more or less intensity depending on the individual and culture.

There is secondary listening or remembered listening. If we remember, we are conscious. There is short-term and long-term consciousness. In any case, consciousness is latent and without memory (however late it might be in manifesting), there is no consciousness.

There is focused listening where attention is directed to communication and learning to listen for specific sounds and to repeat them.

There is global listening where attention is open to the field of undifferentiated fluctuating sounds.

As focal listening gains in importance, global and primary listening lose the foreground and only returns in initiatory or unfamiliar situations such as entering a room full of people speaking a foreign language.

As sounds are reified into language and communication—as we learn reading, 'riting, and 'rithmitic (taught to the tune of a hickory stick), primary listening recedes.

So what?

We have lost that initial rush as we entered the world and made our first cry. Can you remember that? How like the big bang might that be?

I remind myself to listen so that I may be here now even though now has already gone.

* * *

Why does listening matter to me? I am a musician – a composer/improviser engaging with sound, form and technology. Technology is enabling us to hear more and do more.

It may not be too long before we will incorporate bionic ears into our human bodies. There is so much more in outer and inner space/time for listening. Bionic ears are any transducers that we can use to amplify the range of our own limited, damaged or non-existent hearing through air, earth, fire, water, and virtuality. I am interested in these technologies because I might want to use the sounds that may be discovered out there and in there. We are absorbing technology back into the body and may find ourselves distant or even close cousins to intelligent robotic forms in the future. I am interested in how robots will hear and listen and make music. Will I be able to engage with them? Play with them? Hear and understand the music? Feel something?

Scientists use listening for data gathering more often than ever before. There are all those waves waving throughout the universe and beyond. There is the memory of the big bang in the microcosm. I wonder how broadly we could extend our individual hearing ranges? We are protected from hearing all the wavings of waves in our own bodies—otherwise we might be overwhelmed by the din if we could hear our heart beating all the time, or blood rushing through arteries, cells dividing, intestinal motions, etc. We do certainly listen to the waves of our own minds. How, though, could we go beyond the onslaught of mental obsessions to the substrate of quiet where phonons might play another kind of tune – a subatomic music?

Listening is an active engagement with other and simultaneously is memory. Will I remember to remember? Is listening ever direct? Or is listening always a reflection that reminds us that we are human?

HIGH AND LOW TECH TELEMATIC MUSIC: A REPORT

Posted on www.deeplistening.org
April 11, 2008

Telematic Circle

CCRMA, STANFORD UNIVERSITY • DEEP LISTENING INSTITUTE, LTD. • CCRMT, MCGILL UNIVERSITY • IEAR, RENSSELAER POLYTECHNIC INSTITUTE • VISTAMUSE, UNIVERSITY OF CALIFORNIA, SAN DIEGO

Telematic Circle, formed in 2007, is an interest group that uses and develops applications for telepresent music performances. The group supports the creation of new art that specifically uses broadband transmission systems as a new medium.

Each institution represented in TC has participated in multi-site concerts over the internet. Significant music-making has occurred with both high tech multi-channel CD quality audio and DVD-quality video transmissions (via various Internet2 software) and low tech audio and video transmissions using iChat AV, Skype, and other applications.

Telematic Circle's interests go beyond the concerns of mono-location musical performance, exploring musical elements unique to telematic performance, such as the unavoidable transmission latency between two distant sites.

The group also supports the technical development of telematic networks for musical purposes, focusing especially on those issues that are not addressed in typical speech conference systems. Current goals include the development of systems with ultra-low latency, sufficient bandwidth to allow immersive multi-video communication channels, and accurate spatial audio reproduction.

Institutions interested in participating and continuing to improve the telematic experience through research, rehearsals, jam sessions, and concerts are welcome to join. Interested institutions should have an Internet2 connection. TC will provide the necessary consultation to establish connection to Circle.

The member institutions of Telematic Circle have significant input to offer to the continual development of this project. By working together, we can create an unparalleled, excellent, and strong network of expertise in music, software, hardware, and performance venue development.

Virtual Sound Exchange

Virtual Sound Exchange is an online project of the Deep Listening Institute, Ltd. It includes a helpline that provides up-to-date information to musicians on how to establish telematic music connections with musicians throughout the world. Expert advice is available on the freeware and shareware applications that can be used for telematic music-making. The site also facilitates a database of musicians wishing to join telematic ensembles. The information on this site is intended to 1) provide telematic music technology consultation for musicians, 2) serve as a resource on telematic music software, and 3) enable the creation of new ensembles, and/or facilitate rehearsals, performance, and information exchanges that can lead to live, virtual, or mixed reality performances.

The Virtual Sound Exchange helpline project grew from the research for and implementation of the Deep Listening Convergence 2007. Deep Listening Institute, Ltd., with technical direction by Scot Gresham-Lancaster, established the helpline and suite of applications to support forty-five musicians from Europe, Canada, and across the USA in a successful virtual online six-month residency culminating in four in-person concerts in upstate New York, June 8-11, 2007.

Virtual Sound Exchange will continue to update and add new applications as they become available. Participation is welcome and will be logged in a database.

Networked Music: Low and High Tech

Presented at the International Computer Music Conference May 5, 2008

Included in *Contemporary Music Review*, Vol. 28 4/5: *Network Performance*, August-October 2009, Pedro Rebelo, ed.

> *"We just want to play music together without all the bother of buying plane tickets and the time it takes to travel."*
>
> Ge Wang, founder of the Stanford Laptop Orchestra

On May 2, 2008, my piece *The Tuning Meditation* was performed with musicians and audiences at both Stanford University and Beijing University—six thousand miles apart. I greeted both audiences via a Skype video feed from Cassis, France. My low-tech video presence was within the high-tech CD-quality audio transmission facilitated by JackTrip, software developed by Chris Chafe, director of CCRMA at Stanford. High-definition video was streamed between the two locations using VLC Video LAN streaming software. The audio was beautifully clear.

Since fall 2007, two groups at Rensselaer Polytechnic Institute—iEAR Studios from the Art Department and CA3RL from the Architecture Department—have collaborated on a weekly basis with CCRMA at Stanford University. These collaborations have allowed for steady development of the telematic medium and has led to the formation of Telematic Circle. The purpose of Telematic Circle is to provide information on how to use telematic technologies and to encourage new partnerships and collaborations using this new medium.

The ANET Summit was organized by Chris Chafe and took place at the Banff Centre (Alberta, Canada) on April 11-12, 2008, providing a forum for papers, demos, performances, and networked jam sessions utilizing the telematic medium.

Deep Listening Institute, Ltd. recently commissioned six composers to write pieces specifically for the telematic medium using JackTrip and iChat AV. These pieces were successfully performed on April 27, 2008 between iEAR Studios (RPI), CCRMA (Stanford), and VistaMuse, CIRCA (University of California, San Diego), another member of Telematic Circle.

In December 2007, a mixed reality performance took place at Northwestern University during the conference of the International Society for Improvised Music. Dancers, performing as avatars in Second Life (an internet-based virtual reality world), were projected on a screen with a real life (RL) dancer performing in relationship to the dancers on screen. The RL dancer moved slowly with great concentration and poise while the avatars zoomed around doing impossible moves on screen. Two musicians performed live on stage while their audio and video sent into SL and shown on screen in SL above the avatars for a SL audience.

* * *

The above examples of networked collaborations are a few of many mixed low and high tech networked performances that I have been engaged with since 1990. The technology used for these collaborations has progressed from video telephone with still images that updated every five seconds; to PictureTel with ISDN lines which had better audio and video that updated every two seconds; to audio only on the Internet with no video (lack of bandwidth) and an eight second audio latency but easier access; to iChatAV with compressed audio and video with minimal latencies (more for the video than the audio); to Internet2, which is plagued with pocket dropouts in addition to latencies; to JackTrip with stable low-latency CD-quality 8-channel audio and UltraVideo Conferencing (from McGill University) for DVD-quality video. Latency has been a dilemma in all types of networked music transmissions. Additionally, there are many other factors to deal with—from CPU power to firewalls, routers, and all manner of arcane IT rigmarole and politics. I call it head-banging and have spent more hours than I care to count testing, checking, and curbing my frustrations.

So why bother?

As networking technology improves through practice and development, the medium will become a new venue for creative musicians and artists. We now are very close to this point; JackTrip has eliminated significant latency for audio and UltraVideo Conferencing has done the same for video.

The rise of technology is inexorable. There is a desire to explore new possibilities. The transmission of audio and video opens the door to a world of otherwise impossible collaborations, a gathering of knowledge for a richer, broader view and exploration of the world. This is the time to dream on.

FROM OUTSIDE THE WINDOW: ELECTRONIC SOUND PERFORMANCE

Presented at the Camargo Foundation
Cassis, France
May 6, 2008

Included in *The Oxford Handbook of Computer Music*, Roger Dean, ed., Oxford University Press, 2009.

> *"All musical instruments are tools that map human motoric input on an acoustic output."*
>
> Godfried-Willem Raes[1]

> *"How can I translate the sense of corporeal fallibility and virtuosity present in acoustic performances into performances of electronic sounds that have no previously established gestural analog?"*
>
> Peter Musselman[2]

Though I have been working with a personal computer since 1983 (and feel, at times, married to the computer), I have remained an outsider to the world of computer music. This is probably because in the 1960's, I eschewed synthesis and found my own way to generate electronic sound. Rather than adding up sine waves to create sounds and cutting and splicing tape together to make a piece out of those sounds to be played back on tape, I found a way that allowed me to perform my music in real-time in the so-called classical electronic music studio. I needed to map my "human motoric input" onto the machine and "feel my corporeal fallibility and virtuosity" in the process.

The San Francisco Tape Music Center was home base in the 1960's for all kinds of musical adventures and experiments for my colleagues and me[3]. The studio consisted of a small variety of electronic test equipment, a large telephone style patch bay, amplifiers, speakers, and two professional Ampex stereo tape machines. The large Hewlett-Packard war surplus vacuum tube test oscillators [Fig. 1] with big frequency dials on the front did not seem inviting for performance. These instruments were made for setting frequencies for scientific tests. Furthermore, there were switches to shift the range of frequency, since the dial could not cover the whole frequency range of the oscillator.

After staring for a long time at the oscillators and wondering how I could make any music with them, an idea popped into mind. My accordion[4] teacher, Willard Palmer[5], had taught me to listen to difference tones, which could be produced by playing an interval in the high register of the instrument and pulling hard on the bellows. I had always wondered how it would be to just hear the difference tones without the generating tones.

I noticed that the oscillator's frequency range went from 1 Hz to 500 kHz – above and below the range of human hearing. I set two of our three oscillators to around 40 kHz and 39,950 Hz. I patched them through to the sound system expecting to hear the difference. At first there was nothing. I thought, "there must be something – maybe the amplitude is too low". After placing line amplifiers in the patch, I heard my first difference tone low, loud, clear, and rich in quality. I was startled, delighted, and thrilled with the 50 Hz sound! It felt rather magical, drawing down this tone from sound vibrations that I could not hear. I touched the dial tentatively and discovered immediately that I could now sweep the audio range by barely turning the dial. "Now", I thought: – "how do I use this to play music?"

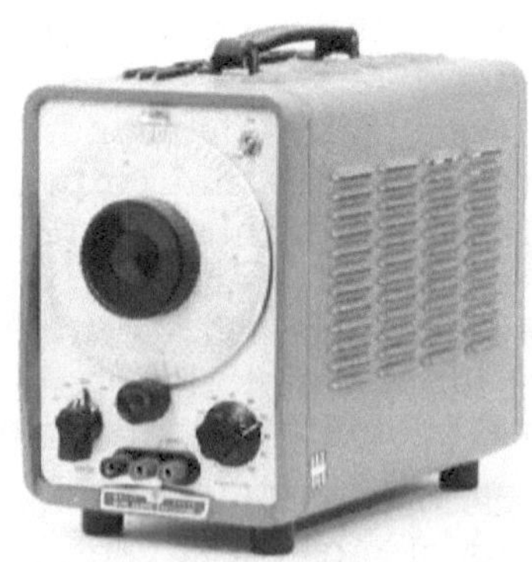

Hewlett-Packard 200CD Audio Oscillator. The large center knob controls frequency (from 5 to 60 Hz) and the small knob on the left multiplies this frequency by powers of 10.

I had discovered tape head delay and that I could use more than one tape machine to add distance between play back heads for longer time delays[6]. I could route the tracks via a patch bay (there were no mixers available then) in a variety of configurations. I fed the output of the oscillators into the first tape machine, listening and tuning the configuration or signal routing to build my performance instrument. The bias frequencies of the tape machines also modulated the sounds I was getting from the heterodyning of the oscillators. I could send sounds into track 1 of the stereo tape, hear both the record head and playback head with the brief delay, then hear the sound come back from a second playback machine when the tape passed over to the distant supply reel. I could patch the tracks back to the first machine so that new loops were created. Feedback and canonical form became core elements of my electronic music.

In my experience with long accordion practice sessions, I had noticed that my hands usually had a very pleasant tingling sensation that I enjoyed – an after effect of mapping "motoric input onto an acoustic output": my fingers extended to accordion keys and buttons which extended to valves so that bellows action could blow air through reeds to make sounds.

Soon, through improvisation, I was creating my first electronic music. In creating my electronic instrument with the oscillators, the huge dials that had seemed so unfriendly to performance now became receivers for the musical knowledge embodied in my hands and fingers. I had created a very unstable non-linear music making system: Difference tones from tones set above the range of hearing manipulated by the bias frequency of the electromagnetic tape recording, feedback from a second tape machine in parallel with newly generated difference tones as I responded instantaneously with my hands on those dials to what I was hearing from the delays and as the sounds were all being recorded on magnetic tape.

I had created a new musical instrument that included my "human motoric input" mapped onto the machine for analog output to speakers. This meant that I could play my electronic music in real-time without editing or overdubbing. The first pieces made at the San Francisco Tape Music Center were called *Mnemonics I-V* (1965). My first electronic music record release was *I of IV*[7] (1966), made at the University of Toronto Electronic Music Studio.

In 1966, the solid-state Buchla modular synthesizer rendered the classical electronic music studio obsolescent[8]. I made some real-time pieces performing the Buchla with my delay system, but missed the sound of the tube oscillators. Transistor oscillators have a very different sound quality and feeling. At the same time, I began to play my accordion with the tape delay system, dragging a couple of Sony 777[9] tape recorders to performance venues for my delay system. I applied what I had learned from playing the oscillators with delays in the studio to my live accordion playing. My interest clearly lay in improvisational real-time manipulation of sound, rather than the use of studio techniques to produce tape music.

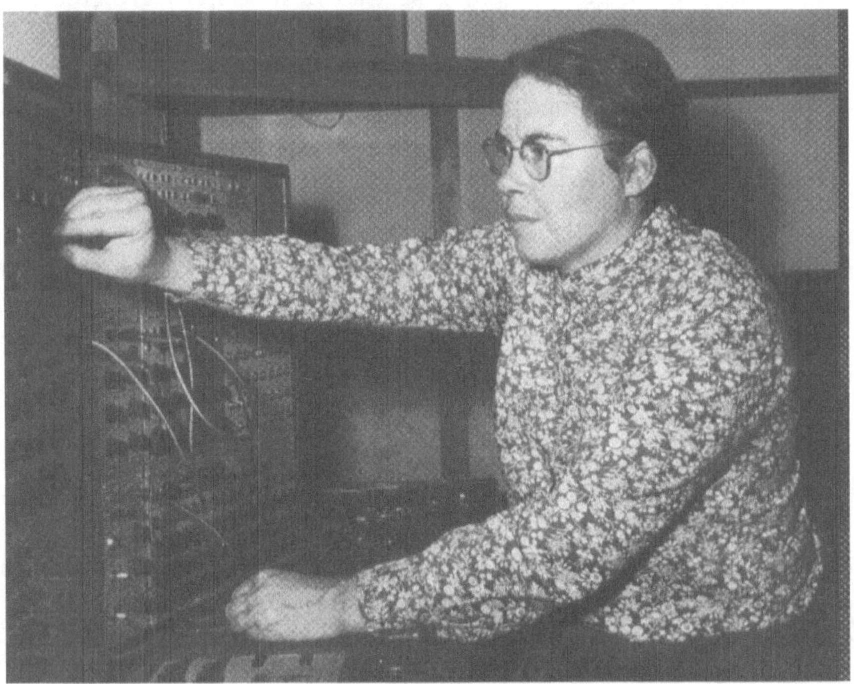

Performing in the studio with Buchla 100-series modular synthesizers.

In 1983, I replaced the tape machines with two Lexicon PCM 42[10] digital delay processors (one for each hand) and called the evolving instrument the Expanded Instrument System (EIS)[11]. In addition to their excellent sound reproduction qualities, the Lexicon PCM 42's had new performance features designed by Gary Hall[12] that were not available with the tape system. The digital delay processors allowed me to capture phrases to loop and modulate, to delay material at oscillating rates with sine and square waves, and to bend pitches by controlling clock time with a variable voltage control. My feet, which controlled accelerator-type pedals, became as sensitive as my hands and fingers had for "motoric mapping to acoustic output." I became very adept at dual foot-controlled pitch bending as I performed new material with my fingers. I wanted more and more delay processors. There was no way to manage all the knobs and switches that I wanted to manipulate while performing, so I eventually adopted a system of computer control of the processors.

Progress of the computer version of EIS slowed until 16-bit, CD-quality sound became more readily available around 1991. I was reluctant to give up the warm sound of the Lexicons just as I had been reluctant to give up the sound of those beautiful tube oscillators of the 60's.

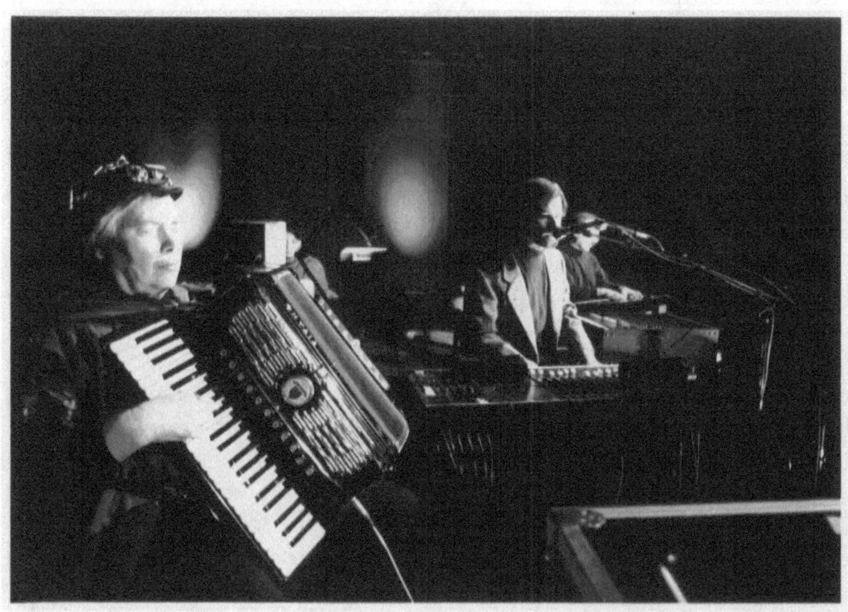

(L-R) Pauline Oliveros, Cornelia Colyer, Peter Ward, and Michael Century performing with the Lightning Box at the Banff Centre, 1990.

During a three-week residency at the Banff Centre in Alberta, Canada in 1990, I worked on a project called the

Lightning Box with programmer Cornelia Colyer[13], out of which came a program that I called super foot. I wanted a tool that could control the Lexicons as though they were controlled by my feet, but that would go beyond what is physically possible with foot pedals. The super foot program modulated the delays as if my feet were moving at impossibly rapid rates and configurations. The first execution of that program was quite thrilling—I had extended my motoric input into the computer and imagined something beyond what I could physically accomplish. This was a start towards what eventually became part of the EIS. I created recipes, or algorithms, for the EIS that could process my human input and the delays themselves. This algorithm-driven computer program controlled what I could not manage alone, though it behaved as though it was still subject to "human corporeality and fallibility". Through my recipes, it assimilated my way of manipulating the knobs and switches and controlling the delays.

I continue to make music in real-time with my accordion and the computerized EIS program. Currently, the program is learning to learn. I want a real-time digital partner that interacts with my input in a humanly motoric way, even though its techniques may be distinctly beyond human capability. It seems important to me, after more than forty years of dealing with my way of making electronic music (both analog and digital), that we need to find a way to work with non-human forms that can present us with musical intelligence and new challenges.

Since 1990, another window has attracted my attention – telematic performance. The history of this odyssey is described in my article "From Telephone to High Speed Internet: A Brief History of My Tele-Musical Performances."[14] Telematic Circle[15] was formed in 2007 as an association of institutions and individuals interested in telematic music performance. Performing with musical partners in different locations opens an entirely new window – a new venue. The space between locations is new territory. How to navigate this space and make it as palpable as performing in the same room is a complex and challenging task.

A collaborative effort between Chris Chafe, director of the Center for Computer Research in Music and Acoustics (CCRMA)[16] at Stanford University, Jonas Braasch, director of the Communications Acoustics and Aural Architecture Research Laboratory (CA3RL)[17] at Rensselaer Polytechnic Institute, Jeremy Cooperstock, member of the Centre for Interdisciplinary

Research in Music Media and Technology (CIRMMT) at McGill University, and myself has begun to made a satisfying realization of telematic performance possible.

Chafe's open-source software JackTrip[18] has provided us with low-latency eight-channel CD quality audio transmission, Cooperstock's UltraVideo Conferencing[19] software gives us DVD-quality video, and Jonas Braasch's ViMic[20] software makes virtual room simulation possible. Using these tools, my improvisation ensemble at RPI, Tintinnabulate, has jammed together with Chafe's SoundWire[21] ensemble for two years. These synergistic sessions have given us an enormous amount of artistic and technical data. The result of some years of exploration from video telephone to the high speed internet has attracted a National Science Foundation grant to research and produce a Robust Distributed Intelligent System for Telematic Applications. This system will incorporate ViMic and the EIS along with an avatar/agent that will be able to give conducting cues to ensembles across the network and learn from the performancer to develop creative solutions in improvisational situations.

For the next two years, Jonas Braasch and I, with Doug Van Nort, postdoctoral research associate, will engage in designing this intelligent system as we continue to make music without partners in the Telematic Circle. The main objective of this work is to improve communications with distant partners and to open the window wider so that all can peek in and participate.

Stay tuned and keep the windows open! I might like to look in.

THE COLLECTIVE INTELLIGENCE OF IMPROVISATION

Presented at the colloquium L'Improvisation: Ordres et Désordres / Faits d'Art et Faits de Sociétié
With Improvisation, Community, and Social Practice (ICASP) research group
Paris, France
January 2009

Creative musical improvisation communicates collective musical intelligence. Whether an individual soloist or an ensemble is improvising, they are mining musical information stored deeply in the collective consciousness of humanity.

Intelligence is the ability to utilize and purpose detectable information or data from inner or outer sources.

Pierre Teilhard de Chardin describes the concept of the *noosphere* in his book The Phenomena of Man[1]. The noosphere is the interconnectedness of human minds—their thoughts, images, and ideas, which surround and permeate the planet like the atmosphere or the biosphere. The noosphere must also be threaded with musical information and sound waves as well as spoken and written thought—human consciousness is primordial and not bound by the alphabetic mind.

When creative musical improvisation happens, it resonates among the musical thoughts and minds of billions of musicians throughout the ages. The creativity that emerges through improvisation carries new combinations and possibilities that are now expanding throughout the world.

Musicians are the harbingers of world community and planetary consciousness through music. There is no need for musicians to speak the same language. They can play together without speaking. They only need to listen to one another to give and receive sound. Their encounters with different musical styles are negotiations and reconciliations of differences. The world music genre has come about through the combination of musical cultures in improvisation, moving through popular, classical, and experimental styles and ideas.

Virtual performance venues have been with us since the advent of recording over 100 years ago. Recording and radio broadcast made it possible to hear music from distant places and cultures, eventually leading musicians around the world to improvise and perform together—musical and cultural handshakes.

Our time is an exciting one where not only can musicians meet and play together in person, but where cybernetics can also allow them to improvise together virtually. The acceleration of technological development is facilitating instantaneous musical encounters and creating new telematic venues for high-quality performances with distant partners. These telematic transmissions can promote reflexive friendships and enlarge the possibilities for world music.

All of these musical friendships contribute to form the *sonosphere*, the sonic envelope of the earth, which resonates within the musical noosphere, mingling frequencies and rhythms and fostering warm feelings that can help unite humanity with the intelligence of evolution—a universal improvisation that is moving ever onward.

On the following pages, I would like to share the scores of a few pieces that are designed to engender creativity and build connections with others and the environment.

Sounding Secret Spaces

When I am creating a piece on stage, the spaces are secret. The secrets are in everybody including in me, until they are sounded. And when they're sounded, the secrets are out. The audience is an instrument too. If I am pure about my listening and creating the sounds that come forth, the audience will feel that and respond to the sound. I am something akin to a high wire artist. The audience is with you, because they perceive the risks and the dangers.

November 2008

Dissolving Your Ear Plugs

For classically trained musicians and anyone else interested.

1. Take some time—no matter where you are—sit down and close your eyes for a while and just listen. When you open your eyes consider what you heard as the "music". Later try to remember what you heard and express it with your instrument.

   Do this practice often until you begin to hear the world as music.

2. Another time—sit down with your instrument and just listen with your eyes closed. As you realize that whatever you are hearing *is* "music". Allow your instrument to enter this musical stream. Stop when the music is over. This is supported improvisation.

3. Listen to a favorite machine and play along with it.

4. Listen to a favorite natural soundscape and play along with it.

Pauline's Solo

Listening to this space I sound the space. Listening to the energy of all who are present I sound this energy. Listening to my listening and your listening I make this music here and now with the assistance of all that there is.

I dedicate this music to a world where peace is more exciting than war.

1992-2008

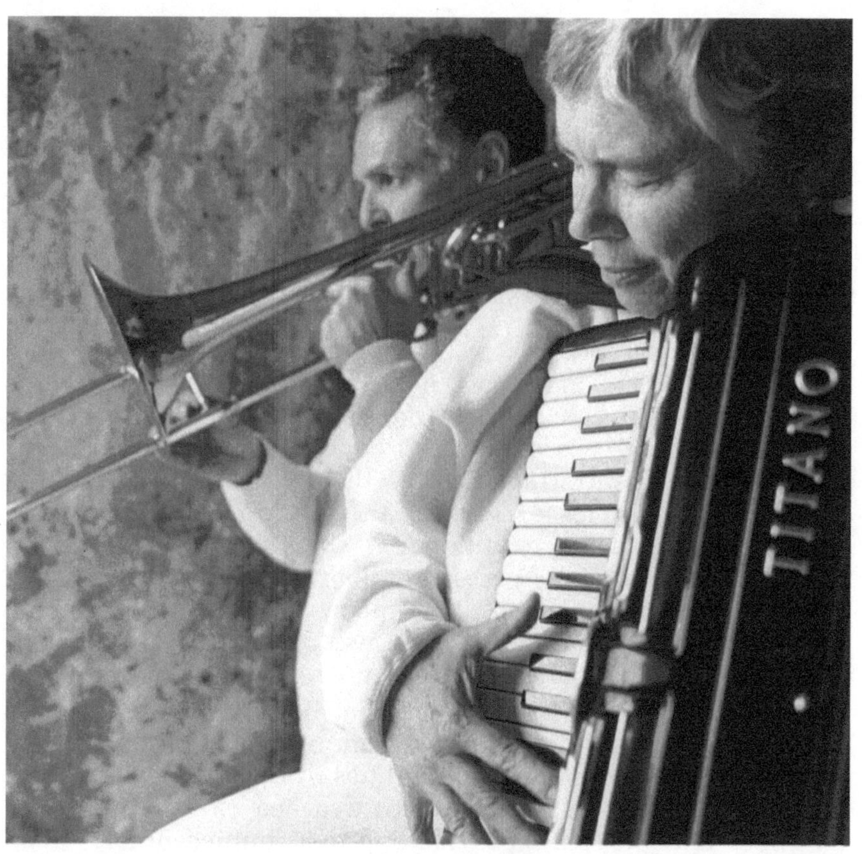

Stuart Dempster and Pauline Oliveros. Photograph by Ronald Chase in his San Francisco studio, April 1990.

AFTWORD

Sounding the Margins invites the question, "What margins are being sounded?" Early on in the book Pauline Oliveros confronts the marginalization of facets of her life and work, her push for women as composers and women's rights, her recognition and encouragement of the margins of society, not only including issues of gender and station but also that of ethnicity and race. Additionally she consistently sounds margins at the edges of access, audibility, beauty, compassion, distance, electro-acoustics, frequency, maximal/minimal, nuance, phrasing, range, relationship, space, spirituality, technology, timbre, transcendence, universe, and more.

Sounding the Margins pushes at boundaries of acoustics and technology, exploring composition and performance by opening up and expanding possibilities through Deep Listening. Grounded in her reality, Oliveros reaches toward an open, spacious, and sacred place sharing her immeasurable Deep Listening experience and gifts with countless musicians and artists. Even with many challenges, Oliveros has broken through the glass ceiling while remaining true to her individuality, realizing her wisdom, and transforming her life experiences into works of beauty, depth, and meaning. She uses her broad-reaching knowledge and understanding to release basic creativity and goodness in others.

As I made my way through *Sounding the Margins* I discovered "Harmonic Anatomy: Women in Improvisation" at the geographic center, or hub. The positioning of "Harmonic Anatomy" arrived at accidentally through chronology, is profound. Here margins that need to be sounded send audible spokes in every direction creating a theme and variations. One can read from the back, front, or middle—even a "Midword" is included. In whatever way one navigates these collected writings Oliveros gives voice not only to her own experience of being on the margins but also voices of many other women grappling with making music in this still too much of a man's world.

Relish in tributes to two important Davids, and quanta of improvisation and listening. Savor topics of attention, auralization, collaboration, evangelism, faith, interaction, and tools. Taste community, electronics, improvisations, nature, network, telematics, and transformations. Make a meal out of adaptive use, borders, change, cybernetic presences, Expanded Instrument System, moon echoes, practice, silence, statements, wireless bodies, and—indeed—the "title track" of *Sounding the Margins*. Dine on such offerings as "Zina's Circle", a piece that even now speaks deeply to me and found its way into my teaching for quite a number of years.

As one who often reads a book from the back, after skimming though *Sounding the Margins'* amazing lists of performances and article notations, I discovered the photo of Pauline Oliveros and me and immediately reflected upon our well-over 50 years of working together. I am forever astonished, blessed, fortunate, grateful, honored, and surprised by the astounding range of musical expression and opportunities that have come forth through our collaborations that have so far transpired. It is with the utmost humility that I write this Aftword, and I do so with the greatest of love and respect.

Stuart Dempster

NOTES AND REFERENCES

BREAKING THE SILENCE

[1] Brand, Juliane, Christopher Hailey, and Donald Harris eds. *The Berg-Schoenberg Correspondence: Selected Letters*. New York. W.W. Norton & Company, 1987.

DEEP LISTENING: BRIDGE TO COLLLABORATION

[1] Catalano, Joe. "Electronic Midwifery: A Videophone Celebration of Pauline Oliveros's *Four Decades of Composing and Community*." Leonardo Music Journal, Vol. 3 (1993): 29-34.

A PERFORMER-CONTROLLED LIVE SOUND PROCESSING SYSTEM: NEW DEVELOPMENTS AND IMPLEMENTATIONS OF THE EXPANDED INSTRUMENT SYSTEM

[1] The Expanded Instrument System is a project of the Pauline Oliveros Foundation and the name "Expanded Instrument System" is trademarked by the Pauline Oliveros Foundation, Inc.

[2] Pauline Oliveros and Panaiotis, "Expanded Instrument System (EIS)," *Proceedings of the International Computer Music Conference*, (Montreal: 1991) pp. 404-407.

[3] Macintosh computers running Opcode's Max programming environment are used. Max allows me to quickly build displays for the performer as well as program higher level functions, such as modulation algorithms and complex multiple control outputs from a single controller.

[4] The first sound processor is always a Lexicon PCM 42 digital delay. Other sound processors are Lexicon PCM 70 or 80 reverberation units and the Reson8 multiple digital signal processor computer running a delay program. The single Reson8 is shared by all musicians through four channels AD/DA

conversion. Other devices, such as an automated Mackie 1604 mixer and Niche ACM MIDI controlled amplifiers, provide for microphone preamplification, gain control and signal routing and mixing.

[5] More technical information can be found on the EIS web site: http://www.artswire.org/pof/EIShome.html

[6] Pauline Oliveros, "Acoustic and Virtual Space as a Dynamic Element of Music," *Leonardo Music Journal*, Volume 5, 19-22 (1995).

[7] Pauline Oliveros, "On Sonic Meditation" and "Meditation Project," *Software for People: Collected Essays 1963-1980* (Baltimore, MD: Smith Publications, 1984) pp. 138-164.

[8] Oliveros writes: "The basis for all of my work as a composer/performer is a practice created for my self which I call Deep Listening. It began with meditation that came to me in 1953: 'Listen to everything all the time and remind yourself when you are not listening.' After 41 years of this practice I am still learning about listening." More information on Deep Listening can be found at http://www.deeplistening.org.

[9] For a description of the Lexicon PCM 42, see Oliveros [6] p. 21.

[10] See Oliveros [6] p. 22.

[11] The LightningBox modulation algorithm was inspired by Oliveros' piece *The Lightning Box*. See Oliveros [6] p. 21.

[12] It may be that the recent addition of digital signal processing to the Max program coupled with an analog to digital input card with frequency response down to zero may allow a solution. Information on David Zicarelli's *MSP* is available at http://www.cycling74.com.

[13] Excerpts from some recent works are at http://www.artswire.org/dgamper.

[14] Oliveros' *Epigraphs in the Time of AIDS* (1994) was commissioned with funding by the Composer's Program of the National Endowment for the Arts. Fullman's *TexasTravelTexture* (1994) was commissioned by the Pauline Oliveros Foundation, Inc. with funding provided by Meet the Composer/Reader's Digest Fund, Inc. and the National Endowment for the Arts.

These two works comprise the CD *Suspended Music* (P0010) (Seattle, WA: Periplum, 1997).

[15] The concert was part of a thirtieth anniversary celebration of the Center for Contemporary Music. An article inspired by the event by David Bernstein can be read at http://www.mills.edu/LIFE/CCM/CCM_Archives.html and a CD of excerpts has been released by Music and Arts. (See Discography)

[16] The Hub is a computer network ensemble whose members (at this performance Chris Brown, Scot Gresham-Lancaster, Tim Perkis, Phil Stone and John Bischoff) are all designers and builders of their own hardware and software instruments. The group electronically coordinates the activity of their individual systems through a central computer, the Hub itself, which received foot pedal data from the EIS and could control the guest EIS station.

[17] Commissioned by Deep Listening Band with support from the Mary Flagler Cary Trust. Premiered August 9, 1997 at the Lincoln Center Out of Doors Festival in New York City by Deep Listening Band and the Joe McPhee Quartet with Rachel Pollack reading from her text.

[18] Quoted with the permission of Kurt Erickson from a personal email dated January 17, 1998.

[19] Quoted with the permission of John Ingle from a personal email dated January 7, 1998.

QUANTUM IMPROVISATION: THE CYBERNETIC PRESENCE
References

Floyd Jr., Samuel. *The Power of Black Music: Interpreting Its History From Africa To The United States*. Oxford University Press, 1995.

Prévost, Edwin. *No Sound Is Innocent: AMM and the Practice of Self-Invention - Meta-musical Narratives: Essays*. Copula, 1995.

Reed, Mark A., and James M. Tour. "Computing with Molecules." *Scientific American*, June 2000.

Notes

[1] Kurzweil, Ray. *The Age of Spiritual Machines: When Computers Exceed Human Intelligence*. Viking Press, 1999.

[2] Luminet, Jean-Pierre, Glenn D. Starkman, and Jeffrey R. Weeks. "Is Space Finite?" *Scientific American*, April 1999.

[3] Cope, David. *Experiments in Musical Intelligence.* A-R Editions, 1996.

QUANTUM LISTENING: FROM PRACTICE TO THEORY (TO PRACTICE PRACTICE)

Notes

[1] Sogyal Rinpoche. Interview. http://www.comngrnd.com/rinpoche.html

[2] Oliveros, Pauline. *Sonic Meditations*. Smith Publications, 1974.

[3] Dempster, Oliveros, Panaiotis. *Deep Listening*. New Albion Records, 1989.

[4] Oliveros, Pauline. *Deep Listening Pieces.* Deep Listening Publications, 1990.

[5] Deep Listening Retreat at Rose Mountain. http://www.deeplistening.org/

[6] Oliveros, Pauline. *Software for People*. Smith Publications, 1984

[7] Three Year Certificate Program. http://www.deeplistening.org/

[8] Ione. *Is This A Dream?* Workshop Manual. Ministry of Maåt, 1997.

[9] Bionic Ear. http://www.medoto.unimelb.edu.au/bei/history1.htm

[10] National Institute of Health Consensus Development Conference on Noise and Hearing Loss

[11] Oliveros, Pauline. *Quantum Improvisation: The Cybernetic Presence*, Improvisation Across Borders Conference, UCSD 1999.

[12] Lee, Virginia. *More Perfect Than Man*, interview with Ray Kurzweil. http://www.comngrnd.com/

[13] Kurzweil, Ray. *The Age of Spiritual Machines: When Computers Exceed Human Intelligence*. Viking Press, 1999.

[14] Lee, Virginia. ibid.

[15] Lee, Virginia. interview with Matthew Fox. http://www.comngrnd.com/fox.html

[16] The term "Chip Monk" was contributed by Stuart Dempster

[17] Hood, Ki Mantle. *Quantum Theory of Music*. The Perfect Beat, 1990.

[18] Petersen, Steven P. *The Quantum Tai Chi*. Empyrean Quest Publishers, 1996.

[19] ibid.

[20] Hood, Ki Mantle. ibid.

[21] Walker, Evan Harris. "The Nature of Consciousness" *Mathematical Biosciences*. pp. 131-178 July 1970.

[22] Petersen, Steven P. ibid.

[23] Zukav, Gary. *The Dancing Wu Li Masters*. New York: Bantam Books 1979

[24] Petersen, P. Steven. ibid.

[25] Weyl, Hermann. *Philosophy of Mathematics and Natural Science*. Athenium 1963.

[26] Fung Yu-Lan. *A Short History of Chinese Philosophy*. The Free Press, 1997.

[27] Dalai Lama. *Ethics for the New Millennium*. Riverhead Books, 1999.

[28] The term "cultural flexibility" was contributed by Abbie Conant in a conversation with the author.

References

Lipsetz, George. *Dangerous Crossroads: Popular Music, Postmodernism and The Poetics of Space*. Verso, 1994.

Morris, Richard. *The Universe, The Eleventh Dimension, and Everything What We Know and How We Know It*. Four Walls Eight Windows, 1999.

Oliveros, Pauline. *The Roots of the Moment.* Drogue Press, 1998.

Wilson, Edward O. *Consilience: The Unity of Knowledge.* Vintage, 1998.

Webliography

http://iias.leidenuniv.nl/oideion/issues/issue2/articles/hood/frame-o.html

http://www.zinezone.com/zones/digital/multimedia/kurzweil/interview6.html

http://ajanta.sci.ccny.cuny.edu/~jupiter/pub/com/baeparts/superstring.html

http://www.angelfire.com/hi2/UFOCHARTS/index.html

http://msnbc.com/news/202284.asp?cp1=1

http://www.neurosonics.com/bgm-kurzweil.html

http://www.comngrnd.com/houston.html

http://www.comngrnd.com/rinpoche.html

http://www.militaryaudiology.org/bang/index.html

http://www.medoto.unimelb.edu.au/bei/history1.htm

http://www.militaryaudiology.org/aric/index.htm

TRIPPING ON WIRES: THE WIRELESS BODY – WHO IS IMPROVISING?

Notes

[1] Baard, Erik. "Cyborg Liberation Front." *Village Voice,* July 29, 2003.

[2] Since I began my work with tape recorders soon after World War Two, I am reminded that this tool was used primarily by the Nazis for gathering intelligence and propaganda. The Nazis

did have portable magnetic tape recorders that were of lesser quality than the studio models. For more information about the history of tape recording see Mullin (below).

[3] Reel to reel tape is measured according to the speed at which it travels from the feed reel to the take-up reel in inches per second, or ips.

[4] Oliveros, Pauline. "Tape Delay Techniques for Electronic Music Composers." in *Software for People: Collected Essays 1962-1981*. Smith Publications, 1984.

[5] Created by Miller Puckette at IRCAM and further developed by David Zicarelli, Max/MSP is a graphical programming environment, which means you create your own software using a visual toolkit of objects, and connect them together with patch cords. The basic environment that includes MIDI control, user interface, and timing objects is called Max. MSP is a set of audio processing objects that do everything from interactive filter design to hard disk recording. For more information on Max/MSP, see the Cycling '74 website (below).

References

Cycling '74. "A Max/MSP Overview." 30 July 2004. http://www.cycling74.com/products/maxmsp_2.html

Missin, Pat. "A Brief History of Mouth Blown Free Reed Instruments." 30 July 2004. http://www.patmissin.com/history/history.html

Missin, Pat. "A Eastern Free Reed Instruments: Mouth Organs With Circular Arrangement of Pipes." 30 July 2004. http://www.patmissin.com/history/eastern.html

Mullin, John. "John (Jack) T. Mullin (1913-99) Recalls the American Development of the Tape Recorder." *Bing Crosby Internet Museum*. Metropolitan Community Colleges, Kansas City, June 1996. http://www.kcmetro.cc.mo.us/pennvalley/biology/lewis/crosby/mullin.htm

Oliveros, Pauline. "Tape Delay Techniques for Electronic Music Composers." in *Software for People: Collected Essays 1962-1981*. Smith Publications, 1984.

Sandberg, Anders. Transhuman Terminology Subpage. 30 July 2004. http://www.aleph.se/Trans/Words/p.html

Toth, Nicholas, and Kathy Schick. "Stone Age," *Microsoft Encarta Online Encyclopedia 2004*. Microsoft Corporation, August 2004. http://encarta.msn.com

Harmonic Anatomy: Women in Improvisation

[1] Cook, Richard M. and Brian Morton. *The Penguin Guide to Jazz on CD: Sixth Edition*. Penguin 2003.

[2] Yaffe, David. "Holding Her Own Among All the Guys." *The New York Times* May 30, 1999.

[3] Jazz Review Magazine. http://www.jazzreview.com

[4] ibid.

[5] Reason Myers, Dana. "The Myth of Absence: Representation, Reception and the Music of Experimental Women Improvisers." PhD diss., University of California, San Diego, 2002.

The Accordion (& the Outsider)

[1] Bernstein, David, ed. *The San Francisco Tape Music Center: 1960's Counterculture and the Avant-Garde*. University of California Press, 2008.

Sounding the Borders

[1] Kurzweil, Ray. "The Law of Accelerating Returns." KurzweilAI.net, March 7, 2001. http://www.kurzweilai.net/meme/frame.html?main=/articles/art0134.html

[2] Gilbert, Scott F. *Developmental Biology*. Sinauer Associates, 2003.

IMPROVISATION IN THE SONOSPHERE

[1] There is no dictionary definition for *Sonosphere,* so what follows is my definition of the word: The Sonosphere is the sonorous or sonic envelope of the earth created by all vibrations caused by natural or technological forces which travel through earth from its core to beyond earth, air, fire and water as waves and phonons to receivers. Receivers are humans and all creatures that perceive and use Earth's biological and technological systems. Vibrations within the range of hearing may be processed consciously or unconsciously; vibrations beyond the range of the human ear are nevertheless received by the body and processed unconsciously or by other inhabitants of the earth and beyond.

[2] *Biosphere* (environment) defines a whole-system model of life on earth. See *The Biosphere,* V. I. Vernadsky, Synergetic Press 1986 or Far West Institute 1998.

[3] *Technosphere* is the term used to define the effects of the technological tools that are guided by human thought. See *Time and the Technosphere: The Law of Time in Human Affairs,* Jose Arguelles, PhD., Bear & Co. 2002.

[4] The Expanded Instrument System (EIS) is a sound-processing program designed by Pauline Oliveros. It has been in development since the late 1950's when Oliveros first began using technology in music performance. See the chapters "A Performer-Controlled Live Sound Processing System" and "The Expanded Instrument System: An Introduction and Brief History" in this book for more information.

PAULINE OLIVEROS IN THE ARMS OF REYNOLS: A COLLABORATION

Notes

[1] Oliveros, Pauline. *Deep Listening: A Composers' Sound Practice.* iUniverse 2005.

[2] Reynols and Pauline Oliveros. *Pauline Oliveros in the Arms of Reynols*. JDK Productions Cream Garden 2001.

[3] Reynols. *Blank Tapes* for amplified blank tapes. Black Bean & Placenta 2000.

[4] Reynols. *10,000 Chickens Symphony* for chicken sounds. Germany: Drone Records 1999.

"the only record in the world where all the participants were killed and eaten afterwards"

[5] Kit Galloway and Sherrie Rabinowitz. http://www.ecafe.com/getty/HIS

[6] Catalano, Joe. "Electronic Midwifery: A Videophone Celebration of Pauline Oliveros' Four Decades of Composing and Community" in *Leonardo Music Journal*, Vol. 3, 1993.

[7] Reynols and Pauline Oliveros. *The Minecxio Connection: Live! At the Rosendale Café*. Roaratorio LP 2000.

Additional References

Gebhardt, Andrew. "Welcome to Minecxio" (interview with Reynols) *The Antioch Review* September 22, 2005.

Warburton, Dan. Interview with Reynols *Paris Transatlantic Magazine* March 12, 2003. http://www.paristransatlantic.com/magazine/interviews/reynols.html

PictureTel is a video monitor with a camera mounted on top and connected for transmission on ISDN high-speed telephone circuit.

Nortek is a collective of Tijuana musicians www.nortek.org.

Maquilopolis (City of Factories) is a film about the women factory workers of Tijuana Mexico with original music by Oliveros. http://www.maquilapolis.com/project_eng.html.

Rosendale Cafe http://www.rosendalecafe.com/.

FROM TELEPHONE TO HIGH-SPEED INTERNET: A BRIEF HISTORY OF MY TELE-MUSICAL PERFORMANCES

[1] Catalano, Joe. "Electronic Midwifery: A Videophone Celebration of Pauline Oliveros's Four Decades of Composing and Community" *Leonardo Music Journal,* Vol. 3. 1993.

[2] This performance is discussed by David Gamper in the chapter "A Performer-Controlled Live Sound-Processing System" in this book.

[3] *Loose Ends/Connections* and Feedback. http://www.turbulence.org/Works/loose/index.html.

[4] *40 Days and 40 Nights* by True Rosaschi. http://www.musicaveritas.com/music/performance/index.html.

[5] AB_TIME Laboratories. http://www.skalen.fr/.

[6] Stover, Chris. "Stuart Dempster: Sedimental Journey." The International Trombone Association *ITA Journal 34,* Issue 2, April 2006.

[7] JackTrip software. http://ccrma.stanford.edu/groups/soundwire/software/jacktrip/.

[8] UltraVideo software. http://ultravideo.mcgill.edu/.

[9] ICAD 2007. http://www.music.mcgill.ca/icad2007/. See also the chapter "Networked Music: High and Low Tech" in this book.

[10] Siggraph. http://www.siggraph.org/s2007/attendees/art/performance.html.

IMPROVISING WITH SPACES

[1] Oliveros, Pauline. *Deep Listening: A Composer's Sound Practice.* iUniverse 2005

[2] See the chapter "Quantum Improvisation: The Cybernetic Presence" in this book.

[3] See the chapter "A Performer Controlled Live Sound-Processing System" in this book.

[4] Oliveros, Pauline. "Acoustic and Virtual Space as a Dynamic Element of Music." *Leonardo Music Journal* Vol. 5, 1995.

[5] Deep Listening Band. http://www.pofinc.org/DLBhome.

[6] See the chapter "Quantum Listening: From Practice to Theory (To Practice Practice)" in this book for an explanation of the listening effect.

[7] Dempster, Stuart, Pauline Oliveros, and Panaiotis. *Deep Listening*. New Albion Records 1989.

[8] The cistern at Ft. Worden in Port Townsend, Washington (70 miles northwest of Seattle) is a 2 million gallon, 186-foot diameter water tank made of reinforced concrete. It has been used for several recording sessions.

[9] Biblioteca National. http://www.bibnal.edu.ar/

[10] Oliveros, Pauline. *Pauline Oliveros and American Voices*. Mode Records 1992.

St. George and the Dragon, for solo accordion in just intonation was recorded in a stone chapel in Pomfret, Connecticut.

[11] Oliveros, Pauline. "Tape Delay Techniques for Electronic Music Composers" in *Software for People: Collected Writings 1963-1980*. Smith Publications/Printed Editions 1983.

[12] Oliveros, Pauline. *I of IV*. Paradigm Records 1966.

[13] Oliveros, Pauline. "Acoustic and Virtual Space as a Dynamic Element of Music." *Leonardo Music Journal* Vol. 5, 1995.

[14] Oliveros, Pauline. *Crone Music*. Lovely Music Ltd. 1989.

Created for the Mabou Mines theater production of *Lear* at the Tribeca Theater in New York. For accordion and EIS.

[15] *Moving Spaces* (2006) created for the 151st meeting of the ASA in 5.1 surround sound.

[16] Vector Based Amplitude Panning (VBAP) is an amplitude panning method which can be used to position virtual sound sources using arbitrary loudspeaker configurations. Developed by Ville Pulkki, implemented in Max/MSP.

[17] Monoverb is a monaural implementation of the Schroeder/Moorer reverb model.

[18] Deep Listening Band. *Troglodyte's Delight*. What's Next 1990.

DEEP LISTENING CONVERGENCE: REPORT

[1] Oliveros, Pauline. *Deep Listening: A Composer's Sound Practice.* iUniverse 2005

"Deep Listening is a practice that is intended to heighten and expand consciousness of sound in as many dimensions of awareness and attentional dynamics as humanly possible. The source for Deep Listening as a practice comes from my background and experience as a composer of concert music, as a performer and improviser. Deep Listening comes from noticing my listening or listening to my listening and discerning the effects on my bodymind continuum, from listening to others, to art and to life."

[2] http://www.skype.com/

[3] http://www.deeplistening.org/site/certificateprogram

[4] http://rockpa.org/special_programs/the-new-york-state-music-fund/

[5] http://www.o-art.org/Scot/

[6] Thorington, Helen. "Interview: Scot Gresham-Lancaster" *Turbulence* July 2007. http://transition.turbulence.org/networked_music_review/2007/07/07/interview-scot-gresham-lancaster/

[7] http://www.internet2.edu/

[8] http://www.apple.com/macosx/features/ichat/

[9] http://www.arts.rpi.edu/

[10] http://www.mills.edu/campus_life/center_for_contemporary_music/index.php

[11] http://skalen.fr/anglais/artisticteam.html

[12] http://www.myspace.com/tintinnabulate

[13] http://ccrma.stanford.edu/groups/soundwire/

[14] http://www.deeplistening.org/site/convergence

[15] http://www.ecamm.com/

[16] http://www.pamela.biz

[17] http://groups.imeem.com/6H3SQa7R,dlconvergence

[18] http://www.basecamphq.com/

[19] Sony Polycomm Soundpoint PC Speakerphones

[20] http://www.lifebridge.org/sanctuary

[21] Dalton, Joseph. "Meditative Music Mines the Depths of Listening." *Albany Times-Union,* June 8, 2007.

THE EXPANDED INSTRUMENT SYSTEM: AN INTRODUCTION AND BRIEF HISTORY

[1] Oliveros, Pauline. "Tape Delay Techniques for Electronic Music Composers" in *Software for People: Collected Writings 1963-1980*. Smith Publications/Printed Editions 1983

[2] Max/MSP is a graphical programming environment for music, audio, and multimedia. http://www.cycling74.com/products/maxmsp

[3] Doyle, Peter. *Echo, and Reverb in Popular Music: Fabricating Space in Popular Recording 1900-1960*. Wesleyan University Press 2005.

[4] Oliveros, Pauline. "Virtual and Acoustic Space as a Dynamic Parameter of Music" in *The Roots of the Moment: Collected Writings 1980-1996*. Drogue Press 1998.

[5] See Webern's *Five Pieces for Orchestra, Op. 10* and Schoenberg's *Five Orchestral Pieces, Op. 16* for musical examples of klangfarbenmelodie.

[6] Lexicon PCM42 digital delay processor. Gary Hall designed and built the PCM42 for Lexicon. The performance parameters and excellent sound are what attracted me to the PCM42. Here is an article by Gary Hall on this device:

Hall, Gary S. "The Max Factor" in *Electronic Musician* June 1, 2002.

[7] Monoverb is a monaural implementation of the Schroeder/Moorer reverb model. See http://maxobjects.com/?v=authors&id_auteur=39

[8] http://www.audioease.com/Pages/Altiverb/AltiverbMain.html

[9] For in depth information on Ville Pulkki, VBAP, and his articles on VBAP see http://www.acoustics.hut.fi/research/cat/vbap/.

My "American Music": Soundscape, Politics, Technology, Community

[1] I say "many worlds" because it depends on the ingredients and who's making the music.

[2] http://www.deeplistening.org

[3] See the chapter "Quantum Improvisation: The Cybernetic Presence" in this book.

[4] Oliveros, Pauline. *Sonic Meditations*. Smith Publications 1971.

[5] See, for example http://www.consciousness.arizona.edu.

[6] This was a forerunner to events such as this: http://ucsdnews.ucsd.edu/newsrel/soc/dhschillerconf.htm

[7] http://www.namelesssound.org. Nameless Sound is directed by David Dove.

[8] The Art Guys—Michael Galbreth and Jack Massing—are artist collaborators who made the resounding vision award that I received: a delightful small sound sculpture. http://www.theartguys.com

[9] You can still hear a lot of cicadas and birds, but not in the density of my own early experience.

[10] http://www.deeplistening.org/site/retreats/faq

[11] Though I must add that you can practice in the urban jungle, too!

[12] On My Lai, see http://www.pbs.org/wgbh/amex/vietnam/trenches/my_lai.html

[13] I should add that, on the railroad you're not only on a track. If you're lucky you'll be sitting in a window seat watching the world go by.

[14] It is a powerful thing for conductors to handle more than one orchestra, no doubt (and it would take a lot of scholarship to trace the impact for orchestras and audiences).

[15] Kurzweil, Ray. *The Age of Spiritual Machines*. Viking Press 1999.

[16] http://www.deeplistening.org/site/convergence

[17] For a description and requirements see http://www.deeplistening.org/site/certificateprogram

[18] You are welcome to join DEEPL anytime. To do so, go to http://groups.google.com/group/deep-l?lnk=srg

[19] Deep listening Institute, Ltd. Newsletter, Fall 2006

[20] http://www.lifebridge.org/

[21] http://www.skype.com/

[22] http://www.iMeem.com/

[23] Deep Listening Band. *Deep Listening*. New Albion 1989.

[24] http://rockpa.org/special_programs/the-new-york-state-music-fund

FROM OUTSIDE THE WINDOW: ELECTRONIC MUSIC PERFORMANCE

[1] Raes, Godfrield-Willem. "Gesture Controlled Musical Instruments: A Practical Report." Ghent University 2007

[2] Musselman, Peter. Welcome address at Mills College MFA Thesis Presentation 2008

[3] Bernstein, David, ed. *The San Francisco Tape Music Center: 60's Counterculture and the Avant-Garde*. University of California Press 2008.

[4] See the chapter "The Accordion (& the Outsider)" in this book.

[5] http://www.willardpalmer.org/

[6] Oliveros, Pauline. "Tape Delay Techniques for Electronic Music Composers" in *Software for People: Collected Writings 1963-1980.* Smith Publications/Printed Editions 1984

[7] *I of IV* was made in July, 1966, at the University of Toronto Electronic Music Studio. It is a real-time studio performance composition (no editing or tape splicing), utilizing the techniques of amplifying combination tones and tape repetition. The combination-tone technique was one, which I developed in 1965 at the San Francisco Tape Music Center.

The equipment consisted of twelve sine-tone square-wave generators connected to an organ keyboard, two line amplifiers, mixer, Hammond spring-type reverb and two stereo tape recorders. Eleven generators were set to operate above twenty thousand cycles per second, and one generator at below one cycle per second. The keyboard output was routed to the line amplifiers, reverb, and then to channel A of recorder 1. The tape was threaded from recorder 1 to recorder 2. Recorder 2 was on playback only. Recorder 2 provided playback repetition approximately eight seconds later. Recorder 1 channel A was routed to recorder 1 channel B, and recorder 1 channel B to recorder 1 channel A in a double feedback loop. Recorder 2 channel A was routed to recorder 1 channel A, and recorder 2 channel B was routed to recorder 1 channel B. The tape repetition contributed timbre and dynamic changes to steady state sounds. The combination tones produced by the eleven generators and the bias frequencies of the tape recorders were pulse modulated by the sub-audio generator.

[8] http://www.synthmuseum.com/buchla/buc10001.html

[9] Sony TC 777
http://www.sony.net/SonyInfo/CorporateInfo/History/sonyhistory-a.html

[10] Lexicon PCM 42 delay processors http://emusician.com/dsp/emusic_max_factor/

[11] See the chapter "The Expanded Instrument System: An Introduction and Brief History" in this book.

[12] http://emusician.com/dsp/emusic_max_factor/

[13] http://www.jstor.org/pss/1575535

[14] In this book.

[15] See the chapter "High and Low Tech Telematic Music: A Report" in this book.

[16] CCRMA, The Stanford University Center for Computer Research in Music and Acoustics is a multi-disciplinary facility where composers and researchers work together using computer-based technology both as an artistic medium and as a research tool. http://ccrma.stanford.edu/

[17] http://symphony.arch.rpi.edu/acoustics/bio.html

[18] JackTrip is a Linux-based system used for multi-machine jam sessions over Internet2. It supports any number of channels (as much as the computer/network can handle) of bidirectional, high quality, uncompressed audio signal steaming: http://ccrma.stanford.edu/groups/soundwire/software/jacktrip/

[19] Jeremy Cooperstock's UltraVideo Conferencing http://ultravideo.mcgill.edu/

[20] ViMic (Virtual Microphone) http://symphony.arch.rpi.edu/~braasj/JonasBraaschResearch.html

[21] http://ccrma.stanford.edu/groups/soundwire/

The Collective Intelligence of Improvisation

[1] Chardin, Pierre Teilhard de. *The Phenomenon of Man*. Translated by Bernard Wall. Harper, 2008.

www.ingramcontent.com/pod-product-compliance
Lightning Source LLC
LaVergne TN
LVHW091028080826
845145LV00002B/390